Kierkegaard and Socrates

A Study in Philosophy and Faith

This volume is a study of the relationship between philosophy and faith in Søren Kierkegaard's *Philosophical Fragments*. It is also the first book to focus on the role of Socrates in this pseudonymous volume, and it illuminates the significance of Socrates for Kierkegaard's thought in general. Jacob Howland argues that in *Fragments*, philosophy and faith are closely related passions. A careful examination of the role of Socrates in *Fragments* demonstrates that Socratic, philosophical eros opens up a path to faith. At the same time, the work of faith – which holds the self together with that which transcends it, the finite with the infinite, and one's life in time with eternity – is essentially erotic in the Socratic sense of the term. Chapters on Kierkegaard's *Johannes Climacus* and on Plato's *Apology* and related dialogues shed light on the Socratic character of the pseudonymous author of *Fragments* and the role of "the god" in Socrates' pursuit of wisdom. Howland also analyzes the *Concluding Unscientific Postscript* and Kierkegaard's reflections on Socrates and Christ in his unpublished papers.

Jacob Howland is McFarlin Professor of Philosophy at the University of Tulsa. He is the author of *The Republic: The Odyssey of Philosophy* and *The Paradox of Political Philosophy: Socrates' Philosophic Trial*, and he has contributed to the *Review of Metaphysics*, *Phoenix*, the *American Political Science Review*, the *American Catholic Philosophical Quarterly*, and the *Review of Politics*, among other journals.

T0381836

Kierkegaard and Socrates

A Study in Philosophy and Faith

JACOB HOWLAND

University of Tulsa

CAMBRIDGE
UNIVERSITY PRESS

University Printing House, Cambridge CB2 8BS, United Kingdom

One Liberty Plaza, 20th Floor, New York, NY 10006, USA

477 Williamstown Road, Port Melbourne, VIC 3207, Australia

314-321, 3rd Floor, Plot 3, Splendor Forum, Jasola District Centre, New Delhi - 110025, India

79 Anson Road, #06-04/06, Singapore 079906

Cambridge University Press is part of the University of Cambridge.

It furthers the University's mission by disseminating knowledge in the pursuit of
education, learning and research at the highest international levels of excellence.

www.cambridge.org
Information on this title: www.cambridge.org/9780521730365

First published 2006

A catalogue record for this publication is available from the British Library

Library of Congress Cataloging in Publication data
Howland, Jacob.
Kierkegaard and Socrates : a study in philosophy and faith / Jacob Howland.
p. cm.
Includes bibliographical references.
ISBN 0-521-86203-5 (hardcover)
1. Kierkegaard, Søren, 1813–1855. Philosophiske smuler. 2. Kierkegaard, Søren,
1813–1855. Afsluttende unvidenskabelig efterskrift. 3. Religion – Philosophy.
4. Socrates. I. Title.
B4373.P453H69   2006
198'.9–dc22   2005027576

ISBN 978-0-521-86203-5 Hardback
ISBN 978-0-521-73036-5 Paperback

The following reprint rights have been granted:
Kierkegaard, Søren; *Philosophical Fragments / Johannes Climacus.* © 1985 Princeton
University Press. Reprinted by permission of Princeton University Press.

Kierkegaard, Søren; *Concluding Unscientific Postscript to Philosophical Fragments* (2 vols.).
© 1992 Princeton University Press. Reprinted by permission of Princeton University Press.

Søren Kierkegaard's Journals and Papers, ed. and trans. Howard V. Hong and Edna H. Hong
(6 vols.). Bloomington: Indiana University Press, 1967–78. Reprinted by permission of
Indiana University Press.

For Bette, Howard, and Monica

Contents

Note on Texts and Translations

In referring to works published under the name of Kierkegaard and his pseudonyms I have employed the following English translations, which are cited parenthetically in the text by page number (including where necessary a short title, e.g., *"Fragments," "Postscript"*).

The Concept of Irony, together with "Notes on Schelling's Berlin Lectures." Trans. Howard V. Hong and Edna H. Hong. Princeton, NJ: Princeton University Press, 1989.

Concluding Unscientific Postscript to Philosophical Fragments. Vol. 1. Trans. Howard V. Hong and Edna H. Hong. Princeton, NJ: Princeton University Press, 1992.

Fear and Trembling. In *Fear and Trembling/Repetition*. Trans. Howard V. Hong and Edna H. Hong. Princeton, NJ: Princeton University Press, 1983.

Johannes Climacus. In *Philosophical Fragments/Johannes Climacus*. Trans. Howard V. Hong and Edna H. Hong. Princeton, NJ: Princeton University Press, 1985.

Philosophical Fragments. In *Philosophical Fragments/Johannes Climacus*. Trans. Howard V. Hong and Edna H. Hong. Princeton, NJ: Princeton University Press, 1985.

The Point of View for My Work as an Author: A Direct Communication, A Report to History. Trans. Walter Lowrie. London: Oxford University Press, 1939.

Material from *Søren Kierkegaard's Journal and Papers*, six vols., ed. and trans. Howard V. Hong and Edna H. Hong (Bloomington: Indiana University Press, 1967–78), abbreviated JP, is cited by entry, volume, and page numbers in the Hong edition and then by arrangement and notation in

Søren Kierkegaards Papirer, ed. P. A. Heiberg, V. Kuhr, and E. Torsting, 20 vols., I–XI.3 (Copenhagen: Gyldendal, 1909–48).

In citing the Danish text of *Fragments* and *Postscript* I have referred to *Søren Kierkegaard: Samlede Værker* [computer file], ed. Alastair McKinnon (Charlottesville, VA: InteLex Corporation, 1992), corrected version of the third edition of *Samlede Værker*, ed. A. B. Drachmann, J. L. Heiberg, H. O. Lange, and Peter P. Rohde, 20 vols. (Copenhagen: Gyldendal, 1962–4).

Platonic dialogues and letters are cited parenthetically in the text by standard (Stephanus) page numbers. Unless otherwise noted, all quotations from Plato are my translations from *Platonis Opera*, five vols., ed. Johannes Burnet (Oxford: Clarendon Press, 1979–82).

Acknowledgments

I have benefited immeasurably from the help and encouragement of my colleagues and students at the University of Tulsa. John Bowlin suggested that I write a book about Kierkegaard and Socrates, and subsequently helped to orient me in the world of Kierkegaard studies. Steve Gardner spent hours with me in animated conversation about Kierkegaard's pseudonymous writings. Russ Hittinger read the manuscript with care and pointed out, among other things, the relevance of the monastic tradition to the concerns of Johannes Climacus. Jane Ackerman organized a brown-bag lecture series in which I gave a presentation on the subject of my book and from which I learned much. Dean Tom Benediktson granted me a sabbatical in the fall of 2003, during which I completed the first draft of *Kierkegaard and Socrates*. Perhaps my greatest debt is to the wonderful undergraduate students with whom I have studied Kierkegaard over the years, including Amy Couch, Anthony Meehan, Alicia Mosier, Jon Novotny, Anthony Quinn, Brandon Rule, Judd Treeman, and Brian White.

Others beyond the walls of my ivory tower have advised and assisted me in important ways. Eva Brann read an early version of the manuscript and gave me a bracing critique. Paul Dry offered sound advice when I was looking for a publisher. Mary Nichols' paper and Denise Schaeffer's comments at the 2005 Southern Political Science Association meeting opened my eyes to some new dimensions of Kierkegaard's understanding of Socrates. C. Stephen Evans and Gordon Marino refereed the manuscript for the Press and saved me from many errors. I owe very special thanks to Gordon and to Cynthia Lund of the Hong Kierkegaard Library at St. Olaf College for hosting the Fifth International Kierkegaard Conference in 2005 and for welcoming me so warmly into the "Kierkegaard family." David Possen, who commented on my paper at St. Olaf, offered much helpful criticism and friendly encouragement. Finally, this book could not have been completed without the love and support of my wife, Jennifer Hayes Howland.

Kierkegaard and Socrates

A Study in Philosophy and Faith

Introduction

During an idle moment in my office at the university, now well over ten years ago, I selected from my bookcase a thin blue hardcover volume that I had never before opened. The book was *Philosophical Fragments* by Johannes Climacus, translated into English by David F. Swenson, and published in 1944 for the American-Scandinavian Foundation by Princeton University Press. Of Climacus, I knew only that he was one of a handful of authorial personae under whose names Søren Kierkegaard published such pseudonymous works as *Either/Or*, *Fear and Trembling*, and *Stages on Life's Way*. Of Kierkegaard, I knew only what little I could remember from a brief encounter in an undergraduate survey course. But Climacus obviously had something to say to me. He talked about the absolute importance of the truth in human life, and he wasted no words in doing so. His insights into the essential nature of Socratic teaching and learning were especially striking. His understanding of Socrates, I thought, was rivaled only by Plato and Xenophon, two authors who had long stood at the center of my philosophical interests. Yet as far as I could tell, the real subject of his book was not Socrates, and not even philosophy. It was religious faith.

There was brilliance in Climacus's writing, and there was ardor. Above all there was mystery. His book was a literary gem as well as a philosophical *tour de force*. It was then and there that I conceived a passion for Kierkegaard's thought, and it was out of this passion that the present study was born.

The book you hold in your hands is about the relationship between philosophy and faith in the thought of Johannes Climacus, and primarily

1

in *Philosophical Fragments*. It does not presuppose that you are a specialist in Kierkegaard or Plato, or even that you have more than a general knowledge of the vocabulary of philosophy. Vast learning, as C. Stephen Evans has noted, is not needed in order to understand Kierkegaard's works.[1] More important is a capacity for wonder. For this book springs from wonder, primarily at the fact that Kierkegaard, a nineteenth-century Danish author who devoted his literary career to promoting the Christian faith, felt himself to be the soulmate of a pagan Athenian who lived and died for philosophy. "I for my part tranquilly adhere to Socrates," Kierkegaard wrote in a reflection on his life and work that was published by his brother a few years after his death. "It is true, he was not a Christian; that I know, and yet I am thoroughly convinced that he has become one."[2]

Kierkegaard, a Christian Socrates – what could this mean? Aren't philosophy and faith opposites? Doesn't philosophy rest on the assumption that reason is by itself sufficient for the achievement of wisdom, while faith, acknowledging the depredations of sin and the weakness of human understanding, humbly embraces divine revelation? If so, how could Socrates – by all appearances a partisan of reason and independent thought – become a Christian? And even if the notion of a Christian Socrates makes sense, would such a person have anything to say to non-Christians?

One cannot attempt to answer these questions directly without presupposing that one already knows what philosophy and faith are. This presupposition is repeatedly challenged in Kierkegaard's pseudonymous works. *Fear and Trembling*, a meditation on the exemplary faith manifested by Abraham when he prepared to sacrifice his son Isaac on Mount Moriah, asks whether *anyone* can understand Abraham's devotion to God (14). And *Philosophical Fragments* suggests that even Socrates did not fully understand the love of wisdom for which he lived and died.

On the most basic level, Climacus's book is a philosophical archaeology of the concepts of "philosophy" and "faith." In *Fragments*, Climacus tries to cut through centuries of "chatter" in order to uncover the original

---

[1] Evans 1983, 2. "It would be tragic," Evans adds," if he [Kierkegaard] became the special property of a band of scholars." The present study falls under the heading of what Evans calls the "literary-philosophical" approach to Kierkegaard, which aims at "an encounter with the text which will be philosophical in what might be termed a Socratic sense" (Evans 1992, 3). It is perhaps worth noting that Poole 1998, which contrasts "blunt readings" of Kierkegaard with those that follow "the deconstructive turn," leaves no room for literary-philosophical readings. Cf. Evans 2004, 63–7.

[2] *Point of View*, 41.

phenomena of philosophy and faith in what he regards as their purest and truest forms – the one exemplified in the speeches and deeds of Socrates, the other both solicited by, and manifested in, the incarnation of God in the person of Christ.[3] Climacus's motivation is easy to discern. In his view, the most important questions we can ask ourselves as human beings – questions about who we are, what we can know, and how we should live – become clear only when we first grasp what is at stake in the alternative of philosophy and faith.

Fragments begins by presenting the guiding presuppositions of philosophy and faith in such a way as to emphasize their mutual exclusivity. According to Climacus, philosophy is founded on the Socratic assumption that knowledge is recollection, or that "the ignorant person merely needs to be reminded in order, by himself, to call to mind what he knows" (9) – a principle that evidently leaves no room for faith. Because Climacus identifies Socrates with this principle, scholarly consensus holds that he is, in the somewhat extreme formulation of Merold Westphal, the "villain" of *Fragments*.[4] But this identification is only the first move in a book full of unexpected twists and turns. Climacus introduces philosophy and faith as competing hypotheses about learning the truth. Yet he also makes it clear that neither philosophy nor faith is reducible to a hypothesis, because neither can be understood without reference to the individual who embraces it as a path to the truth. One therefore cannot answer the question "What is philosophy?" without first asking the ontologically prior question "Who is the philosopher?" To fail to recognize this priority is to obscure the passion that is essential to Socratic philosophizing and the existential transformation that is central to faith. Because Climacus is well aware of this problem, neither philosophy nor faith is what it first appears to be in *Fragments*. This becomes obvious as the inquiry unfolds. While philosophy is supposed to rest on the assumption that knowledge is already latent in our souls, Climacus will make much of Socrates' frank admission that he does not even know himself (Plato, *Phaedrus* 229e–30a).

---

[3] One would not be mistaken to detect here an anticipation of the attempts of Heidegger, who never fully acknowledges his debt to Kierkegaard, to dig beneath the sediment of philosophical tradition and to penetrate the veil of idle talk in order to uncover original phenomena.

[4] Westphal 1996, 121. Westphal adds that *Fragments* identifies Socrates with "the speculative collapsing of the difference between the divine and the human," whereas *Postscript* presents him as the "hero" who challenges Hegelian, speculative philosophy. This, too, expresses the scholarly consensus; cf. most recently Rubenstein 2001. A closer reading, however, suggests that Socrates is already an antispeculative hero in *Fragments*. Cf. Allison 1967/2002, 3.13.

And while Climacus introduces faith as a "happy passion," it turns out to involve terror and struggle.

Although the opposition between philosophy and faith is never entirely overcome in *Fragments*, it nonetheless begins to break down almost as soon as it is formulated. This is in large part because Climacus chooses to convey what is meant by philosophy not merely by examining its fundamental presuppositions, but also by attending to the figure of Socrates as he is depicted in the dialogues of Plato. This procedure gives rise to a certain interpretative tension, because Socrates' philosophical practice is in important respects at odds with the hypothesis of philosophy with which the book begins. Climacus makes it clear, however, that philosophy is a way of life, from which it follows that it cannot be evaluated in abstraction from the speeches and deeds of the philosopher.[5]

In sum, *Fragments* develops dialectically, which is to say that the careful reader is obliged continually to rethink earlier assumptions and expectations in the light of later developments. Climacus initially leads us to anticipate that he will attack philosophy in the name of faith, but he goes on to show that genuine or Socratic philosophy and faith are siblings whose family resemblance rests on certain fundamental analogies. In this important respect, *Fragments* echoes the intellectual tradition initiated by Thomas Aquinas in the *Summa Theologiae*, in which faith is seen not as the negation but as the perfection of reason.

Yet Climacus is otherwise no Thomist. While Thomas's thought reflects the philosophical sobriety of Aristotle, Climacus gives voice to the divine erotic madness of Plato. He identifies passion as the central element of both philosophy and faith, and he sees both as distinct expressions of what we might as a preliminary approximation call love. According to Climacus, faith is a passion analogous to the erotic or romantic love between a man and a woman. This is an insight advanced also by Johannes de Silentio in *Fear and Trembling*; as we shall see, *Fragments* develops the analogy between faith and love in a way that complements Silentio's thought. At the same time, Climacus embraces Socrates' claim, as set forth in the Platonic dialogues, that philosophy is rooted in eros. But

---

5 Socrates is thus more than "an ideal type or metaphor" in *Fragments* (Perkins 1994, 1). Nor is he "transformed into a promulgator of a philosophy, that by a stereotypical exaggeration is presented as encapsulating the entire tradition of Greek humanities," a role in which he supposedly "provides the negative counterpart to the Christian embodiment of God" (Petersen 2004, 46–7). It is more precise to say that "'the Socratic' way of thinking" or philosophical *hypothesis* "includes the whole of the (Platonic) idealist tradition, up to Hegel and his successors" (Rudd 2000/2002, 2.257).

what exactly is eros, a phenomenon that manifests itself in ways ranging from sexual longing to the love of wisdom? Although Socrates wrestles at length with this question, Climacus claims that he is never fully able to answer it. Eros is difficult to grasp because it is fundamentally ambiguous. It is simultaneously human and divine, "objective" as well as "subjective": it comes from without just as much as it springs from within, and pulls the soul upward no less than it drives it forward.

According to Climacus, Socrates follows his passion for wisdom to the point where he is forced to acknowledge the intractable mystery of the divinity to which eros opens him up – a divine other without which he is less than whole. The experience of eros thus leads Socrates implicitly to admit the failure of his philosophical quest for wisdom and self-knowledge. For this very reason, however, Climacus sees Socrates as the proper judge of his own attempt in *Fragments* to "go beyond" philosophy by developing the hypothesis of faith (111). What is more, it is precisely Socrates' knowledge of eros – knowledge just as ambiguous as his celebrated knowledge of ignorance – that qualifies him to judge Climacus's accomplishment. If philosophical eros opens up a path to faith, faith also reflects the structure of eros. For in striving to hold together elements that seem to be poles apart – the self and that which transcends it, the finite and the infinite, one's life in time and eternity – the work of faith is essentially erotic in the Socratic sense of the term.

Although Socrates' philosophical eros stands at the center of Climacus's consideration of the relationship between philosophy and faith, scholars have paid little attention to its role in *Fragments*.[6] This is all the more surprising because Socrates' erotic nature is reflected in Climacus's own passions and convictions.[7] In particular, the exemplary openness Climacus displays in *Fragments* to the claims of both philosophy and faith is itself rooted in a Socratic love of thinking and longing for wisdom. The literary critic Bakhtin remarks that, in his novels, Dostoyevsky strove to express "fidelity to the authoritative image of a human being."[8] This phrase nicely describes what is at stake in *Fragments* as well, which is itself a kind of philosophical novel in that its author – who writes, among

---

[6] Even Daise 1999, which reads *Fragments* and *Postscript* as Socratic exercises in indirect communication, does not examine the significance of the figure of Socrates *within* these texts.

[7] Cf. Muench 2003: "in his two books... [Climacus] giv[es] what I contend is one of the most compelling performances we have of a Socratic philosopher at work since Plato put Socrates himself on stage" (140).

[8] Quoted by Richard Pevear in his Forward to Dostoyevsky 1994, xix.

other things, about himself – is Kierkegaard's literary creation. Climacus offers us a profound reflection on two such authoritative images, those of Socrates and Christ, while presenting in his own paradoxical person a unique attempt to live one's life in fidelity to *both* of them. By Climacus's own admission, he ultimately falls short of his goal.[9] But this does not diminish our ability to learn from his example. To think with Climacus about what it means to be human is an undertaking that must appeal to all those – regardless of their particular philosophical or faith commitments – in whom the human condition arouses wonder.

No less important, *Fragments* is noteworthy as a corrective to the critical interpretation of Socratic philosophizing initiated by Friedrich Nietzsche and developed by twentieth-century European philosophers. In the *Birth of Tragedy*, which appeared almost thirty years after the publication of *Fragments*, Nietzsche presents Socrates as the originator of a great and consequential error – "the unshakable faith that thought, using the thread of causality, can penetrate the deepest abysses of being, and that thought is capable not only of knowing being but even of *correcting* it."[10] It is this misplaced optimism, the ultimate fruits of which can be seen in the seemingly unlimited ambition of natural science and technology, that in Nietzsche's view cuts us off from rejuvenating and healing contact with the life-giving yet fundamentally unintelligible core of reality he called "the Dionysian." Nietzsche's critical appraisal of Socrates and Plato (or more precisely, of Socratism and Platonism), as well as his attention to pre-Socratic poetry and philosophy, are echoed and extended in the work of Martin Heidegger.[11] These themes lie at the root of the thought of the Frankfurt School philosophers Horkheimer and Adorno, who argue that the Socratic quest for knowledge (which they trace back to Homer's Odysseus) is inseparable from the "totalitarian" attempt to dominate the

---

9 If he "does not make out that he is a Christian," Climacus writes in *Postscript*, this is only because "he is, to be sure, completely preoccupied with how difficult it must be to become one" (617). But perhaps such claims should not be taken at face value. See Lippitt 2000 with ch. 10 below, 205–08.

10 Nietzsche 1967, 95, emphasis in original.

11 See in this connection David Farrell Krell's Introduction to Heidegger 1975, 10: "In his *Introduction to Metaphysics*...focusing on the question of the meaning of *to on* [being], Heidegger describes his own task as one of 'bringing Nietzsche's accomplishment to a full unfolding.' That means following Nietzsche's turn toward early Greek thinking in such a way as to bring the possibilities concealed in *eon* [the form of *on* in the dialects of the pre-Socratic philosophers Heraclitus and Parmenides] to a radical questioning."

objects of knowledge, including ourselves as well as nature.[12] And they are most recently reflected in the deconstructionist interpretation of Plato exemplified in the work of Jacques Derrida, who presents Socrates as a purveyor of intellectual snake-oil – one who vainly promises to make intelligible that which is intrinsically resistant to the charms of philosophical reason.[13]

Because Climacus is also engaged in an exploration of the limits of Socratic philosophizing, one might have expected him to criticize Socrates along the lines laid out by Nietzsche and followed by his philosophical heirs. Far from condemning Socrates in *Fragments* as an arrogant partisan of reason, however, Climacus discerns in his speeches and deeds the capacity of philosophy to know its own limits, and therewith to acknowledge the impenetrable mysteriousness of ourselves as well as the world we inhabit. And far from associating Socrates with totalizing ambition, Climacus presents himself, in what turns out to be an essentially Socratic gesture, as a thinker who offers merely a fragment or scrap of philosophy at a time when the loudest voice in the fields of philosophy and theology was that of Hegelians claiming to be able to embrace all of thought and being in a single system.

In *Kierkegaard and Socrates*, I have attempted to make the nature of Climacus's project and its implications clear enough to be understood by educated amateurs while also saying something important to scholars of philosophy and religion. Students of the Platonic dialogues may hope to understand Socrates better after reading this book, because Climacus's reflection on what he calls the "paradoxical passion" of philosophical eros sheds new light on the erotic core of Socratic philosophizing. Students of Kierkegaard may hope to gain an appreciation of the seminal importance of Socrates to his thought. And anyone who seeks greater clarity about either philosophy or faith will learn much from Climacus's remarkable understanding of their relationship.

The plan of the present study is straightforward. The first chapter introduces Climacus by examining the way in which Kierkegaard himself intended to introduce him in his unfinished intellectual biography of the author, *Johannes Climacus*. Subsequent chapters take the reader step by step through *Philosophical Fragments*, with attention to its literary and

---

[12] Horkheimer and Adorno 1991. The original title of *Dialektik der Aufklärung* was *Philosophische Fragmente*.
[13] Derrida 1981.

rhetorical dimensions (including poetic analogy, humor, and irony) as well as its philosophical ideas and arguments. There is a pause early on to explore Socrates' relationship to the inscrutable divinity he calls "the god" and the nature of his philosophical eros as these are presented in some of Plato's major dialogues. The book concludes with a chapter on Climacus's presentation of Socrates in his sequel to *Fragments*, the *Concluding Unscientific Postscript to Philosophical Fragments*, and with a brief epilogue.

There were many different literary representations of Socrates in antiquity, primarily including those of Aristophanes, Plato, and Xenophon, and readers may wonder which Socrates they will encounter in this book. It is important to note in this connection that Climacus views Socrates through the lens of the Platonic dialogues. He does not ask whether the character of Socrates in the dialogues is an accurate representation of the historical Socrates, nor is this a question with which we need be concerned here.[14] Unless otherwise indicated, any mention of "Socrates" in the following pages should accordingly be understood to refer to the protagonist of the Platonic dialogues.[15]

The reader should also bear in mind the peculiar interpretive challenges posed by Kierkegaard's pseudonymous writings. These writings leave the clear impression that one must work to earn whatever wisdom they might contain. Reading the pseudonymous works is in this respect like reading a Platonic dialogue or talking to Socrates. Not coincidentally, both Plato and Socrates tend to keep others guessing when it comes to their own opinions. Kierkegaard accomplishes the same thing by writing pseudonymously, and he has a good pedagogical reason for doing so: the

---

[14] In contrast, Kierkegaard makes much of this question. He begins his dissertation by stating that "it is necessary to make sure that I have a reliable and authentic view of Socrates' historical-actual, phenomenological existence with respect to the question of its possible relation to the transformed view that was his fate through enthusiastic or envious contemporaries" (*Concept of Irony*, 9).

[15] The question remains whether it is possible to distinguish between the philosophy of Plato and that of the character of Socrates in the Platonic dialogues. As we shall see, Climacus criticizes Plato's understanding of Socrates in *Fragments* and makes the distinction between them explicit in *Postscript* (n. on 206–7). Yet insofar as Climacus bothers to offer a textual basis for his picture of Socrates, he moves freely between dialogues that Kierkegaard, following Schleiermacher, regards as belonging to both the "early" stage of Plato's "development" (e.g., the *Apology*) and the "later" stage of "authentic Platonism" (e.g., the *Theaetetus*; cf. *Concept of Irony*, 123 with *Fragments*, 10–11). Following Climacus, I have ignored the putative authorial chronology of the dialogues in attempting to flesh out the nature of Socratic philosophizing. Howland 1991 offers a scholarly justification of this practice; cf. Cooper 1997, xii–xv.

mere fact that he himself holds a certain opinion should be of no interest to his readers, whose primary task is think for themselves.[16]

At the very end of *Concluding Unscientific Postscript*, there appears "A First and Last Explanation" signed by "S. Kierkegaard." In this explanation, Kierkegaard admits that he is the author of the pseudonymous works. Yet he observes that his relationship to the likes of Johannes Climacus "is even more remote than that of a poet, who *poetizes* characters and yet in preference is *himself* the *author*." This is because he has "poetically produced the *authors*, whose *prefaces* in turn are their productions, as their *names* are also." Thus in the pseudonymous books, he declares, "there is not a single word by me."[17] In accordance with this declaration, and out of respect for Kierkegaard's "wish" and "prayer" that "if it should occur to anyone to want to quote a particular passage from the books . . . he will do me the kindness of citing the respective pseudonymous author's name, not mine,"[18] I have treated Climacus, and not Kierkegaard, as the author of *Fragments* and *Postscript*. This has not prevented me from attributing to Kierkegaard those writings to which he has not attached a pseudonym.[19]

A final word on pronominal usage. As neither Plato nor Kierkegaard employed gender-neutral pronouns, it would be potentially misleading and, to my ear, disruptive for me to switch between "he" and "she." With some misgivings, I have therefore chosen to employ the traditional pronoun "he" even in contexts where "he or she" is to be understood, as for example in speaking without qualification of the philosophical learner or the faithful follower.

[16] Alastair Hannay notes that "pseudonymity 'scrambles' the author–reader link in a way that allows the writings to enjoy a genuinely independent existence, letting them become considerations in the mind of the reader, to do there whatever they have it *in themselves* to do" (Hannay 2001, 175–6, emphasis in original). Niels Thulstrup observes that *Fragments* resembles both "a Platonic dialogue" and "a classical drama in five acts" with "two main actors, Socrates and Christ" (Kierkegaard 1962, lxvii–lxviii). Cf. the discussion of "Socratic midwifery" in the pseudonymous authorship at Taylor 1975, 51–62.

[17] *Postscript*, 625–6, emphases in original. Compare Plato's assertion that "there is no writing of Plato, nor will there be, but the things now said to be his are of a Socrates grown beautiful and young" (*Second Letter*, 314c).

[18] *Postscript*, 627.

[19] See ch. 1 and Epilogue. Nor have I refrained from occasionally noting connections between Climacus's thought and that of Johannes de Silentio – something Climacus himself does in *Postscript* (see, e.g., 261–2, 264–8).

1

Johannes Climacus, Socratic Philosopher

The relationship between philosophy and religious faith is the central theme of two of Kierkegaard's pseudonymous volumes. *Philosophical Fragments, or A Fragment of Philosophy*, by Johannes Climacus, edited by S. Kierkegaard, was published in 1844. *Concluding Unscientific Postscript to Philosophical Fragments: A Mimical-Pathetical-Dialectical Compilation, An Existential Contribution*, also by Johannes Climacus, edited by S. Kierkegaard, appeared two years later, in 1846. These are the only works by Climacus in the Kierkegaardean corpus.[1]

Kierkegaard first mentions the name of Climacus in connection with the speculative philosophy of G. W. F. Hegel (1770–1831), whose followers, including theologians as well as philosophers, played a leading role in the Danish intellectual scene of the day.[2] In a journal entry dated January 20, 1839, he writes: "Hegel is a Johannes Climacus who does not storm the heavens as do the giants – by setting mountain upon mountain – but climbs up to them by means of his syllogisms."[3] Hegel ascends to the "heaven" of absolute knowledge stepwise, on the basis of a series of philosophical arguments. This occurs in his *Phenomenology of Spirit*, which

---

[1] The Hongs claim that *Johannes Climacus*, which Kierkegaard did not finish, is also by Climacus (*Philosophical Fragments/Johannes Climacus*, xv–xvi). The book has no stated author, however, and so "inhabits, as it were, a limbo of anonymity" (Dunning 1994, 209).

[2] On the Hegelians J. L. Heiberg and H. L. Martensen and their influence in Denmark, see Stewart 2003, 50–69. Stewart argues against the assumption that the Danish academy was dominated by Hegelians. He notes there were a number of "anti-Hegelians" in Denmark, that only Heiberg was a "full-fledged" Hegelian, and that the Danish Hegelians "never formed an organized or coherent school" (69).

[3] JP 1575, 2.209–210 (II A 335).

he envisions as furnishing the natural or prephilosophic consciousness with a "ladder" to the "absolute" beginning of his philosophical system – the standpoint of absolute spirit and absolute knowing.[4] Kierkegaard's allusion to the rebellious giants of Greek myth who made war on Zeus after the defeat of the Titans hints that, in his view, Hegel's philosophical ascent is both hybristic and illegitimate – a point to which we shall return in due course.

But who is Johannes Climacus, or John of the Ladder (from the Greek *klimax*)? This was the name given to the late sixth- and early seventh-century author of one of the most well-known books of Eastern Christendom, *Scala paradisi* (*The Ladder of Divine Ascent*).[5] Climacus was a hermit monk who became Abbot of the central monastery at Mt. Sinai and was later made a saint of the Eastern Church. *The Ladder* was written for his fellow monks, and it describes thirty steps – corresponding to Jesus' age at the time of his baptism – by which one living the ascetic life may ascend to union with God. *The Ladder* thus makes use of an image with an already long history. Jacob dreams that he sees angels ascending and descending a ladder that stretches from earth to heaven (Genesis 28:12). In the New Testament, Jesus explicitly identifies himself as the ladder of Jacob's dream (John 1:51). And in *The Rule of Saint Benedict*, the great guide to monastic life that predates the writings of St. John Climacus by perhaps half a century, Benedict explains to his fellow monks that the ladder of Jacob's dream is nothing other than "our life in the world, which, if the heart be humbled, is lifted up by the Lord to heaven." On the ladder thus construed, going up is actually going down, in that "we descend [from God] by exaltation and ascend [to God] by humility." Benedict also emphasizes that the goal of monastic discipline is to become a whole human being, in whom action and thought are in harmony. "The sides of the same ladder," he writes, "we understand to be body and soul, in which the call of God has placed various degrees of humility or discipline, which we must ascend."[6]

The union with God that St. John Climacus envisions is philosophical, insofar as it involves the fulfillment of our longing for understanding. *The Ladder* describes an intellectual encounter with God who is the Word that is reminiscent of a memorable moment in the *Confessions* of St. Augustine – the moment when Augustine and his mother Monica for

---

[4] Hegel 1977 (hereafter cited parenthetically in the text, by paragraph), §26 and §808.
[5] Climacus 1982, hereafter cited parenthetically in the text.
[6] Delatte 1950, 101.

one fleeting instant touch eternal wisdom (9.10). Like Augustine's experience, the encounter of which Climacus speaks is one in which "what God has said is mysteriously clarified" (288). This is the first point one should keep in mind in thinking about the resemblance between *The Ladder*'s author and the author of *Fragments* and *Postscript.* The second is that St. John Climacus's ladder begins and ends in love. Just as the love of God and the longing to come into God's presence motivates the ascent (74, 81), the ladder ends with the experience of God as love. Climacus furthermore introduces and concludes the thirtieth and final step of the ladder by quoting 1 Corinthians 13:13: "Remaining now are faith, hope, and love, these three. But the greatest of these is love." Love is greatest because it "never falls, never halts on its way, never gives respite to the man wounded by its blessed rapture." And he adds that "Love, by its nature, is a resemblance to God, insofar as this is humanly possible. In its activity it is inebriation of the soul. Its distinctive character is to be a fountain of faith, an abyss of patience, a sea of humility" (286).

Kierkegaard's Climacus is a philosopher, which implies that *his* ladder is thought, not religious faith. Yet he resembles the saint whose name he shares in that he, too, is a faithful lover of the kind of truth that promises to make us whole. He presupposes that human beings can ascend to knowledge of this truth, and that passion is essential to doing so. What is at issue, then, is not *whether* the truth is accessible, but *how:* what is the nature of the ladder by which we are to make our ascent? In *Fragments,* in which the Hegelians' systematic assault on the truth provides a foil for his own inquiry, Climacus asks whether it is philosophy or religious faith that furnishes this ladder. This question is really twofold. Is the passion that makes the truth attainable the love of wisdom – the passion Socrates called eros? Or is it the passion of faith – a passion that is itself made possible by the love of God for man? And what *is* the truth? Is it God, the living Word, or is it the nonliving being of which the philosophers speak?

Even this brief statement of Climacus's inquiry in *Fragments* suggests that he is a philosopher who is unusually self-conscious about the possible limits of philosophy and open to the competing claims of religious faith. Kierkegaard himself confirms this suggestion in a surprising way, for Climacus is unique among the pseudonymous authors in that we possess an intellectual biography of him. Kierkegaard wrote *Johannes Climacus, or De Omnibus Dubitandum est: A Narrative* about the time *Either/Or* was in press (i.e., around 1842–3), but left it unfinished and unpublished.[7]

---

[7] Hannay 2001, 198.

The portrait he draws in *Johannes Climacus* is nevertheless essential for our understanding of the author of *Fragments* and *Postscript*.[8]

TRUTHFUL PHILOSOPHY: THE HARMONY
OF SPEECH AND DEED

In his unpublished papers, Kierkegaard makes it clear that *Johannes Climacus* was to be a polemic against modern philosophy.

> The plan of this narrative was as follows. . . . by means of the profound earnestness involved in a young man's being sufficiently honest and earnest enough to do quietly and unostentatiously what philosophers say (and he thereby becomes unhappy) – I would strike a blow at [modern speculative] philosophy. Johannes does what we are told to do – he actually doubts everything. . . . When he has gone as far in that direction as he can go and wants to come back, he cannot do so.[9]

Kierkegaard's polemical aim is never fully realized in *Johannes Climacus*, for the narrative breaks off shortly after Climacus begins to doubt without the aid of traditional philosophical theses. As his reference to Climacus's "honest and earnest" character suggests, however, there is more to *Johannes Climacus* than polemic. The young Climacus runs into trouble because he takes the philosophers at their word. This may be naïve, but it should not distract us from the fact that his philosophical disposition is in important respects exemplary. While *Johannes Climacus* does not produce positive "results" in the form of philosophical theses, the contrast between Climacus and those who are reputed to be philosophers allows Kierkegaard to underscore certain essential characteristics of the true philosopher.

---

[8] Evans cautions against taking *Johannes Climacus* as an intellectual biography of the author of *Fragments*. He notes that: 1) *Johannes Climacus* was left unfinished and unpublished; 2) it gives us "only the third-person testimony of Kierkegaard about Climacus"; 3) we have no "real basis" for assuming that its subject is identical with the author Climacus; and 4) it provides a picture of Climacus as "a young innocent who seems far removed from the mature, self-confident, if somewhat enigmatic, author of *Philosophical Fragments*" (Evans 1992, 9). Although 1) reminds us that *Johannes Climacus* may offer only a provisional treatment of its subject, this is not directly relevant to the question at hand. Point 2) seems to miss the mark: Kierkegaard is in fact the omniscient narrator of *Johannes Climacus*, and as such, his testimony is presumably unimpeachable. As for 3), the fact that the subject of *Johannes Climacus* and the author of *Fragments* share the same name at the very least invites us to reflect on their possible similarities. When we do so, I suggest, we shall find that the resemblance between the two is so strong as to leave little doubt that, in spite of the differences of age and maturity Evans notes in point 4), they are one and the same.

[9] *Philosophical Fragments/Johannes Climacus*, 234 (*Pap.* IV B 16). The bracketed words are the Hongs' addition.

Johannes Climacus is introduced by two epigrams. Appropriately, one is from a philosophical treatise and the other is from scripture. Both, however, anticipate a theme that will be developed in the text itself, that of the harmony of speech and deed, or, more broadly, the integrity of life and thought.

The first epigram, from Spinoza's *On the Emendation of the Understanding*, distinguishes "real doubt" from "such doubt as we see exemplified when a man says that he doubts, though his mind does not really hesitate" (115). Spinoza here calls attention to the common difference between what men say and what they do with regard to the matter of doubt. As we shall see directly, Climacus – whose life, as much as is possible for a human being, *is* thinking – takes it for granted that a philosopher's words will match his thoughts.

The second epigram is from 1 Timothy 4:12: "Let no one despise your youth." The rest of 4:12 reads as follows: "... but be an example of the believers in speech, in conduct, in charity, in spirit, in faith, in purity." Although Kierkegaard omits the latter words, they are crucial for understanding the epigram. In this passage, Paul advises Timothy that he can overcome the common prejudice against youth by exemplifying Christian belief in the integrity of his words, actions, thoughts, and feelings. If, as seems likely, Kierkegaard presents Johannes Climacus as an example of the harmony of speech and deed that Socrates calls for, what does it mean that he compares him with "the believers" or "the faithful" (*tōn pistōn*) to whom Paul refers? Climacus, one surmises, is in Kierkegaard's eyes the philosophical counterpart of the faithful Christian. He is "faithful" in the sense that his conduct displays his fidelity to a philosophical ideal of integrity or inner harmony – a harmony of thought and existence, or, in Kierkegaardean terms, of "ideality" and "actuality," that is apparently no longer to be found among philosophers.

That current philosophy is distinguished by the dissonance of speech and deed is made clear in the note to the reader that constitutes the immediate sequel to the epigrams. In this note, Kierkegaard observes that the narrative form of *Johannes Climacus* will scandalize those who suppose "that philosophy has never in all the world been so close as it is now to fulfilling the task of explaining all mysteries." Such readers will deplore Kierkegaard's choice to provide a narrative rather than "hand[ing] up a stone to culminate the system." But those who agree that "philosophy has never been so eccentric as now, never so confused despite all its definitions," will applaud his attempt to "counteract the detestable untruth that characterizes recent philosophy, which differs from older philosophy by having discovered that it is ludicrous to do what a person himself said he would do or had done" (117).

Kierkegaard takes aim here, if not at Hegel himself, then at least at some of his followers.[10] The philosophical validity of Hegelianism as a systematic articulation of reality that explains "all mysteries" (including those of religion) lies in its completeness, yet the system is still incomplete. The system is furthermore supposed to reflect the self-development of Reason, which is conceived as Spirit (*Geist*) – an independently existing, living "subject" rather than an inert "substance" (Hegel 1977, §23, §25). Yet Kierkegaard likens the system to a structure of stone. As such, it is a dead letter – a speech that stands apart from life as it is actually lived. Philosophical ideality thus conflicts with actuality: what the Hegelians say is at odds with what they do. It is this situation that Kierkegaard characterizes as "the detestable untruth" of recent philosophy. The truth of a philosophy, he implies, cannot be estimated independently of the conduct of the philosopher who espouses it. If speculative philosophy is "untrue" it is not because it is objectively inaccurate as a representation of reality (a claim Kierkegaard does not make in *Johannes Climacus*), but because its practitioners act "falsely" in that their deeds do not accord with their words. Conversely, it would seem that a philosophy is true only if one is true to *it*. To be a true philosopher is not merely to espouse philosophical doctrines, but to live a philosophical life. To be true in this sense, Kierkegaard notes, is the mark of "older philosophy."[11]

While it is not immediately evident what "older philosophy" Kierkegaard is thinking of, its practitioners certainly include Plato's Socrates, whose commitment to living up to his own words was evidenced by his willingness to die rather than to cease philosophizing (cf. Plato, *Apology* 37e–38a). In his 1841 dissertation, Kierkegaard notes that "theory and practice in him [Socrates] were in harmony" – a claim he bases on the nature of love as embodied in the character of Socrates in Plato's *Symposium*.[12] In a journal entry from 1849, Kierkegaard observes

---

[10] Stewart 2003, 238–81 takes pains to distinguish Hegel's thought from that of Martensen and his students, whom he sees as the real target of Kierkegaard's polemic in *Johannes Climacus*.

[11] For further discussion of this Kierkegaardean understanding of truth, see Rudd 1993, 54–67. Rudd notes that "truth is a relatedness to reality, an openness to it, which enables reality to become manifest, to find expression" (65). Viewed in this light, " 'truth' can be attributed not only to ideas, but to attitudes: not only to beliefs but to the spirit in which they are held; not only to propositions, but to human lives" (56).

[12] *Concept of Irony*, 51.

that Socrates "had no doctrine, no system and the like, but had one in action."[13] And in an entry from 1854, the year before his death, he writes: "[H]ow true and how Socratic was this Socratic principle: to understand, truly to understand, is to be. For us more ordinary men this divides and becomes twofold: it is one thing to understand and another to be. Socrates is so elevated that he does away with this distinction…"[14]

The Socratic theme of the philosopher's truth or integrity is memorably articulated in Plato's dialogue *Laches,* with which Kierkegaard was familiar.[15] In this dialogue, Socrates discusses the nature of courage with two Athenian generals, Laches and Nicias. Although inexperienced in philosophical conversation, Laches is willing to speak with Socrates because he has had a chance to observe his courage on the battlefield. Laches explains his view of the harmony of *logos* (speech) and *ergon* (deed) as follows:

> I might seem to someone to be a lover of speech and, in turn, a hater of speech [*misologos*]. Whenever I hear a man discussing virtue or some wisdom who is truly a man and worthy of the speeches that he is uttering, I rejoice extraordinarily upon seeing that the speaker and the things said are suitable and harmonious with each other…. When such a one gives voice, therefore, he makes me rejoice and seem to anyone to be a lover of speech… but he who does the contrary of this man pains me, all the more the better he seems to me to speak, and makes me seem to be a hater of speech.[16]

Laches' notion of being worthy of the speeches that one utters is precisely the criterion that Kierkegaard employs in judging the philosophical fashions of his day. Kierkegaard's choice of the narrative form in writing *Johannes Climacus* makes perfect sense in this light. For narrative is the form proper to biography, and Kierkegaard's attention to the life of Climacus is motivated in large part by his desire to defend "truthful" philosophy.

YOUNG CLIMACUS

The Introduction to *Johannes Climacus* describes Climacus's nature and upbringing. Virtually the first thing we learn about him is that he was "ardently in love… with thinking." His soul was moved by a kind of love

[13] JP 4275, 4.212 (X.2 A 229).
[14] JP 4301, 4.222 (XI.1 A 430).
[15] Cf. *Concept of Irony*, 54.
[16] *Laches* 188c–e. I have used the translation of James H. Nichols, Jr., in Pangle 1987, 240–68.

that others might easily have mistaken for the erotic love (*Elskov*) young men feel when they are captivated by a woman's beauty. "It was his delight to begin with a single thought," Kierkegaard writes, "and then, by way of coherent thinking, to climb step by step to a higher one, because to him coherent thinking was a *scala paradisi*." In ascending and then descending the ladder of thought, "his blessedness seemed to him even more glorious than the angels" (118–19).

This description of Climacus is in several ways strongly reminiscent of Socrates. Climacus is moved by a passion for thought that is akin to erotic love. In the Platonic dialogues, Socrates regularly identifies philosophy with erotic love. In the *Republic*, he introduces the philosopher as a lover of wisdom whose longing for the sight of truth resembles the passion of men who love boys in the bloom of youth (474c–75a). In the *Phaedrus*, Socrates presents philosophy as a divine erotic madness that is initially nourished by the sight of physical beauty and that ultimately carries the soul up to the beings above the roof of the cosmos (245b ff.). And in the *Symposium*, Socrates puts in the mouth of the priestess Diotima the teaching that eros, an intermediate divinity (*daimōn*) that links the human and divine spheres and binds together the realm of becoming with that of being, is itself a lover of wisdom (*philosophon*: 204b). Socrates also on more than one occasion uses the image of a ladder, or something like it, to describe the movement of philosophy. In the *Republic*, he employs an image that is structurally equivalent to a ladder – that of the Divided Line – to represent both the levels of reality the soul traverses in its ascent to knowledge of the Ideas and the Good and the powers of the soul that cognize reality (509d–11e). Socrates' account of the erotic, dialectical movement of thought up and down the Line (511b–c) is echoed in Kierkegaard's remark that Climacus found "unparalleled joy" in "the up-and-down and down-and-up of thought" (119). And in the *Symposium*, Diotima compares the philosophical and erotic ascent of the soul from beautiful things to the Beautiful itself to the manner in which one climbs "rising stairs" (211c).

Another link with Socrates is forged by Kierkegaard's description of Climacus's relationship with his father. When he was a boy, his father would play games with him in which he fashioned whole worlds in speech by means of his "omnipotent imagination." These games taught him to relish the "ambrosia" of imaginative discourse. In school, the rules of Greek and Latin grammar also captured Climacus's imagination and opened up new intellectual spaces. But it was in listening to his father, who, like Socrates, was an expert in dialectical debate, that he developed a sense for "the sudden" and "the surprising" in argument. His father would allow his opponent to state his case fully, and then would strike like a shark: "in an instant, everything was turned upside down; the explicable was made inexplicable, the certain doubtful, the opposite was made obvious." This is also a common experience of Socrates' interlocutors, some of whom as a result become dissatisfied with philosophical dialogue.[17] Climacus, however, is affected by his father in the opposite way, for he comes to appreciate more fully the importance of attending to "the step-by-step process of thought" (120–4).

Climacus's life had "a rare continuity," in that "the repose of intuition and the interchange of dialectic .... delighted the child, became the boy's play, the young man's desire" (123). His "whole life was thinking," yet this "by no means weakened his belief and trust in actuality"; "the ideality by which he was nourished was so close to him, everything took place so naturally, that this ideality became his actuality, and in turn he was bound to expect to find ideality in the actuality all around him" (124). Oddly, this expectation was not undermined by his father's depression and excessively low self-estimation. Climacus's "trust in actuality," which had not yet been diminished by much experience of the world, was, if anything, strengthened by the fact that his father did not make his knowledge seem like something glorious, but "knew how to render it as unimportant and valueless as possible" (125). Climacus's inwardness, however, meant that he "was and remained a stranger in the world" (119) – much like Socrates, whose philosophical intensity gave him an air of "strangeness" (*atopia*) that is often remarked upon in the dialogues of Plato.[18] Kierkegaard repeats this phrase almost verbatim a few pages later: Climacus entered the university, took his qualifying exams, turned twenty, "and yet no change took place in him – he was and remained a stranger to the world." He furthermore "never betrayed" his views to others, because "the erotic in him was too deep for that" (123). This suggests that the fidelity and depth of his love of wisdom kept him a stranger to others in that it prevented him from forming worldly attachments that might compromise this love. In this, too, Climacus resembles Socrates, whose unvarying arguments were meant to please his unchanging beloved, philosophy, and who preferred that "the great majority of human beings disagree with me and contradict me than that I, although I am only one

---

[17] Plato, *Euthyphro* 11b, *Meno* 79e–80b.
[18] *Theaetetus* 149a (cited by Climacus in *Fragments*, 10), *Alcibiades I* 106a, *Symposium* 207e; cf. *Phaedrus* 230c.

person, should be out of harmony with myself and contradict myself"
(Plato, *Gorgias* 482a–c).

In sum, Climacus's nature and upbringing combine to form a character that is in certain respects perfectly suited for philosophical reflection. He is a lover of intellectual exercise with a keen sense of logic and dialectical argument, and he is confident about the power of thought to reveal the higher mysteries of life. It is not surprising that *Fragments* and *Postscript* present the protagonist of the Platonic dialogues as the unsurpassable model of philosophical excellence, for the very qualities that make Climacus an eager and adept thinker also establish his close kinship with Socrates.

EVERYTHING MUST BE DOUBTED

Johannes Climacus narrates Climacus's attempt to enter into philosophy, about which he initially makes the most charitable possible assumptions. Climacus regards philosophy as a well-established discipline populated by great minds, but two obstacles impede his entry into this discipline. First, Climacus's exalts the great thinkers of his time to such an extent that he does not dare to read their books: he was "fearful that the major thinkers would smile at him if they heard that he, too, wanted to think, just as fine ladies smile at the lowly maiden if she has the audacity of also wanting to know the bliss of erotic love." Second, his "whole orientation of mind" in any case "made him feel uncomfortable about reading." When he did chance to read a "recent philosophical work," he felt "disappointed and discouraged" because the investigation was invariably incomplete and insufficiently rigorous. When tempted by a title, "he would go to the book gladly and expectantly, but, lo and behold, it would discuss many other things, least of all that which one would have expected." Perhaps not coincidentally, Socrates has a similar experience when he eagerly takes up Anaxagoras's books in the expectation that he will learn how Mind arranges all things for the best, only to discover that the author explains things in purely physical or material terms. In any case, the effect is the same: Climacus, like Socrates, responds to his disappointment by taking counsel with himself and trying to think things through on his own (cf. Plato, *Phaedo* 97b–100a). Climacus's disposition insures that the ideas of others do not imprint themselves upon his soul in the form of an accepted teaching, but rather serve merely as occasions for his own active reflection. Yet he is still charmingly ignorant of the value of this Socratic turn of mind. Although he was all the more happy "the less others had assisted in his thinking," he "truly considered it a great thing to be able, as were the others, to toss about in the multiple thoughts of multiple thinkers" (129–31).

The explicit subject of Climacus's reflections in *Johannes Climacus* is the question of how philosophy begins. This question, which thematizes what Climacus is doing as he himself tries to begin to philosophize, is one upon which he stumbles by "fate." He picks up from the conversations of others "one thesis that came up again and again, was passed from mouth to mouth, was always praised, always venerated" – a thesis that was also usually connected with becoming a philosopher. That thesis, we later learn, is *De omnibus dubitandum est* (Everything must be doubted), an assertion that articulates Descartes' central methodological imperative but that is also propounded by Hegel.[19] That everything must be doubted became "a task" for Climacus's thinking – a task that he would not let go until he had thought it through, "even though it were to cost him his life" (131).

Part One of *Johannes Climacus*, in which Climacus "begins to philoso-phize with the aid of traditional ideas" (127), narrates his largely unsuc-cessful attempt to understand three common philosophical theses: "(1) philosophy begins with doubt; (2) in order to philosophize, one must have doubted; (3) modern philosophy begins with doubt" (132). Clima-cus examines these theses in order to "shed some light on the connection between *de omnibus dubitandum est* and philosophy and thereby more or less brighten his prospects of entering into philosophy" (144). Part Two, which describes Climacus's attempt to think on his own the proposi-tion that everything must be doubted, breaks off after only a few pages. For this reason, and because Climacus's development as an independent thinker is essentially completed by the end of Part One, the second part of *Johannes Climacus* will not concern us in what follows.

In general, Climacus's attempts to approach philosophy by way of doubt establish the imprecise and therefore thoughtless character of the theses propounded by the philosophers. Climacus first wonders, for example, whether the apparently merely historical and contingent claim that modern philosophy begins with doubt (the third thesis) is actually an essential or "eternal" claim about philosophy as such. If beginning with

---

[19] Cf. Hegel 1974, 1.406 (quoted by the Hongs in *Philosophical Fragments/Johannes Climacus*, 311 n. 45): "Philosophy must, generally speaking, begin with a puzzle in order to bring about reflection; everything must be doubted, all presuppositions given up, to reach the truth as created through the Notion [*Begriff*]."

doubt is crucial for philosophy as such, the third thesis collapses into the first, namely, that philosophy itself, and not just *modern* philosophy, begins with doubt. In that case, the obvious implication of the third thesis – that what came before modern philosophy is also philosophy – is misleading (134). The first thesis, on the other hand, seems essential but turns out on closer examination to be historical. For if philosophy begins with doubt, there must be something within philosophy that it doubts, which implies a polemic against an antecedent philosophical principle (144–5). The philosophers, in sum, "confused historical and eternal categories in such a way that when they seemed to be saying something historical they were saying something eternal," and vice versa (134).

Climacus's reflections about the beginning of the quest for wisdom anticipate the inquiry he will undertake in *Fragments*, wherein he supposes that this beginning is provided either by Socratic recollection or by divine revelation. In the former case, the beginning is eternal in that it is in principle accessible to all human beings at all times; in the latter, it is paradoxically both historical (because revelation is a historical event) and eternal (because what is revealed is the truth that stands outside of time). The philosophers' confusion of historical and eternal categories accordingly puts Climacus in mind of Christianity, whose "claim that it had come into the world by a beginning that was simultaneously historical and eternal had caused philosophy much difficulty" (134–5).

As interesting as the foregoing insights may be, only part of what *Johannes Climacus* has to teach us about philosophy is contained in Climacus's reflections. To borrow Laches' terminology, the ergon of the book – its action, or *how* Climacus goes about philosophizing – is at least as significant as its logos or argument. As we have seen, the book exhibits a harmony of action and argument in that its explicit theme, how philosophy begins, is dramatically exhibited in Climacus's own attempt to begin philosophizing. And just as the opening pages of the book counsel us to evaluate the speeches of philosophers in the light of their deeds, *Johannes Climacus* invites us to view its own logos in the light of its ergon. For it is especially in the action of its protagonist that *Johannes Climacus* sheds light on the beginnings of philosophy.

CLIMACUS COMES OF AGE

We are already familiar with the beginnings of philosophy in Climacus's soul. Climacus at one point remembers that "the Greeks taught that philosophy begins with wonder" (145). This turns us in the right direction: it would be more true to say that Climacus begins with wonder than with doubt, for he starts to philosophize by wondering about the meaning of certain philosophical theses pertaining to the role of doubt in philosophizing. But Climacus is capable of philosophical wonder only because he approaches the mysteries of thought with reverence, and his soul is open to these mysteries only because he is already familiar with the rigorous pleasures of thinking. To advance these sorts of considerations is to call attention to the "subjective" beginnings of philosophy, and in particular to raise the question of the character one needs in order to philosophize. This is a question about which Socrates was deeply concerned, as is clear, for example, from his extensive discussion of the philosophic nature in the fifth and sixth books of Plato's *Republic* (474c–504a). It is one that Kierkegaard raises indirectly when he notes Climacus's growing frustration with the philosophers, who "only needed to outline . . . vaguely" matters that were "so hard for him to think" (139). Finally, it is also a question that Climacus himself ultimately confronts explicitly.

At one point, it occurs to Climacus to ask about the relationship of "the single individual" to the thesis that philosophy begins with doubt. His soul "pregnantly ponder[s]" this matter through a kind of internal dialogue (147). The image of psychic pregnancy is Platonic: as Climacus notes in *Fragments* (10–11), Socrates represents himself as a midwife who helps to relieve the souls of young men of their labor pains and to examine the quality of their offspring (*Theaetetus* 148e–51d). The image underscores Kierkegaard's Socratic sense that philosophizing is an active process of deeply personal significance, for those who have given birth have the most intimate attachment to the offspring they bring forth by their intense labor. That Climacus is pregnant also suggests that the problem of how a philosophical thesis can come to have meaning for the individual is a particularly fruitful one. Climacus hears a philosopher who claims that anyone who wishes to give himself to philosophy must embrace the thesis that philosophy begins with doubt, but who says "not a single word concerning how one is to go about doing this [i.e., doubting]" (148). How can the individual actually make use of this thesis?

Climacus next hears that philosophy has three beginnings, "absolute," "objective," and "subjective." The reference is to the Hegelian system. As we have seen, Hegel attempts to provide the subjective beginning of philosophy – defined as "the work of consciousness, by which this elevates itself to thinking or to positing the abstraction" (149) – in the *Phenomenology of Spirit*, which is supposed to furnish the individual with a ladder to the absolute beginning. Only once he has ascended this ladder is the reader in a position to enter the system proper, starting with the objective beginning of "absolutely indeterminate being" in the *Logic*.

Climacus recognizes that the beginning with which he must concern himself is the subjective one: whereas only those who had already become philosophers are in a position to reflect about absolute and objective beginnings, the subjective beginning was "certainly the one with which the individual started from not having been a philosopher to become a philosopher" (149). But this overview of the three beginnings of speculative philosophy raises the additional question of whether "to elevate oneself" and "to doubt" are supposed to be identical. To doubt is to call into question an antecedent philosophical principle, whereas to elevate oneself implies no such negative historical relationship (150). Does philosophy then have three beginnings, or four?

Still more important, Climacus asks himself whether the thesis that philosophy begins with doubt is like a metaphysical or mathematical thesis, to the truth of which the "personality" of the speaker does not matter, or like a religious or ethical thesis. For Climacus, the question concerns what authorizes one to enunciate a thesis. For a mathematical thesis to retain its essential truth, it is necessary only that the person who is supposed to enunciate it have mathematical talent – the proof of which is his ability to enunciate the thesis correctly. Thus, "if a two-year-old child could be taught a mathematical thesis, it would be essentially just as true in the child's mouth as in the mouth of Protagoras." The situation is otherwise with respect to religious and ethical theses:

If we taught a two-year-old child to say these words, 'I believe that there is a God,' or 'Know yourself,' then no one would reflect on these words. Is talent itself, then, not the adequate authority? Do not religious and ethical truths require something else, or another kind of authority, or, rather, what do we actually call authority, for we do, after all, make a distinction between talent and authority? If someone has enough talent to perceive all the implications in such a thesis, enough talent to enunciate it, it does not follow that he himself believes it or that he himself does it, and insofar as this is not the case, he then changes the thesis from a religious to a historical thesis, or from an ethical to a metaphysical thesis. (152–3)

The foregoing insight will prove decisive in Climacus's approach to philosophy and religion in *Fragments* and *Postscript*. Metaphysical theses, including the doctrines of speculative philosophy, are like mathematical theses in that their adequacy is to be judged in objective terms alone. What matters is only what the thesis itself says. Like bearer bonds, they are indifferent to the character of the individual who holds them, and are just as sound in the hands of "a rich man or a poor man . . . a thief or the legitimate owner" (152). The adequacy of a religious or ethical thesis, however, derives not simply from *what* it says, but also from *who* says it. Religious and ethical theses must also be considered subjectively, or from the point of view of ergon as well as logos: such theses become genuinely religious or ethical depending on whether the actions of the speaker are in harmony with his words or at odds with them. One who writes a life of Jesus but does not believe that Jesus is Lord and does not act in accordance with this belief, writes historically but not religiously. One who writes a treatise on the nature of the good but whose beliefs and actions express personal indifference to what he has written, writes metaphysically but not ethically. In each case, the writer may have talent, and may even have adequately articulated the truth from an objective standpoint, but nonetheless lacks the active and passionate commitment that is required to confer religious or ethical authority on what he says.

Climacus observes that the thesis "philosophy begins with doubt" cannot belong to the absolute or objective philosophy, but must rather belong to the subjective beginning of philosophy. It therefore cannot be a metaphysical thesis and cannot make claims to philosophical necessity, "as any thesis in the absolute and objective philosophy does." Climacus concludes that its nature must be that of religious and ethical theses: "the person who was supposed to enunciate it . . . had to have authority" (153). The person who tells another that philosophy begins with doubt is worth listening to only insofar as he has himself begun with doubt. Furthermore, although Climacus does not make the point, that philosophy begins with doubt *must* be an ethical thesis in the mouth of a philosopher: he has chosen philosophy over other pursuits, and cannot consistently regard it as a matter of indifference whether one philosophizes or not.

Climacus is nevertheless ultimately forced to conclude that doubt cannot be the way into philosophy, because that would destroy the continuity of philosophy itself. One who receives from a teacher the thesis that philosophy begins with doubt is thereby obliged to doubt his teacher's teaching. In this way, "he would not have the slightest benefit from his predecessors but would have either the prospect of becoming the absolute monarch in philosophy . . . or the prospect of ending up the same way as his great predecessors" (155). Beginning with doubt either excludes one from the tradition of philosophy or annihilates that tradition; in either case, "this beginning was a beginning that kept one outside of philosophy" (156). Climacus has now encountered for himself what Kierkegaard earlier called "the detestable untruth" of the philosophers, who enunciate a thesis that they themselves fail to act upon.

Having established that doubt lies outside of philosophy (contrary to the first and third theses), Climacus turns finally to the second thesis, namely, that "in order to philosophize, one must have doubted." Perhaps, he reflects, doubt prepares one to begin philosophizing. Up to this point, Climacus had sought to attach himself as a follower to a philosophical teacher, and it occurs to him that this preparation might be just the sort of initiation that a master might demand of a novice. Yet he is now disturbed by the thought that "he who doubts elevates himself above the person from whom he learns" (158). This thought forces him to rethink his initial assumptions about teaching and learning:

When the master positively orders the follower to do something, it certainly is easier for the follower, because then the teacher assumes the responsibility. The follower, however, thereby becomes a less perfect being, one who has his life in another person. But by imposing something negative, the teacher emancipates the follower from himself, makes him just as important as himself. The relation of teacher and follower is indeed cancelled. (158–9)

Climacus regards the emancipation of the follower as "something elevated and noble," and therefore something highly desirable (158). He is now prepared to "do everything" on his own responsibility, "even though I could have wished to remain a minor for yet a while longer, even though I could have wished that there would be someone to give me orders" (159). To do everything on one's own responsibility, however, is to approach philosophy in just the way that Socrates, who claimed not to be a teacher but merely a midwife of others' thoughts, insisted one ought to. Climacus has truly come of age as a Socratic philosopher.

Johannes Climacus poses the question of how philosophy begins. It never explicitly answers this question, because Climacus never succeeds in arriving at an adequate understanding of the various theses he entertains about the beginning of philosophy. I have suggested, however, that the book at least *shows* Climacus beginning to philosophize, even if it does not explain exactly how it is possible for him to do so. There is nevertheless one potential problem with this claim: while it presupposes that Climacus is at some point actually engaging in philosophy, Climacus himself begins by distinguishing between his own thinking and philosophy proper. And although the insincere and contradictory pronouncements of those who are reputed to be philosophers ultimately lead him to bid them "farewell forever" (165), he persists in viewing philosophy as an exalted discipline into which he hopes someday to be worthy of initiation. *Johannes Climacus* thus leaves unanswered the question of how we are to understand philosophy. If Hegelian, speculative thought is not philosophy, what is?

The specification and exploration of the nature of philosophy are tasks that Climacus himself will take up in *Fragments*. As we have seen, however, *Johannes Climacus* encourages us to think about philosophy in the most concrete terms. Like the dialogues of Plato, *Johannes Climacus* focuses our attention on what it means for an individual to live a philosophical *life*. The framework in which Kierkegaard reflects upon philosophy – a framework embraced by Climacus himself, as will be amply evident in his comparison of philosophy and faith in *Fragments* – is a Socratic one, in which the fundamental issue is what constitutes the life most worth living for a human being (cf. *Apology* 38a).

Keeping in mind its essentially Socratic character, it is clear that *Johannes Climacus* is not merely polemical. In a positive vein, it helps us to understand the beginning of philosophy in the specific sense of what is required for genuinely philosophical thinking. Indeed, this is a major unspoken theme of the book. Our reading has brought to light a number of insights in this connection.

First of all, Climacus is moved by an erotic love for thinking that is akin to Socratic eros. Kierkegaard's emphasis on this dimension of Climacus's character suggests that passion is essential for philosophy. Climacus will explicitly insist on this point in *Fragments*. It remains to be seen what relationship this passion, as Climacus understands it, bears to eros as it is presented by Socrates in the Platonic dialogues.

Second, and closely related to the importance of eros, is the notion of philosophical fidelity or "truth" that Kierkegaard develops in *Johannes Climacus*. True philosophy is a harmony of speech and deed that is rooted in passion. To be a philosopher is to live a philosophical life, which entails that, whatever else a philosophy is, it must be livable. A logos that cannot be actualized as ergon in the life of an existing individual is not philosophical at all. So, too, one who loves philosophy so little that his actions are unfaithful to his best understanding does not deserve the name "philosopher."

Finally, *Johannes Climacus* teaches that the adequacy or "essential truth" of certain philosophical theses – specifically, religious and ethical ones – depends upon the "authority" of the person who enunciates them. It is still unclear, however, whether authority in Climacus's sense, involving as it does passionate conviction, moral sincerity, and integrity, is a sufficient condition for philosophical truth or only a necessary one. Does the philosophical disclosure of truth depend only on the intellect and character of the philosopher, or is something more required – perhaps including divine assistance? This is a matter with which Socrates, no less than Climacus, was essentially concerned, and it is one to which we shall return in the following pages.

2

Climacus's Thought-Project

On the title page of *Philosophical Fragments, or A Fragment of Philosophy* we find three questions: "Can a historical point of departure be given for an eternal consciousness; how can such a point of departure be of more than historical interest; can an eternal happiness be built on historical knowledge?" Climacus explores these questions within the framework of a hypothetical understanding of the difference between philosophy and religious faith. This framework is provided by two diametrically opposed assumptions about our access to the truth: (1) We can learn the truth by means of reason alone (the Socratic or philosophical hypothesis), and (2) We can learn the truth only with divine aid (the hypothesis of religious faith). *Fragments* initially appears to be a philosophical deduction, or logical development, of the implications of these assumptions – a deduction that ultimately presents the reader with a choice between Socratic philosophizing and Christianity.

In *Fragments*, however, first appearances often deceive. Climacus's "deduction" unfolds in the space between philosophy and religion, a space that we are at pains to characterize given the direct and fundamental opposition between these two that emerges in the course of the inquiry. On the one hand, Climacus seems to arrive at Christianity through philosophical reasoning about the conditions under which learning can take place, if one assumes that the truth is not accessible by means of the unaided intellect. On the other, he repeatedly insists that the elements of the religious hypothesis are known through divine revelation and cannot be discovered by philosophical thought. Climacus is evidently well aware of the contradiction between what he says and what he seems to be doing. Indeed, he works hard to keep us suspended between the philosophical and religious hypotheses. His use throughout the book of the term "the god" (*Guden*) is a case in point. Climacus never calls Christ by name in *Fragments*, and first mentions Christianity only at the end of the book (109). In *Postscript*, he explains that he wished to avoid an expression whose meaning had been obscured by speculative thought (362–3). Another reason may be Climacus's desire to show that the Christian understanding of God – as opposed to other possible understandings – follows necessarily from the assumption that the truth must be revealed to us.[1] In any case, "the god" is Climacus's term for the divine teacher of the religious hypothesis. Yet it is also a Socratic term, as Climacus reminds us when he calls attention to the seminal role of the god (*ho theos*) in Socrates' philosophical quest (10). In speaking of "the god" Climacus thus manages to adopt an initially neutral stance with respect to the two hypotheses, while at the same time provoking thought about the relationship between Socrates' god and the god of the religious hypothesis.

The ambiguity of Climacus's undertaking will be a major theme in our study of *Fragments*. An overview of the main lines of Climacus's argument will help to flesh out this ambiguity and to orient us as we begin our reading.

Fragments has five main chapters as well as a Preface, an Appendix, an Interlude, and a concluding Moral. While the book has no obvious overarching structure, it is useful to divide it roughly into two halves. In Chapters One through Three, Climacus develops the hypothesis of faith; in Chapters Four and Five, he examines the nature of faith.

Climacus introduces himself in the Preface of *Fragments* as a mere pamphleteer who has nothing to do with systematic thought. Although the tone of the Preface is humorous and ironic, Climacus nevertheless tells us some important things about himself.

In Chapter One, Climacus lays out his "thought-project": he will explore how it is possible for us to learn the truth if we cannot do so

---

[1] Because Climacus presents Christianity as a *consequence* of this assumption, it is misleading to connect the hypothesis of faith from the outset with the theology of the New Testament, as Nielsen 1983 does (see, e.g., 14 and 21). Climacus does not introduce the incarnation until Chapter Two; in general, the religious concepts he introduces in Chapter One, including sin, the moment, and rebirth, apply to the Hebrew Bible as well as the Christian. With regard to rebirth, consider Genesis 17:5 ("And you shall no longer be called Abram, but your name shall be Abraham . . .") and 32:29 ("Said he, 'Your name shall no longer be called Jacob, but Israel, for you have striven with beings divine and human, and have prevailed'").

by means of philosophical inquiry. (What Climacus means by "the truth" is discussed later in this chapter.) Philosophy is rooted in the assumption that every human being already possesses, in the form of reason, the condition for understanding the truth. According to Climacus, the implications of this assumption were worked out to perfection by Socrates. Socrates represented the individual's access to the truth by means of the intellect as the soul's "recollection" of what it once knew. Of course, the precondition for attempting to recollect something is the conviction that it has been forgotten. Socrates therefore concentrated on reminding others that they were actually ignorant of what they thought they knew.

Strictly speaking, Socrates never taught anyone anything; he served only as an occasion for others to learn the truth on their own. That this was the most he could do is suggested by the metaphor of recollection: I can try to remind you of what you have forgotten, but if you are going to remember it, you must do so for yourself. According to Climacus, the philosopher can do no better than to imitate Socrates by aiding others to recover their own independence and responsibility as thoughtful human beings, or, as Climacus puts it, to "give birth to themselves." If anyone presents himself as anything more than an occasion for others to learn on their own – anything more than an intellectual midwife – then he is actually less than a philosopher, because he puts obstacles in the way of their independent advance toward the truth.

Although Climacus treats Socrates with great respect, he devotes most of *Fragments* to developing the implications of the assumption that we humans *lack* the condition for understanding the truth. In that case, he argues, we are "untruth," and cannot learn the truth unless both it and the condition for understanding it are provided by a teacher who must, by definition, be more than human. If we are untruth, we must have become so through our own fault – in other words, through sin. The divine teacher, whom Climacus calls simply "the god," must therefore transform the learner by redeeming him from sin.

In Chapters Two and Three, Climacus continues to spell out the consequences of assuming that we can learn the truth only with divine assistance. The god can transform the learner who is untruth only by means of a revelation that springs from love and takes the form of incarnation. For there is an absolute difference, Climacus maintains, between the unredeemed learner and the god, a difference that the god can successfully "annul" only by revealing himself in human form.

In becoming incarnate, the god becomes absolutely equal to the lowest human being. But the god is then nothing other than the absolutely paradoxical unity of absolute difference and absolute equality. Because this absolute paradox cannot be grasped by the understanding, it must be apprehended by faith, which is a passion that answers to the god's love for the learner. The learner must therefore become a "follower" in order to receive the truth from the god. Socrates, Climacus suggests, has an intimation of the absolute paradox in wrestling with the paradoxes of self-knowledge and self-love. Yet in general, the learner is at least as likely to reject the paradox as to embrace it. In the Appendix that follows Chapter Three, Climacus explores the "offense" that philosophers in particular are inclined to feel in the face of the absolute paradox.

The last four sections of *Fragments* explore the nature of faith and the different sorts of challenges that have confronted those who seek to acquire it. In Chapter Four, Climacus asks whether the follower who is historically contemporary with the incarnate god has any advantage with respect to faith over those who come later. The Interlude that follows is a critical reflection on the claim that speculative thought reveals the necessity of the past – a claim that, in Climacus's view, makes faith impossible and prevents us from grasping its true character. In Chapter Five, Climacus examines the situation of historically noncontemporaneous followers, who can know of the god's incarnation only through the report of others. Because everyone is equally contemporaneous with the eternal god, and because the individual can acquire faith only through an immediate relationship to the god, Climacus concludes that the decision of faith is essentially equally difficult at every period of human history.

The Moral with which *Fragments* concludes appears to be no less ironic than the Preface, for it contains no clear lesson whatsoever. Instead, it paradoxically suggests that Climacus has written *Fragments* with the intention of presenting it to Socrates – even though Socrates would seem to be utterly incapable of evaluating Climacus's thought-project, insofar as the project assumes that he is untruth.

The problem of the ambiguity of Climacus's thought-project may now be stated more clearly. On the philosophical hypothesis, the teacher is no more than the occasion for learning on one's own. The Socratic learner may thus be said to give birth to himself as a knower of the truth. On the hypothesis of faith, however, the learner can be reborn only in the god and through the agency of the god. Out of love for the learner, the god gives the condition for understanding the truth by descending into the world (as in the person of Jesus Christ); apart from this descent, the ascent of the learner to the truth would be impossible. As St. John

Climacus taught, Christ *is* the ladder of divine ascent, and the teacher *is* the teaching.

In sum, there appears to be a gap between philosophy and faith that cannot be bridged insofar as each denies the essential claim of the other. From the perspective of faith, philosophy is simply untruth. It is a prideful and sinful delusion that is not merely "outside" but also "polemical against" the truth (15). In practical terms, then, one cannot think one's way into faith; there is no philosophical ladder that can be climbed to its standpoint. For philosophy, on the other hand, it is faith that is untruth because its basic premise is self-contradictory. Hence there is no ladder of faith by which one could climb up to philosophy. For how could anyone who begins by believing in the absurdity of the absolute paradox ascend by its means to the standpoint of reason?

Although the preceding characterization of the relationship between philosophy and faith is suggested by the text of *Fragments*, it renders Climacus's project incoherent. As we have already noted, Climacus's approach is neither exclusively philosophical nor exclusively religious, and he seems to be open to the claims of *both* philosophy and faith. *Fragments* thus challenges the reader to explain the conditions of its own possibility.

Fortunately, *Fragments* provides the reader with the resources to meet this challenge. In particular, The Moral calls into question the assumption that there can be no common ground between philosophy and faith. In The Moral, Climacus first claims to have gone beyond Socrates, and then goes on to wonder whether what he has articulated is "more true" than the Socratic hypothesis (111). What must be assumed in order for this question to make sense? If the Socratic or philosophical hypothesis is true, it would seem that one cannot go beyond it to anything that is "more true." Climacus furthermore maintains that all attempts within philosophy to go beyond Socrates actually result in falling short of him. If the Socratic hypothesis is not true, however, the radical opposition between philosophy and faith that we have just reviewed would seem to leave no room for its being anything other than what Climacus calls "untruth." Yet the claim that something might be "more true" than the Socratic hypothesis implies that the latter is not simply untruth, insofar as it partakes of truth at least to some degree.

This is not all. Climacus declares in The Moral that, without the conceptions of faith, the consciousness of sin, and the like, "I really would not have dared to present myself for inspection before that ironist who has been admired for millennia, whom I approach with as much ardent enthusiasm as anyone" (111). "That ironist" is obviously Socrates.

Climacus thus imagines that Socrates *himself* could meaningfully entertain the question whether he has articulated something superior to the Socratic hypothesis. Once again, however, this would be impossible if Socrates were simply untruth – in which case he could not possibly judge Climacus's writing – or if the Socratic hypothesis were simply true – in which case it would make no sense to talk of something "more true." Socrates evidently occupies a position in between irremediable ignorance and wisdom, and enjoys an openness to religious as well as philosophical claims, that Climacus's conflicting hypotheses do not seem to allow for.

The relationship between philosophy and religious faith is evidently more complex than meets the eye. If we need divine assistance to learn the truth, it would seem that we cannot ascend to the truth by way of philosophy. But The Moral seems to leave open the possibility that we *can* ascend by way of philosophy, if not to faith itself, then at least to an understanding of the necessity of faith.

It may be helpful to frame the questions raised by The Moral in terms of the image of the ladder. A ladder is composed of both discrete and continuous elements: the steps are discontinuous, yet the ladder as a whole is held together by two continuous, parallel beams. If philosophy and faith are not separated by an unbridgeable abyss, does Climacus envision the possibility that one might lead to the other by means of a series of steps, as if by way of a ladder? If so, is this passage a relatively smooth and continuous one, or are these steps more like leaps? And if philosophy ultimately opens one up to faith, might it even be possible that, under certain conditions, *both* philosophy *and* faith could in their own ways lead to the truth – perhaps because, like the sides of a ladder, they are somehow both parallel and joined to each other?

We may hope to find answers to these questions only by thinking carefully about what Climacus has written. Let us begin with the Preface, in which Climacus implicitly connects his own philosophical endeavor with that of Socrates.

INTRODUCING CLIMACUS

If the title of his book leaves any doubt that Climacus intends to take aim at systematic philosophy, and to employ an ironic tone in doing so, this doubt is removed by the Preface. The Preface is unusual in that it introduces the book's author, but says almost nothing about the book itself. As Climacus makes clear, he is concerned that the reader will misunderstand him, in particular by confusing him with a speculative philosopher.

By posing the question of Climacus's philosophical identity, the Preface opens up the larger question of what it is to be a philosopher. In addressing this question, *Fragments* will speak to one of the central issues of *Johannes Climacus*. Given what the latter book tells us about Climacus's experience with the philosophers, it is not surprising that he takes a polemical approach to this matter when he begins to write in his own name. In alluding more than once in the Preface to the problem of the distinction between sophists and philosophers – a matter that was of special concern to Plato – Climacus presents himself as a kind of latter-day Socrates amid a crowd of sham philosophers. That he does so with self-deprecating irony only strengthens his identification with Socrates.

Climacus begins the Preface by noting that "what is offered here is only a pamphlet... without any claim to becoming part of the scientific-scholarly endeavor in which one acquires legitimacy" (5). In the case of speculative philosophy, as we know from *Johannes Climacus*, authority consists in the talent correctly to enunciate metaphysical theses. The legitimacy of the philosopher, Climacus now suggests, derives from the exercise of authority through participation in the construction of the system, and must accordingly be "acquired." He claims that his "accomplishment" – the pamphlet before us – is "in proportion to my talents" (5); as he points out, however, one could never acquire legitimacy through the production of pamphlets, no matter how many one wrote.[2]

Since Climacus lacks philosophical legitimacy, the question arises why one should pay any attention to him at all. This question can be answered only by an alternative account of philosophical legitimacy and authority, which is precisely what he goes on to offer in *Fragments*. This means that Climacus must, at least for a while, rely on the good faith of the reader. To those who might be inclined to regard this as an unjustifiable imposition, he could reasonably observe that speculative philosophy makes still greater demands on one's good faith. The truth of the system can be assessed only once one has ascended to the level of "objective" and "absolute" philosophy. To say that this is a long and arduous task would be an understatement, given that, in *Johannes Climacus*, Climacus was personally unable to find the ladder that would allow him to make this ascent.

---

[2] This accurately reflects Hegel's own view of the matter. "Unless it is a system, a philosophy is not a scientific production. Unsystematic philosophizing can only be expected to give expression to personal peculiarities of mind.... apart from their interdependence and organic union, the truths of philosophy are valueless." Hegel 1975, 20 (Introduction to the *Encyclopedia Logic*, §14).

Climacus claims to be "a loafer" not only by inclination, but also, as he goes on to explain, for good reasons. *Apragmosunē* (literally "inactivity," and specifically withdrawal from public life) "is a political offense in any age, but especially in a time of ferment"; nonetheless, if "someone's intervention made him guilty of a greater crime simply by giving rise to confusion – would it not be better for him to mind his own business?" (5). The opposite of *apragmosunē* is *polupragmosunē*, "being a busybody." In Plato's *Republic*, for example, Socrates and his companions find that justice is "doing one's own business and not being a busybody" (*mē polupragmonein*: 433a). "Doing one's own business," however, does *not* mean loafing and doing nothing in the public sphere. For Socrates, it means that each citizen will attend to his proper work in the city (cf. 441c–d). In identifying minding one's own business with *apragmosunē*, Climacus thus ignores the middle ground between not participating at all in public life and meddling in the affairs of others. This must be kept in mind as we consider the two contrasting models or patterns of intellectual life Climacus goes on to offer us: perhaps neither of these models captures the middle ground opened up by Socrates.

"It is not given to everyone to have his intellectual pursuits coincide happily with the interests of the public," Climacus writes. "Did not Archimedes sit undisturbed, contemplating his circles while Syracuse was being occupied, and was it not to the Roman soldier who murdered him that he said these beautiful words: *Nolite perturbare circulos meos* [Do not disturb my circles]?" "One who is not that fortunate," he adds, "should look for another prototype [*Forbillede*]" (5–6). The second model he offers is that of Diogenes the Cynic, who rolled his tub around the city during Philip of Macedon's siege of Corinth so that he would not be "the one and only loafer among so many busy people." Climacus adds that such conduct is not sophistical "if Aristotle's definition of sophistry as the art of making money is generally correct," nor can it occasion misunderstanding: just as Diogenes could never be regarded as "the savior and benefactor of the city," no one would "dream of attributing world-historical significance to a pamphlet" (6).

This is puzzling. Is Archimedes "fortunate" in that his intellectual pursuits do in fact coincide with the interests of the public, as the context seems to suggest? Or is he an example of the *apragmosunē* that Climacus recommends in the event that such a happy coincidence is absent? In either case, Climacus evidently regards himself as following the example of Diogenes, whose pointless and clownish behavior contrasts sharply with Archimedes' serious intellectual work. What is more, the contrast between Diogenes and Archimedes seems intended to illustrate the difference between the indolent loafer Climacus and the hard-working speculative philosophers. Mathematics resembles metaphysics, and therefore systematic philosophy, in that the "essential truth" of its theses may be judged independently of any reference to the character of the one who enunciates them (*Johannes Climacus*, 152). And just as Archimedes contemplates circles he has drawn in the sand, speculative philosophers contemplate truth in the form of the circular philosophical system that they have constructed.[3]

If the foregoing suggestion is on the mark, the Archimedes anecdote implies that speculative philosophy is at least as irrelevant to "the interests of the public" as Climacus's pamphlet. For the circumstances of Archimedes' death suggest that the Syracusan mathematician is absurdly detached from the emergency that confronts his community – so much so that his ignorance of the "facts on the ground" causes him to lose his footing in the real world. That something similar is the case with the Hegelians is suggested by Climacus's later comment that devotion to the system ends with one's "flip[ping] over" (6), like a man who attempts to walk on his head. Notwithstanding Climacus's claim to be a mere pamphleteer, it is the Hegelians who – in detaching thought from existence and speech from deed – most obviously possess only a fragment of philosophy.

The buffoonery of Diogenes, however, is clearly not the only alternative to Archimedean abstraction. By intentionally providing us with opposing extremes, Climacus seems to call attention to an unspoken middle ground. Both Syracuse and Corinth were under siege in Climacus's examples. The middle ground would be a serious way of thinking (unlike Diogenes' tub-trundling) that takes account of the "time of ferment" in which we live and the exigencies of our existence (unlike Archimedes' timeless mathematical speculation). It would be a way of "doing one's own business" as a philosopher that does not also ignore one's business as a human being and citizen. The prototype for this middle ground, in which philosophizing and existing do not fall apart from each other, would seem to be Socrates – who according to Cicero was "the first to call philosophy down from the heavens and set her in the cities of men" (*Tusculan Disputations*, 5.4.10–11), and who in the sequel will provide Climacus's model for philosophy per se.

---

[3] "Each of the parts of philosophy is a philosophical whole, a circle rounded and complete in itself.... The whole of philosophy in this way resembles a circle of circles." Hegel 1975, 20 (Introduction to the *Encyclopedia Logic*, §15).

Our reading of *Johannes Climacus* has already given us ample reason to regard Climacus as a Socratic philosopher. In the Preface of *Fragments*, moreover, Climacus explicitly identifies himself with Socrates when he states that "I . . . have no learning to offer . . . 'scarcely enough for the one-drachma course, to say nothing of the big fifty-drachma course' (*Craty-lus*)" (8). Paraphrasing Plato's *Cratylus* 384b–c, Climacus recalls Socrates' claim to be ignorant about the relationship between names and the beings they name because he has been able to attend only the one-drachma course offered by the sophist Prodicus. With similar irony, Climacus says nothing about the prototype of Socrates and claims only to be following the laughable example of Diogenes, a rival of Plato whose cynicism was a kind of decayed Socratism. All the same, he has harsh words for the "higher lunacy" and "irrational exaltation" of speculative philosophy, which he associates with those who are "singularly stupid by nature" (6). He particularly fears being misunderstood by such people, which would "prevent a kind and well-disposed reader from unabashedly looking to see if there is anything in the pamphlet he can use." Being misunderstood in this way would be akin to the situation of the citizens of Fredericia, who read in the newspapers that fire engines raced down their streets, although there is in truth only one fire engine and "not much more than one street." "But of course," Climacus adds, "my pamphlet seems to be least reminiscent of the beating of an alarm drum, and its author least of all inclined to sound an alarm" (7).

Should we take Climacus at his word? Although he claims to mind his own business so as not to give rise to confusion, he implicitly compares the situation in which he and his readers find themselves to that of the besieged cities of Syracuse and Corinth. Such circumstances would seem to require at least the sounding of an alarm, if not also the assistance of a "savior" and "benefactor." Socrates, moreover, regards *himself* as a benefactor of Athens precisely because he responds to what he sees as a moral and intellectual crisis by sounding the alarm. "No greater good has ever come to be for you in the city than my service to the god," he asserts at his trial, "for I go around doing nothing but persuading you, both younger and older, neither to care for your bodies and money more than, nor as vehemently as, how your soul will be as excellent as possible" (*Apology* 30a–b). Nor is it clear that Climacus can avoid causing confusion in any case, especially since he has good reason to think that he may be misunderstood by at least some readers. For all of these reasons, one suspects that Climacus's "pamphlet" may be more – perhaps much more – than it claims to be. While he and his readers do not confront the physical danger of an invading army, could it be that, like the gadfly Socrates, Climacus intends to awaken his readers to a crisis that is moral and intellectual in nature? Could at least part of the danger faced by his likely readers – whom one must suppose to have at least some interest in, and acquaintance with, philosophy – follow from speculative philosophy itself, "the howling madness of the higher lunacy" (6)?[4]

The last paragraph of the Preface connects Climacus still more closely with Socrates. Climacus begins by telling us that one should not seek to know his opinion. If he, in fact, has an opinion (and one should note that, unlike the speculative philosophers, he makes no claim to possess *knowledge*), what it is can be of no interest to anyone else. His next remark clarifies why this should be so. "To have an opinion," he writes, "is to me both too much and too little; it presupposes a security and well-being in existence akin to having a wife and children in this mortal life" (7). This is ironic: Climacus has just given his opinion about having opinions, which presupposes that at least this sort of self-reflective opinion might be of interest to us. Nevertheless, his analogy suggests that opinions, properly speaking, are intimately related to the one who holds them. They reflect the nature and circumstances of one's own existence; unlike bearer bonds, they therefore lose whatever validity they may have when transferred from their rightful owners. I may, and of course do, have opinions that I have received willy-nilly from others, but in that case they are not *my* opinions. This is why Climacus's opinion can be of no interest to us.

What *might* interest us, Climacus implies, is the nature of his existence as a thinker. If his inner life is indeed of interest – presumably because an acquaintance with it, like his opinion about opinions, might contribute something to our self-knowledge – Climacus must be more than a buffoon and a loafer. And so it is: it turns out that "in the world of spirit" he is actually "up and about night and day and yet has no fixed income" (7), which suggests that the "security and well-being in existence" that allows others to have an opinion is purchased at the price of wakefulness. Climacus's reason for telling us this, as well as for warning us against

---

[4] In its combination of humorous playfulness with seriousness, its irony, and its focus on eros, the *Cratylus* is a kind of philosophical satyr-play, a dramatic genre that combined comedy and tragedy (cf. Howland 1998, 162). While the suggestion cannot be developed here, perhaps Climacus's association of himself with the figure of Socrates in the *Cratylus* should be taken as a clue to the essentially satyric nature of his own enterprise. Cf. his observation in *Postscript* that "existence . . . is just as pathos-filled as it is comic" (92).

taking opinions from others, must be to wake us up to our own spiritual indolence. Having an opinion, he explains, makes possible "domestic bliss and civic esteem, the *communio bonorum* [community of goods] and the concordance of joys" (7). In other words, opinions – including the academically well-established ones of the speculative philosophers – not only reflect security and well-being, but also serve it. Climacus, however, introduces us to another, more dangerous kind of service, one that is reminiscent of Socrates' service to the god. "I have trained myself and am training myself always to be able to dance lightly in the service of thought," he writes, "as far as possible to the honor of the god [*Guden*] and for my own enjoyment." "Do I have any reward for this?" he asks. "Do I myself, like the person who serves at the altar, eat of what is set on the altar? . . . That is up to me. The one I serve is good for it." (7).

Not having opinions, it should be noted, does not preclude doing precisely what Climacus does in *Fragments*, namely, formulating hypotheses on the basis of which one can construct ladders of coherent thoughts. Ascending and descending these ladders, we recall, was something in which the young Climacus was always passionately interested (*Johannes Climacus* 118–19). As his service to thought literally consists in philosophical inquiry, dancing must be an image of inquiry. Climacus implicitly contrasts the musical, orderly motion of inquiry with the stability, or, perhaps better, the immobility that makes it possible to have an opinion. This immobility is exemplified by those who resist philosophizing as well as by those who believe that they have already arrived at the goal of wisdom. The former group includes the Platonic character Meno, whose name (*Menōn*) means "standing still," and whose fundamental challenge to the very possibility of philosophical inquiry will serve as Climacus's introduction to Socrates' principle that learning is recollection (see the next section). The latter includes the Hegelians, who claim to achieve wisdom in the form of the system. In emphasizing his devotion to inquiry as such, Climacus, like Socrates, calls attention to the middle ground between ignorance and wisdom wherein human life unfolds and philosophizing takes place (cf. *Symposium* 204b).

Climacus claims to dance in the service of thought, to the honor of the god, and for his own enjoyment. He philosophizes both because it gives him pleasure and out of something like a sense of reverence for the divine. As we shall see, Socrates' philosophical activity has similar roots.[5]

---

[5] See the next section, as well as ch. 3.

But who is "the god" in whose honor Climacus dances? One might initially suppose that this is the god of the hypothesis of religious faith that he develops in *Fragments*, that is, God plain and simple. But Climacus later cites Plato's *Theaetetus* in support of the claim that that "Socrates . . . was a midwife examined by the god himself," and moreover one whom "the god forbade . . . to give birth."[6] "The work he [Socrates] carried out," he adds, "was a divine commission (see Plato's *Apology*)" (10). Perhaps Climacus dances in honor of Socrates' god, the god of the philosophical hypothesis. We may note in this connection that, in *Postscript*, Climacus describes Socrates as "a solo dancer to the honor of the god" (89). To complicate matters further, Climacus concludes the Preface by swearing "by the gods" (*per deos*: 8). Nor does his question whether "I myself, like the person who serves at the altar, eat of what I set on the altar" (7) help to clarify the issue at hand. While Climacus implies that he sets forth his intellectual labor in *Fragments* as a sacrificial feast, he leaves us in the dark about whose altar he serves, and, if he himself is nourished by this feast, of which portion(s) – the philosophical or the religious – he partakes.

Climacus intentionally leaves to the reader the most fundamental judgments about what he has written. He makes it clear that we cannot rely on him to do our thinking: he dances alone, as he says, because "every human being is too heavy for me." His own dancing partner is "the thought of death," a thought that underscores his sense of the urgency of philosophical inquiry as a personal response to human finitude.[7] He is nothing more than a midwife of thoughts: like Socrates, he has "no learning to offer" the reader (8), nor, one presumes, would his understanding that we are responsible for our own opinions allow him to offer his learning if he did have any. One thing is clear: at issue in *Fragments* is not merely thinking, but living a philosophical life. For Climacus, as for Socrates, living and thinking are one. "The only thing I am able to do for thought," he writes, is to "stake my own life"; "all I have is my life, which I promptly stake every time a difficulty appears" (8). So, too, when at the end of the book Climacus imagines coming before Socrates, he envisions presenting for Socrates' "inspection" not *Fragments* – as one might have expected – but "myself" (111).

---

[6] Cf. *Theaetetus* 150c.

[7] Cf. Evans 1992, 25: "Bringing death into the picture not only personalizes the issue, but makes it clear that disinterested contemplation may not be appropriate. . . . Climacus will not take any other person as 'dancing partner,' neither as objective authority nor devoted disciple. Since no one else can die for me, no one else can decide the meaning of life for me either."

THE THOUGHT-PROJECT

The Philosophical Hypothesis

"Can the truth be learned? With this question we shall begin" (9). The first line of the first chapter of *Fragments* announces that the present inquiry concerns the subjective beginning of philosophy, now understood not as a specific academic discipline (as in *Johannes Climacus*) but simply as the attempt to learn the truth. Yet the thoughtful reader begins with more questions than the one Climacus states.

First, it is not immediately clear how Climacus's question serves as a beginning. The question suggests that *Fragments* will ask whether the truth can be learned, but what follows is instead a hypothetical inquiry into what must be the case if one assumes that the truth *can* be learned.

Second, what sort of truth does Climacus have in mind? As he never explicitly addresses this question, one must infer the answer from the context. In the first part of Chapter One, labeled "A.," Climacus explores the Socratic hypothesis about learning the truth. In this context, "the truth" is the kind of truth with which Socrates was concerned. The question about truth was, Climacus writes, "a Socratic question or became that by way of the Socratic question whether virtue can be taught – for virtue in turn was defined as insight" (9). In the Platonic dialogues, Socrates seeks the truth about virtue, about how we should live and what will make our souls as excellent as possible, and therefore the truth essentially embraces self-knowledge as well as knowledge of the good. Needless to say, this kind of truth will be useless to anyone who is not willing to conduct his life in accordance with it. The inquiry in *Fragments* relies on this Socratic notion of the truth, as it defines, at least in general terms, the goal of learning with which Climacus is concerned throughout.[8]

The "Socratic-Platonic" context within which Climacus initially raises the question of the truth helps to explain why he does not entertain the possibility that the truth is unattainable.[9] To suppose that the truth is

---

[8] Rudd 2000/2002 remarks that "the 'Truth' which Climacus is concerned with is essential, eternal Truth; the truth about the ultimate nature of reality, about the Good.... The assumption he does make is that there is an Ultimate or Absolute, and that the Good for humans consists in bringing themselves into an appropriate relation with it" (2.258). Cf. Roberts 1986, 18: "The 'truth' in question here is an ethical and religious one, the fulfillment of the pupil's being as human. So that if the pupil does not have this truth he is in a sense not himself." Evans 1992, 28 follows a similar line.

[9] The expression "Socratic-Platonic" is the Hongs': *Philosophical Fragments/Johannes Climacus*, 278 n. 13.

unattainable is to embrace the unexamined life, and for Socrates this is simply not a viable option for a human being (cf. *Apology* 38a). Climacus seems to agree with Socrates that a distinctively human life, a life worth living, requires the presupposition that – one way or another – we can learn the truth.

There is one additional assumption, however, that we require in order meaningfully to compare the philosophical hypothesis about learning the truth with the religious hypothesis. This assumption is that the soul is immortal – not in the sense that it has existed and will exist for all time, but in the sense that its essential being lies somehow outside of time, in eternity. For Socrates, Climacus writes, "my *eternal* happiness . . . is given retrogressively in the possession of the truth that I had from the beginning without knowing it" (12, emphasis added). That learning the truth confers happiness is either a foundational assumption of the Socratic enterprise, or may be directly inferred from the premises that happiness consists in virtue and that being in possession of the truth is a necessary and sufficient condition for virtue. That learning the truth confers *eternal* happiness requires the additional assumption that the soul is immortal in the sense specified previously.

Note that Climacus does not bother to articulate the assumptions underlying the assertion that learning the truth confers eternal happiness. He simply takes it for granted that Socrates endorses these assumptions. We may conclude that *Fragments* is not a philological work, which is to say that Climacus is not concerned to establish that his interpretation of Socrates is textually well founded. A philosophical point in favor of this procedure is that it emphasizes ideas rather than their pedigree, and is consistent with Climacus's view that no one should hold an opinion simply because it happens to be held by another. Yet *Fragments* is also not a philosophical work in the traditional sense. As commentators have noted, Climacus pays little attention to constructing sound arguments.[10] This is presumably because philosophical argument cannot establish what he considers to be the most important theses, such as the soul's immortality or the existence of God (cf. 39–44). Rather, Climacus is interested in thinking through certain ideas – ideas that pertain to learning the truth and achieving eternal happiness, and that, in the first instance, he has come to associate with Socrates through reading Plato. There is, however, no philological or philosophical necessity that we accept *any* of these ideas. We shall return to this point in due course.

[10] Rudd 2000/2002 (see esp. 2.261–2); Roberts 1986, 49–60.

According to Climacus, a paradox articulated by Meno in Plato's dialogue of the same name (*Meno* 80d) prompts Socrates to formulate the philosophical hypothesis about learning the truth. Climacus paraphrases Meno's paradox, which concerns how we are to seek the truth, as follows: "A person cannot possibly seek what he knows, and, just as impossibly, he cannot seek what he does not know, for what he knows he cannot seek, since he knows it, and what he does not know he cannot seek, because, after all, he does not even know what he is supposed to seek." In the face of this challenge, Socrates advances the principle "that all learning and seeking are but recollecting." By this means, he manages to go between the horns of Meno's dilemma. We stand in the middle ground between ignorance and wisdom: we neither know the truth (because we have temporarily forgotten it) nor are we simply ignorant of it (because we can call it to mind once again). It follows that all learning takes place through one's independent efforts to bring the truth to mind. "The ignorant person merely needs to be reminded in order, by himself, to call to mind what he knows," for "the truth is not introduced into him but was in him" (9). A teacher is accordingly nothing other than an occasion for one to learn by one's own efforts; "nor is the teacher anything more, and if he gives of himself and his erudition in any other way, he does not give but takes away" (11).

The principle that learning is recollection is also, Climacus claims, the basis for a Socratic "demonstration" of the immortality of the soul (9–10). In the *Meno*, however, Socrates' sole support for the claim that the soul is never destroyed (although it has often died and been reborn), and that it has learned all things prior to this mortal life, consists in an appeal to the authority of certain "wise" priests and priestesses as well as certain "divine" poets (81a–b). Nor does Socrates insist on the truth of what he has heard from these priests and poets (86b–c). These features of the text cast doubt on whether we should understand the principle of recollection literally. What is more, immortality in the sense of sempiternity or never-ending duration – the sense in which Socrates employs the term in speaking of the soul with Meno – cannot without argument be identified with immortality in the sense of eternity. The same point can be made with respect to Socrates' inquiry into the question of the soul's immortality in Plato's *Phaedo*, an inquiry that has immediate relevance because it takes place on the day Socrates dies.

Socrates' alleged demonstrations of immortality in the Platonic dialogues are evidently of little interest to Climacus. In fact, he ultimately acknowledges that *no* philosophical demonstration of the soul's immortality is possible, and that what matters is Socrates' passionate fidelity, as expressed in the conduct of his life, to this uncertain thesis.[11] More important, Climacus suggests that what underlies Socrates' discussion of the soul's immortality is an intuition that the soul's essential being resides in eternity. The connection Socrates draws between immortality and recollection seems to reflect this intuition. In both the *Meno* and the *Phaedo*, Socrates ties the possibility of philosophy to the immortality of the soul. It is in the *Phaedo*, however, that his reason for doing so becomes fully apparent. Immortality entails that the soul can exist in separation from the body. According to Socrates, the perturbations of the body keep the soul from grasping the things that truly are, including the Just itself, the Beautiful, and the Good – for these are known only to one who, "using pure thought [*dianoia*] by itself, tries to track down each of the beings pure and by itself" (66a). In other words, the soul, which exists in time at least insofar as it is conjoined with a body, nevertheless has a natural affinity for the eternal truth, the longed-for union with which it can fully realize only after death liberates it from the body (cf. 66e–67a). Socrates' talk of the immortality of the soul thus expresses, to adopt the language of the guiding questions of *Fragments*, the latent eternality of consciousness. For Socrates – and as we shall see, for Climacus as well – an existing human being is a paradoxical combination of the temporal and the eternal.[12]

The key to Socrates' pedagogy as well as to his entire ethical orientation is the principle that learning is recollection. It follows from this principle that the teacher, like "any point of departure in time," is no more than "something accidental, a vanishing point, an occasion" (11). Socrates accordingly has companions, but no students, and he engages in dialogue, but does not lecture. He does not attempt to fill the minds of

---

[11] *Postscript*, 173–4. Socrates poses the question of immortality hypothetically: "he stakes his whole life on this 'if'; he dares to die, and with the passion of the infinite he has so ordered his life that it might be acceptable – *if* there is an immortality" (*Postscript*, 201, emphasis in original).

[12] In some dialogues Plato makes explicit the eternity of the beings or Ideas, while in others he merely suggests it. The divine craftsman of the *Timaeus* fashions time as an image of eternity in the course of constructing the cosmos after the model of unchanging being (38b–c). In the *Phaedrus*, Socrates assigns the things that truly are to the region beyond the roof of the rotating heaven. The beings thus seem to stand outside of time. Cf. *Phaedrus* 247c–e with the remark of Griswold 1986, 89: "These Beings are pictured as immutable, stable in every way, eternal, soulless, and separate from the spheres of genesis, motion, and life (hence they are 'above the heavens' and 'outside' the cosmos cared for by the soul)."

others with his own thoughts, for to do so would be to impede their learning by claiming an intellectual authority that no human being legitimately possesses in relation to anyone else. Instead of providing answers, he asks questions, "for the ultimate idea in all questioning is that the person asked must himself possess the truth and acquire it by himself" (13).

Socrates' actions express absolute fidelity to his fundamental insight. With "wonderful consistency," Climacus writes, "Socrates remained true to himself," persisting in being merely an intellectual midwife "because he perceived that this relation is the highest relation a human being can have to another." "And in that," Climacus adds,

> he is indeed forever right, for even if a divine point of departure is ever given, this remains the true relation between one human being and another, if one reflects upon the absolute and does not dally with the accidental but with all one's heart renounces understanding the half-measures that seem to be the inclination of men and the secret of the system. (10)

Because he is unfailingly guided by his insight that the single individual is the one and only authority with respect to the truth, Socrates remains true both to himself and to others. Especially commendable is the "rare magnanimity" that led him to "philosophiz[e] just as absolutely with whomever he spoke" – "rare in our day...when every second person is an authority," even though "no human being has ever truly been an authority or has benefited anyone else by being that or has ever really managed successfully to carry his dependent along" (11–12).

For Climacus, Socrates' exemplary magnanimity is rooted in a self-knowledge that is accessible "if one reflects upon the absolute." Socrates is remarkable because he truly understands what it is to be human: "in the Socratic view, every human being is himself the midpoint, and the whole world focuses only on him because his self-knowledge is God-knowledge." No less remarkably, Socrates adheres to this understanding absolutely, forsaking "half-thoughts...higgling and haggling...[and] claiming and disclaiming," with all of which "one does not go beyond Socrates...but simply remains in empty talk" (11). Indeed, the essential nature of philosophy is exemplified in Socrates' grasp of the principle of recollection and its implications. Climacus maintains that there is no way to go beyond Socrates within the domain of philosophy, "even though we use many and strange words, even though in our failure to understand ourselves we suppose we have gone beyond that simple wise man" (19). It is true that Socrates did not have a system, but the claim that objective authority resides in the system betrays a misunderstanding of the fundamental presupposition of philosophy. This presupposition is summed up in the statement that "every human being is himself the midpoint," which must be understood both ethically and intellectually: a philosophical truth that I cannot come to possess through my own efforts, and in accordance with which I cannot live, is not philosophical at all. Speculative philosophy, as *Johannes Climacus* has already shown, fails on both accounts.

As we have seen, *Fragments* begins with three questions about the acquisition of an eternal consciousness and eternal happiness. It is now reasonably clear how the Socratic or philosophical hypothesis about learning responds to these orienting questions. The principle that learning is recollection implies that there is a historical point of departure for an eternal consciousness (a consciousness in possession of the eternal truth), but that this point of departure has merely historical interest. It is important to emphasize that time has no ultimate significance on the philosophical hypothesis: I "rest" in the truth that emerges from within me, which is to say that I rest in eternity. From the vantage point of eternity, I could not find, "even if I were to look for it," the moment in which I discovered that the truth is in me, for in eternity "there is no Here and no There but only an *ubique et nusquam* [everywhere and nowhere]" (13). Here Climacus has occasion to criticize Plato from the perspective of Plato's Socrates. Understood Socratically, Plato's "beautiful" and enthusiastic devotion to his friend and teacher Socrates is an "illusion" and "a muddiness of the mind": the fact that I have learned from Socrates or Prodicus or a maidservant, or "that the teaching of Socrates or of Prodicus was this or that," cannot "have anything but historical interest for me, because the truth in which I rest was in me and emerged from me" (12).

The assertion that self-knowledge is God-knowledge is nevertheless difficult and deeply ambiguous. One way to interpret this statement is to understand God-knowledge as the knowledge of eternal being and truth. To know oneself is to know what is eternal, both because the soul is itself somehow eternal (although it also exists in time) and because the truth that is in the soul and available for recollection is eternal truth. One could state the same point in terms of transcendence and immanence. The eternal, unchanging truth transcends the instability and evanescence of mortal existence, but the insight that makes philosophy possible is that the truth is also immanent or latently present within our souls, and thus available for recollection. Philosophy is the attempt to ascend to transcendent being and truth by bringing to consciousness, and thinking through, this immanence.

There is, however, another (and indeed opposite) sense in which, for Socrates at least, self-knowledge may be God-knowledge. At the same time as he sets forth the Socratic view that the individual must both possesses and acquire the truth by himself, Climacus calls attention to the important role of "the god" in Socratic philosophizing. He notes that Socrates "was a midwife examined by the god himself" who "forbade him to give birth" (and here he quotes from Plato's *Theaetetus*, 150c), and he adds that "the work he [Socrates] carried out was a divine commission (see Plato's *Apology*)" (10). Is the god who examines Socrates or the god who commissions his examination of others (assuming, as Climacus seems to, that these are one and the same) a mere occasion for Socrates to learn the truth on his own, or something more? In the *Apology*, the dramatic setting of which is Socrates' public trial, Socrates traces the origin of his philosophical activity to the oracle of the god at Delphi. He tells the jury that he was prompted to interrogate his fellow Athenians by the oracle's affirmation that no one was wiser than he (21a ff.). But does the oracle teach Socrates something that he could not have learned on his own because it was not immanent in his soul? If so, Socrates' reliance on the god would call into question the representation of philosophy as recollection. In that case, Socrates' self-knowledge would be God-knowledge in the sense that at least part of the truth, and thus of what he needs to know in order to achieve self-knowledge, is not accessible through his own efforts but must be *given* to him by the god.

Climacus says nothing about the role of the god in Socrates' philosophical quest until Chapter Three, and even there his remarks are largely suggestive. Yet his immediate acknowledgment of the importance of the god makes his presentation of Socrates and the philosophical hypothesis no less ambiguous that his self-presentation in the Preface. In a word, Climacus makes it clear the Socratic hypothesis about learning the truth – a hypothesis that is intended to express the guiding presupposition of philosophy as such – may in fact be inadequate as a characterization of Socrates' *own* philosophical activity. In implicitly calling attention to this problem, Climacus also indicates that he expects his readers to reflect on Plato's characterization of Socrates in the dialogues.

Whether the oracle of the god is indeed more than a mere occasion for Socrates to learn the truth can only be determined by an examination of the *Apology*. If we find that the god acts as more than an occasion, we will have to rethink Climacus's distinction between the philosophical and religious hypotheses. What role would faith then play in philosophy, and how might we characterize this faith? We shall investigate these issues in due course.[13] We now turn to Climacus's characterization of the hypothesis of religious faith.

The Religious Hypothesis

On the philosophical hypothesis, "the temporal point of departure is a nothing, because in the same moment I discover that I have known the truth from eternity without knowing it, in the same instant that moment is hidden in the eternal" (13). Climacus now entertains a different presupposition about the moment when I awaken to my eternal consciousness. Suppose this moment were to have "such decisive significance that for no moment will I be able to forget it, neither in time nor in eternity, because the eternal, previously nonexistent, came into existence in that moment": how would we then characterize the process of learning the truth (13)? This question guides Climacus in developing the hypothesis of religious faith.

The principle of recollection maintains that "basically every human being possesses the truth," in which case the moment of awakening (which Climacus refers to henceforth simply as "the moment") is in itself insignificant. If the moment is to have "decisive significance," however, then the transcendent truth cannot also have been immanent in our souls prior to that moment: "the seeker up until that moment must not have possessed the truth, not even in the form of ignorance ... indeed, he must not even be a seeker" (13). Climacus clarifies this statement when he later says that "the condition for understanding the truth is like being able to ask about it – the condition and the question contain the conditioned and the answer" (14). This is a crucial presupposition of Socratic inquiry, which supposes that someone who has been reminded of his own ignorance will be able to ask meaningful questions and thereby advance toward knowledge. A person who could not do this even if he *did* acknowledge his own ignorance "has to be defined as being outside the truth (not coming toward it like a proselyte, but going away from it), or as untruth" (13).

Meno's paradox, as we have seen, denies that we possess the condition for learning the truth. Whether Socrates' principle of recollection is to be understood literally or metaphorically, it answers this paradox by affirming our possession of the condition for learning the truth and articulating its nature. One who is untruth, however, lacks this condition. On the religious hypothesis, then, the principle of recollection cannot

[13] See ch. 3.

be used to escape Meno's paradox. How is one who is untruth to be reminded of what he has never known, and what would be the use in reminding him?

Climacus begins to answer the latter question by considering what sort of teacher would be required. As on the philosophical hypothesis, the teacher is in the first place an occasion for recollection. Yet the teacher does not help the learner to recollect that he actually does know the truth. Rather, he helps the learner to call to mind his untruth. Climacus insists that the learner must discover his untruth on his own. Here, "the Socratic principle applies... I can discover my own untruth only by myself, because only when *I* discover it is it discovered, not before, even though the whole world knew it" (emphasis in original). But while the philosophical and religious hypotheses agree that understanding of any sort requires the learner's active effort, they differ with respect to the question of how such effort can result in the acquisition of the truth. Note that the consciousness that one is untruth is not in itself an understanding of the truth; on the contrary, it is a recognition that one is "definitely excluded from the truth." On the religious hypothesis, the teacher must therefore bring to the learner the truth as well as the condition for understanding it (which in any case contains the truth, inasmuch as "the condition and the question contain the conditioned and the answer"). This means that the teacher must be more than a mere occasion for the learner to discover the truth on his own. Since no learning can take place if the learner lacks the condition, the teacher, "before beginning to teach, must transform, not reform, the learner." As no human being is capable of doing this, "it must be done by the god himself" (14–15).

Climacus's religious hypothesis allows him to define key religious concepts, all of which are already familiar from scripture, in terms of teaching and learning. If the learner lacks the condition for learning the truth, Climacus asserts, he must have initially possessed it and then lost it: God (here the word is not *Guden*, "the god," but *Gud*) would not have created him without it, for otherwise he would have been created as an animal rather than a human being.[14] But "the god" could not have deprived him of this condition, for this would be a contradiction, nor could he have lost it by accident, as the condition is essential to his God-given nature.[15]

[14] Once again, Climacus, like Socrates, rejects without argument the supposition that human beings are simply not meant to understand the truth.

[15] Cf. Roberts 1986, 19: this point may be compared to Socrates' notion that "it is inconceivable that one person should be caused by another to lose his virtue." As Evans 1992 notes, Climacus "is rejecting the coherence of what some philosophers have called 'moral luck'" (36).

He must thus have lost the condition "due to himself"; "he himself has forfeited and is forfeiting the condition," which reiterates that he is not merely outside the truth but polemical against it. Climacus calls *sin* the state of being untruth through one's own fault, and it is of sin that the teacher, who is the god himself, "prompts the learner to be reminded." Because he is excluded from the truth through his own free action, he is "unfree" and "bound." Like the forgetfulness that Socratic recollection hopes to remedy, sin is a falling away from truth, but it is curiously not one that the individual can remedy on his own (15).[16]

Climacus illustrates his understanding of sin by the analogy of a child who has enough money to buy either "a good book" or "one toy." Having chosen to buy the toy, he can no longer exchange it for the book. "And so it was also once, when man could buy freedom and unfreedom for the same price, and this price was the free choice of the soul and the surrender of the choice" (note on 16). Because sin involves choice, it springs from the will; the choice of sin, however, entails a corruption of the will and the intellect that makes subsequent free choice impossible.[17] Climacus's implicit comparison of sin with the child's choice of a mere toy as opposed to a good book sheds further light on the matter. A good book (does Climacus have in mind *the* Good Book?) contains the possibility of expanding one's understanding and thereby of growing and maturing; the sinner forfeits this possibility, however, by childishly choosing immediate self-satisfaction.

In the moment of awakening to the truth the learner liberates himself from the bondage of sin. He cannot free himself by an act of will, however, because in that case the moment would not gain decisive significance (15–16). The teacher who sets him free should thus be called a *savior* and a *deliverer*, for he saves the learner from himself and delivers him from his self-imprisonment. He is a *reconciler*, for he "takes away the wrath that lay over" the guilt that the learner incurred by forfeiting the condition with which he was created. He is also a *judge*, for he holds to an accounting the learner to whom he has entrusted the condition – something the teacher cannot do on the philosophical hypothesis, for, although he can evaluate

[16] Rudd 2000/2002 notes, however, that we cannot take at face value the religious hypothesis' "apparent claim that we have simply lost all contact with the Truth.... Being 'outside the Truth' must be interpreted as 'being polemical against the Truth'...and one can hardly polemicise against something if one is wholly unaware of it" (2.264–5).

[17] The phenomenon of losing one's freedom to choose by making bad choices was not unknown to the ancient Greeks, although they lacked the Christian conception of sin. Cf. Aristotle, *Nicomachean Ethics* 1114a3–21.

the learner's progress, "he must be Socratic enough to perceive that he cannot give the learner what is essential" (17–18).

As for the learner, he becomes a "follower" in relation to the divine teacher, and he becomes a *new* person when he turns from untruth to truth. Since being in untruth means that "he was continually in the process of departing from the truth," this turning is *conversion*. His sorrow over his former state is *repentance*, and the change in him, which is like the transition from "not to be" to "to be" that is experienced in birth, is *rebirth*. Finally, the unique and unforgettable moment in which he receives the condition and the truth is "short," "temporal," and "passing," yet it is "decisive" and "filled with the eternal." Its special name is *the fullness of time* – an allusion to Galatians 4:4, "When the fullness of time was come God sent forth his son" (18–19).[18]

In concluding the first chapter of *Fragments*, Climacus imagines that someone might accuse him of not having invented his thought-project. He is quite ready to admit the justice of this accusation. As we have seen, philosophy is essentially nothing other than, and can never be anything other than, Socratic philosophizing. For this reason, the claim of the speculative philosophers (among others) to go beyond Socrates is effectively an admission of their lack of self-knowledge. Something similar obtains in the case of faith. According to St. John Climacus, the ladder to the Absolute is nothing other than Jesus Christ, for ascent to God takes place through the imitation of Christ.[19] St. John Climacus is thus in the deepest sense not the author of *The Ladder of Divine Ascent*: everything he writes in his book was taught to him by Christ. For his part, Kierkegaard's Climacus wonders how the religious hypothesis could have occurred to any human being. The notion of being reborn, he maintains, cannot have occurred to anyone who has not already been reborn, just as, by analogy, the notion of birth can only occur to one who has already been born (20). But just as one who has been born did not invent birth, so, too, one who becomes aware of his rebirth in the moment did not invent the moment (21). Hence no human being, much less Climacus himself, has invented the religious hypothesis. "This oddity," Climacus writes, "enthralls me exceedingly, for it tests the correctness of the hypothesis and demonstrates it" (22). If Socrates once and for all

[18] Note, however, that "the moment" is used in several ways in *Fragments*. It may designate the historical time of the divine teacher's appearance, the time at which the learner receives the condition, or the divine teacher himself (Roberts 1986, 17 n. 2).

[19] Climacus 1982, 74.

establishes the philosophical hypothesis, it is God who establishes that of faith.[20]

Has Climacus refuted the philosophical hypothesis? Climacus claims that we have learned through divine revelation that we need divine revelation in order to learn the truth, yet he must be aware that his alleged demonstration has fatal flaws. As Anthony Rudd observes, "it would be hard to prove that any particular idea, however strange, was too strange for a human being to have invented"; in fact, Climacus himself has "shown how we might have invented Christianity under our own steam, precisely by trying the experiment of negating all the normal assumptions of our thinking."[21] Climacus's "demonstration" notwithstanding, we remain in the no-man's land between the philosophical hypothesis, which views the ostensible revelations of God precisely as unself-conscious human inventions, and the religious hypothesis, which regards philosophy as arrogant blindness.

Must we view Climacus's claim that he is the author of neither the philosophical nor the religious hypothesis as a rhetorical gesture?[22] Climacus clearly intends to provoke the speculative philosophers, who claim to go beyond faith as well as beyond Socrates. Hegel, of course, did no see himself as a mere imitator: according to his *Phenomenology*, the story of the incarnation of God is actually an imitation, in the form of religious imagination or "picture-thinking," of the activity of Spirit or self-conscious Reason (Hegel 1977, §788). If Hegel goes beyond faith, it is only insofar as he deconstructs it by translating its mysteries into the conceptual language of philosophy.[23] The first chapter of *Fragments*, however, suggests

---

[20] Evans 1992 notices that "even this argument on Climacus' part may be part of his borrowing, since it so clearly reflects the traditional Christian claim that Christianity is rooted in a divine revelation, not in human philosophizing" (17).

[21] Rudd 2000/2002, 2.260, 261. Cf. Roberts 1986, 21–3.

[22] Rudd 2000/2002 sees this claim as part of a broad and indirect strategy to show his readers that Christianity cannot in fact be approached as a "hypothesis" or a "set of propositions" because it is "an existence communication [i.e., pertaining to the transformation of one's way of life] and not a body of doctrine" (2.273; cf. 2.259–62). The same insight, I would suggest, applies to *Fragments'* presentation of Socratic philosophizing. Nielsen 1983 also discerns a rhetorical dimension in the alleged demonstration: "Climacus practices the art of noticing, of being struck by, the all-too-familiar. When he lets himself be struck, the result is not instant religiousness but a freshening of wonder at seeing something familiar for the first time, and the proof here is an expression of that wonder" (25).

[23] Cf. Hegel 1974, 1.76–9: "Philosophy thinks and conceives of that which Religion represents as the object of consciousness, whether it is as the work of the imagination or as existent facts in history. . . . Philosophy permits full justice to be done to the content

that speculative philosophy is an unself-conscious and therefore inferior imitation of *both* Socratic philosophizing *and* Christian faith. Yet
Climacus's intention is not simply polemical. He evidently strives to imitate Socrates' magnanimity by reminding the speculative philosophers
of their lack of self-knowledge. In so doing, he offers them an occasion
to climb down from the "empty talk" and presumption of philosophical
abstraction and, in the same motion, to ascend to the level of Socratic
ignorance. For inasmuch as Socratic ignorance is the philosophical analogue of spiritual *kenōsis* or self-emptying, *Fragments* is a ladder in the
Benedictine tradition – one that is ascended only by the downward movement of humility.

Climacus's initial presentation of the philosophical and religious
hypotheses suggests that they are fundamentally incompatible and
unbridgeable. On both hypotheses, the teacher reminds the learner that
he is ignorant of the truth. As Climacus notes, however, this is the "one
and only analogy" between the two (14). On the philosophical hypothesis, the learner who discovers ignorance in himself can also find the truth
within himself, so that ideally the teacher delivers the learner *to* himself.
On the religious hypothesis, however, the learner can find only untruth
within himself, so that the task of the teacher is to deliver the learner *from*
himself. Climacus expresses the contrast as follows:

Just as the person who by Socratic midwifery gave birth to himself and in so
doing forgot everything else in the world and in a more profound sense owed
no human being anything, so also the one who is born again owes no human
being anything, but owes the divine teacher everything. And just as the other
one, because of himself, forgot the whole world, so he in turn, because of this
teacher, must forget himself. (19)

The pedagogy of the Socratic midwife is thus directly at odds with that of
the divine teacher. Viewed from the perspective of the religious hypothesis, the philosophical midwife, who is himself untruth, further enslaves
the learner by encouraging a false independence of thought. Viewed
from the perspective of the philosophical hypothesis, on the other hand,
the religious notion of a divine teacher encourages a slavish dependence

of Religion through the speculative Notion [*Begriff*], which is thought itself. . . . Thus
Religion has a content in common with Philosophy, the forms alone being different;
and the only essential point is that the form of the Notion should be so far perfected as
to be able to grasp the content of Religion. The Truth is just that which has been called
the mysteries of Religion."

on illegitimate authority. The truth of either hypothesis is the untruth of the other.

Nor does it seem to be possible to think one's way out of the philosophical hypothesis and into the religious hypothesis, or, conversely, to come back to Socratic recollection once one has embraced the decisive significance of the moment. On the religious hypothesis, one sinks into unfreedom "by forgetting that God is" (17). Whether or not the philosophical hypothesis is correct, "that God is" is unfortunately not something that can be recollected Socratically. One who originally possesses the condition for understanding the truth "thinks that, since he himself is, God is" (20). He correctly assumes that self-knowledge is at bottom knowledge of the eternal truth, and that in this sense God can be found within himself. Such a one will have no need or occasion to recollect that "God is" in the sense in which the religious hypothesis intends these words to be understood. He who has lost this condition, however, is untruth, which is to say that his own being provides no access to God or the eternal truth. Yet "he must of course think this about himself [i.e., that since he himself is, God is], and recollection will be unable to help him to think anything but this" (20). If, however, one has embraced the decisive significance of the moment, there is no returning to philosophy: "the break has occurred, and the person can no longer come back and will find no pleasure in recollecting what remembrance wants to bring him in recollection" (19).

In the remaining chapters of *Fragments*, Climacus uses the philosophical hypothesis as a kind of foil against which the elements of the religious hypothesis may be more clearly discerned. Given the apparently total incompatibility of the two hypotheses, this fact might lead one to assume that Climacus himself has decisively broken with philosophy. As we have already seen, however, The Moral with which *Fragments* concludes argues strongly against this assumption. In The Moral, Climacus presents himself and his project "for inspection" before Socrates, equipped as he is with the "new" and potentially "more true" concepts of faith, sin, the moment, and the god in time. That he has "gone beyond" Socrates, he claims, is "apparent at every point," yet it seems that he hopes to have done so in a Socratic manner: "to go beyond Socrates when one nevertheless says essentially the same as he, only not nearly so well – that, at least, is not Socratic" (111). The Moral and the Preface are thus matching bookends for *Fragments*, insofar as Climacus continues to regard Socrates as *the* touchstone for the adequacy of thought. If even the religious hypothesis is potentially Socratic, and if Socrates can meaningfully "inspect"

that hypothesis, there must be something in the nature of Socratic philosophizing (and so of philosophy as such) that allows it to bridge the
seemingly unbridgeable opposition between philosophy and faith. And
this means that the philosophical hypothesis as set forth in Chapter One
of *Fragments* does not adequately capture the nature of philosophy.[24]

This is not all. Like Socrates, Climacus stands in a place that is not
fully described by either hypothesis. Had he been unable to set aside the
preconceptions that he himself attributes to philosophy, he would have
rejected the religious hypothesis either directly or by trying to assimilate
faith to philosophy after the manner of the Hegelians. Nor does his deep
appreciation of the religious hypothesis and its implications prevent him
from doing justice to the essential nature of philosophy as exemplified
by Socrates.

The understanding of Socrates that Climacus expresses in The Moral
suggests that Climacus continues to remain open to the claims of both
philosophy and faith because he is in essential respects a Socratic philosopher. He is devoted to philosophy as a way of life in which deed harmo-
nizes with speech, he has no doctrine and emphasizes questions rather
than answers, and he insists that we think for ourselves. Perhaps most
important, he has a passion for thinking that is akin to Socratic eros, and
in serving thought he honors "the god." But what is the role of the god in
Socratic philosophizing? How is philosophical passion or eros – which for
Socrates leads the soul through immanent truth to transcendent being
and divinity, and which draws the young Climacus up the *scala paradisi*
of coherent thought – connected with the god? These questions become
more pressing in subsequent chapters of *Fragments*, in which Climacus
turns directly to the topic of love. It therefore makes sense for us to pause
in order to address these matters directly.

Near the very beginning of Chapter One, Climacus notes that "the
work he [Socrates] carried out was a divine commission (see Plato's
Apology)" (10). If Climacus refers to the *Apology* as a whole rather than

[24] It also means that there are reasons to doubt the claim of some authors that *Fragments*
and *Postscript* are intended to show the vanity of philosophy (cf. Mackey 1971, 168 and
Thompson 1973, 146, quoted at Evans 1983, 4–5). Allison 1967/2002 and Mulhall
1999 point out that Christianity's emphasis on the existential transformation of the
follower makes it resistant to conceptualization, but the same could be said of Socratic
philosophizing as a mode of subjective thinking (see, ch. 10). Rather than showing
the vanity of philosophy as such, Climacus forces us to rethink our preconceptions
about what philosophy *is*. Cf. Roberts 1986, 5: "Certain thought-processes might be . . . a
procedure for personal transformation; or . . . a means of seeing the world aright . . . . [or
even] a means of spiritual awakening."

singling out a specific passage, this is presumably because there are many passages in the dialogue that support his claim.[25] Indeed, Socrates' relationship to the god is a central theme, if not *the* central theme, of the *Apology*. What does the *Apology* reveal about this relationship? Is the god more than an occasion for Socrates to engage in the independent, erotic pursuit of wisdom? Pursuing these questions should help to shed light on Climacus's understanding of the relationship between philosophy and religious faith. Conversely, reading the *Apology* with special attention to the problem of faith may help us to gain a deeper understanding of Plato's Socrates. It is to the *Apology*, then, that we now turn.

[25] The Hongs cite 21–23b and 28e–30 (*Philosophical Fragments/Johannes Climacus*, 278 n. 13), both of which are discussed in the following chapter. But one might also mention 30a ("Know well, then, that the god orders this [i.e., that I philosophize]") and 32c ("I have been ordered to do this [i.e., to philosophize] by the god . . . in every way that any other divine allotment has ever ordered a human being to do anything whatsoever").

3

Platonic Interlude

Eros and the God

Johannes Climacus tells the story of a young man who is ardently in love with thinking. For Climacus, philosophy begins with passion. Passion gives birth to his attempt to philosophize, and it has the power to confer authority upon philosophical claims. Climacus recognizes that the essential truth of certain sorts of claims cannot be independently assessed, but depends instead on what one might call the existential commitment of the philosopher. The authority of a religious or ethical thesis derives not simply from the intellectual talent of the one who enunciates it, but also from his willingness to believe and to do what he says. *Johannes Climacus* thus suggests that the truth of a philosophy as a representation of reality is less important than the truth of a *philosopher*, or the fidelity with which he lives up to his understanding of things.

As we have seen, *Fragments* echoes these notions of truth and authority. In his Preface, Climacus associates himself with Socrates, who (he suggests) was able to hold philosophizing together with existing in a way that eluded both Archimedes and Diogenes, and that continues to elude the speculative philosophers. Yet Climacus also leads us to ask whether authority – philosophical talent wedded to existential commitment – is all that one needs in order to attain the truth. This question comes up especially in connection with the god who examines Socrates and orders him to philosophize as a "divine commission" (10). Socrates' philosophical passion draws him toward the truth, but what role does the god play in his quest for wisdom? Does the god act as more than an occasion for Socrates to learn the truth? If so, does Socrates have a kind of faith?

Plato's *Apology of Socrates* presents a unique opportunity to reflect on the foregoing issues, and, more generally, on the origins of philosophy. In the

Apology, Socrates is on trial as a result of his public, philosophical activity. He is accused of failing to show due reverence to the gods of Athens and introducing new divinities into the city. For these and other reasons, he also faces the third charge of corrupting the young. Yet Socrates does not confine his defense speech to the refutation of these specific charges. Instead, he uses his trial as an opportunity to try to explain and to justify his philosophizing to his fellow Athenians.

Even so, Socrates must take into account the fact that the only essential question before the court is whether the gods and laws of Athens permit philosophy as he practices it. For the jurors, the city comes first. In its juridical capacity, the court embodies the authority of the gods that protect the city as well as the *nomoi* – the written and unwritten laws, customs, and traditions that sustain it. The crimes of which Socrates stands accused are furthermore simultaneously religious and political. Offenses against the protecting gods of Athens threaten the well-being of the community itself, while the alleged corruption of the young is evidenced, not only by the disputatious impertinence they have picked up through imitating Socrates, but especially by their apparent impiety.[1]

Under the circumstances, Socrates must try to provide a defense of philosophy in religious as well as political terms. This is precisely what he does. He argues that he philosophizes for the well-being of the city and its citizens (30a–b). What is more, he repeatedly asserts that he has been commanded to philosophize by "the god." The context of these assertions seems to imply that this god is Apollo, whose divinity is customarily acknowledged by all Greek cities (23b; cf. 28e, 29d, 30a, 30e, 33c). Socrates' defense is thus designed to present his philosophical activity in such a way that, when viewed from within the civic horizons of Athens, it will come to light not merely as permissible but as obligatory.

Socrates' claim that his philosophizing is divinely authorized is, however, called into question by the ambiguity of his defense speech. For one thing, he never actually names the god who commands him to philosophize. The god's identity thus remains a mystery throughout the *Apology*.[2] Socrates also speaks in a manner that raises doubts about the sincerity of some of his claims, and in doing so he poses a riddle that

---

[1] See *Apology* 26b with Xenophon, *Memorabilia* 1.2.40–47. Aristophanes' *Clouds*, which was produced in Athens twenty-four years before Socrates' trial, attributes to the influence of Socrates the gross impiety of the young Pheidippides.

[2] Why this should be so is unclear. Climacus will argue that Socrates is ignorant of who or what the god is. See ch. 5.

continues to puzzle scholars today. In particular, it remains uncertain whether Socrates' quest for wisdom reflects his obedience to the god, or merely expresses his own peculiar longing to know. In the latter case, philosophy would be nothing more than a projection of subjectivity – an activity that is explicable only in terms of the impulse to philosophize, however inwardly compelling it may be.[3] In the former, it would be a task that responds to something outside of the psyche of the philosopher, and one whose character is genuinely obligatory insofar as it comes to him as a divine command. In one instance, philosophy is a spontaneous activity that is answerable only to itself. In the other, philosophy answers to the god.

In my view, neither of the aforementioned alternatives is wholly persuasive, for Socrates is serious about *both* the human *and* the divine origins of his philosophical quest. His explanation of his philosophizing is necessarily ambiguous because the origins of philosophy are neither simply human nor simply divine, and neither simply identical with, nor simply other than, oneself. Philosophy has two roots: it is answerable to, and authorized by, the god, but also by what Socrates calls eros. It is possible for philosophy to spring from both roots simultaneously, because both work together in such a way that neither has priority: while the god arouses eros, it is eros that opens the soul to the god. Eros does so because is not simply human desire. Rather, it is a daimonic or intermediate passion that binds the human with the divine and the self with that which transcends it. The daimonic structure of eros reflects the immanence of transcendent truth in our souls that makes philosophical recollection possible. At the same time, however, the daimonic nature of eros makes Socrates receptive to the guidance of the god – guidance that is crucial for his philosophic quest, but that is neither available nor explicable in terms of recollection. In this way, eros is also a ground of faith.

SOCRATES' FAITH

In Greek as in English, the title of the *Apology of Socrates* (*Apologia Sōkratous*) is ambiguous: it is unclear whether the defense speech (*apologia*) contained in the dialogue is *by* Socrates or *on behalf of* him. The title also contains the hint of a Platonic pun: is the *Apologia* also an *Apollo-logia*,

---

[3] Socrates' talk of the god would furthermore be mere courtroom rhetoric. Yet as Climacus notes (*Fragments*, 10–11), Socrates also relates his philosophical activity to "the god" in the extrajudicial context of the *Theaetetus* (150c–d).

a speech of Apollo? As we shall see, Socrates' assertion that he was commanded to philosophize by the oracle of Apollo at Delphi allows him to claim that, in speaking for himself, he speaks for the god, or, what is the same, that the god speaks for him. The title of the *Apology* thus prepares us for the very ambiguity we are about to investigate.

In the *Apology*, Socrates does not begin by attempting to refute the charges against him. Instead, he addresses the "slander" of his "first accusers," men who have for many years been spreading the tale that Socrates "ponders the heavenly bodies, and has investigated everything under the earth, and makes the weaker speech stronger." These rumors, which may in large part be traced back to the public performance of Aristophanes' *Clouds* at Athens in 423 B.C.E, suggest that Socrates does not acknowledge the gods in accordance with custom or convention (*nomos*), which is to say that he does not worship the gods of Athens (18b–d).

In order to defend himself against these first and, as he asserts, more dangerous accusers (18c), Socrates attempts to explain how he became the object of slander. He offers a brief philosophical autobiography designed to show that he is on a mission imposed upon him by the god at Delphi, and he attributes the legal charges he now faces to the rumors that have grown up around him as a result of this mission. Socrates' autobiographical narrative of the origins and effects of his philosophical activity (20d–24b) thus forms the foundation of his defense speech in the *Apology*.

Socrates is prompted to speak about the origins of his public philosophizing in the following way. Having denied that he possesses the knowledge attributed to him by Aristophanes or taught by sophists such as Gorgias, Hippias, and others, he imagines that someone might ask, as we would say today, "But then, Socrates, what is your story?" Socrates admits the justice of the question, as well as the suspicion from which it arises, namely, that his behavior differs from that of the many. He states that he will tell "the whole truth" about his activity, even though to some he may seem to be "playing" (20c–d). This is not the only time Socrates refers to the impression that he is being playful. He later observes that some will find unpersuasive his story about being commanded to philosophize by the god at Delphi because they think that he is speaking ironically (*eirōneuomenōi* 37e). Yet he states in that context as well that he is telling the truth.

Why does Socrates predict that some may doubt the veracity of his story about the god? Part of the answer is that he speaks vaguely about, and sometimes even seems to identify himself with, the god he supposedly obeys. In the face of this fact, scholars have tended to take one of two paths. Some neglect passages that provoke doubts about the sincerity of his religious obedience (e.g., 28d–29a and 37e–38a, both of which are discussed in this chapter), while others, just as Socrates predicted, dismiss his story as an instance of his habitual irony or at best a pious fiction.[4] In either case, Socrates cannot be understood to be telling "the whole truth," as he insists he is: the former approach ignores an important part of what he actually says, while the latter denies the truthfulness of his story as a whole. The challenge before us is to see whether we can make sense of Socrates' claim that he tells "the whole truth" while accepting the fundamental ambiguity of his self-presentation.

Socrates begins his philosophical autobiography by explaining that his reputation and the slander against him have arisen because he has a "certain wisdom" that could perhaps be called "human wisdom." In any case, he is not wise in any wisdom greater than the human sort; whoever claims he has such wisdom "is lying and speaks so as to slander me." As witness to his wisdom – "if indeed it is wisdom" – and to what sort it is, Socrates offers "the god, the one in Delphi." His companion Chaerephon inquired of the Pythia, the priestess of Apollo at Delphi, whether anyone was wiser than Socrates, and "the Pythia replied that no one was wiser." While Socrates must have enjoyed a reputation for wisdom before Chaerephon's visit to Delphi, he does not claim to have been engaged in *philosophy* prior to that visit. In fact, he says nothing at all about his prior activity. Socrates thus makes it clear that his companion's visit to Delphi was the beginning of his philosophical quest as he himself understands it.[5] Since Chaerephon is now deceased, Socrates says that Chaerephon's brother will bear witness to the truth of what he has said (20d–21a).

One peculiarity of Socrates' introductory remarks deserves immediate mention. Socrates not only puts forward the god at Delphi as his witness,

---

4 Examples of the former are Brickhouse and Smith 1989 and Reeve 1989. Examples of the latter are Taylor n.d., 160 and Hackforth 1933, 101–04; cf. the skeptical reading of West 1979.

5 Although it lies beyond the scope of this inquiry, one should compare the *Apology*'s account of the beginning of Socrates' quest for wisdom with *Phaedo* 95e–102a and Plato's *Parmenides*, the earliest Platonic dialogue in internal or dramatic chronology. The *Symposium* relates how Socrates acquired his knowledge of eros, a field in which he claims special expertise (177e); it is noteworthy that he attributes this knowledge to the teaching of a priestess (see the section "Eros and the Soul").

but he even implies that his story is properly the god's story – "for the speech I will speak is not mine, but the speaker I will refer you to is a trustworthy one" (20e). Yet the god, whose name is never mentioned, is not (and cannot be) a witness in the literal and legally satisfactory sense. The god's meaning is mediated by a priestess, whose words are in turn reported by Socrates as reported by Chaerephon, for whose report yet another person must vouch. How can the god bear witness for a human being if human beings must first bear witness for the god? The distinction between the human and the divine is never a sharp one in Socrates' defense speech.

The difficulty of untangling divine speech from human speech is further complicated by the fact that the god communicates by means of an oracle. This means that the jurors lack direct access not only to what the god said, but also to what the god *meant*. The pre-Socratic philosopher Heracleitus aptly remarked that "The lord whose oracle is at Delphi neither speaks nor conceals but signifies" (frag. 93). "Know Thyself" was inscribed in or on the temple at Delphi, as if to emphasize that an oracle from the Pythia was a provocation to thought, and especially to self-reflection – and woe to those who couldn't take a hint. Herodotus tells us that Lydia fell to Persia because Croesus the Lydian did not stop to think about the possible meanings of the oracle that "if he made war on the Persians he would destroy a mighty empire" (1.53). So, too, Oedipus's fulfillment of the terrible oracle he received from the priestess went hand-in-hand with his failure to question what he thought he knew about his own identity. Socrates is wiser than Croesus or Oedipus because he regards the oracle as a riddle and an occasion for introspection: "I am conscious that I am not wise, either much or little. So whatever does he [the god] mean in asserting that I am the wisest?" This riddle must be taken seriously, for it would be irreverent to suppose that the god is ignorant or lying: "Surely he is not saying something false, for that is not sanctioned for him." What Socrates thinks he knows about himself seems to conflict with what he thinks he knows about the god. Hence he cannot be certain about either sort of knowledge. "For a long time I was perplexed," he confesses, "as to whatever he was saying" (21b).

Socrates finds that it is not easy to separate himself from the god. Because he seeks to understand the god, he must examine himself; because he seeks to understand himself, he must investigate what the god means. Furthermore, because the god at Delphi signifies but does not speak, to say what he means is the task of the recipient of his oracle. In the present instance, it is Socrates who must interpret the Pythia's statement and thereby speak for the god.[6] He sets about doing so, as he says, "very reluctantly" (21b). His plan is to find someone wiser, and thus to refute the divination by showing that "this man is wiser than I" (21c). This is a shocking proposal: if the oracle is false, it would seem to follow either that the god has lied or that he is more ignorant than Socrates. This reflection may help to explain Socrates' reluctance, for his behavior runs the risk of seeming impious. It would be rash to suppose, however, that he intends to prove that the god has spoken falsely, for that goal pre-supposes a degree of certainty about who he is and what the god means that Socrates obviously lacks. Rather, in his perplexity, he seems to envi-sion his relationship to the god as a kind of dialogue, within which the refutation of the original "assertion" that no one is wiser than Socrates might lead to a clarification of the meaning of the oracle.[7]

As it turns out, Socrates fails to find anyone wiser, and this very failure helps to clarify what the god means. The first man he talks to, a politician, proves not to be wise, even though he seems to himself and others to be so. "Probably neither of us," Socrates concludes, "knows anything noble and good." Yet he does not let matters rest there, for he then tries "to show him [the politician] that he thought he was wise, but was not" (21c). While this additional step might seem irrelevant to Socrates' aim of understanding the meaning of the oracle, it actually contributes to that attempt. If the man had at any point been able and willing to recognize his own ignorance – which he was not – he would have proved to be no less wise than Socrates, for he, too, would then have been "conscious that [he is] not wise, either much or little." In the event, however, Socrates reasons that he is wiser than the other man in one respect: "he thinks he knows something when he does not know, while I, just as I do not know, do not think I know, either" (21d). "No one is wiser than Socrates" could have been a roundabout way of saying that all human beings are utterly ignorant, but the failure of others to do what Socrates has done – namely, to recognize their own ignorance – helps to establish that this is not what the god had in mind.

As Socrates continues to examine men reputed to be wise, he increas-ingly incurs hatred, from which eventually arises the slander put forth by his first accusers (21d, 22e–23a). Yet he persists, because "it seemed

---

[6] Cf. Vlastos 1991, who notes that Socrates' commitment to critical reason does not con-flict with his commitment to obey divine commands issued through supernatural signs, "because only by the use of his own critical reason can Socrates determine the true mean-ing of any of these signs" (171).

[7] Cf. Reeve 1989, 22–3.

to be necessary to regard the matter of the god as of the greatest importance" (21e). In fact, his understanding of his relationship to the god
changes fundamentally over the course of his examinations. At some
point, Socrates becomes a devoted servant of the god, and he begins to
see the interrogation of his fellow Athenians as a kind of heroic quest.
He brings to mind the trials of Heracles and Odysseus in speaking of his
"wandering" as the performance of "certain labors." Still more striking
is the fact that, whereas Socrates initially intended to "refute" the oracle,
he now labors "in order that the oracle would turn out to be *unrefuted*"
(22a, emphasis added).

Socrates goes on to question the poets and the craftsmen. Like the
most highly esteemed politicians, the latter deem themselves to be wise
in matters of which they turn out to be ignorant – including in particular
"the greatest matters." Asking himself "on behalf of the oracle" whether
his knowledge of ignorance is preferable to their condition, Socrates
answers both himself and the oracle that "it profits me to be just as I am"
(22d–e). The god, he concludes, meant to say through the oracle that
"human wisdom is worth little or nothing." He used Socrates' name so
as "to make me an example [*paradeigma*], as if he should say 'this one of
you, human beings, is wisest, who, like Socrates, has come to know that
he is in truth worth nothing with respect to wisdom.'" Socrates tells the
jury that his devotion to the god has not ceased; to this day, he continues
to examine anyone he supposes to be wise, and is consequently in great
poverty through the neglect of his own affairs (23b–c).

What explains Socrates' new understanding of the oracle and of his
relationship to the god? For one thing, his examination of others has
made him aware of several points that had earlier escaped his notice. He
now knows that others lack his knowledge of ignorance, and he knows
that he is to this extent wiser than they are. But he has also learned that he
can learn from the god, or, as he says, that "[it is] really the god [who] is
wise" (23a). In these ways, he has grown wiser in the course of examining
the meaning of the oracle. Perhaps this fact has led him to conclude that
it is wise for one who seeks wisdom to serve the god.

Socrates' devotion to the god is a theme to which he returns frequently
in the *Apology*. The god, he says, orders him to philosophize and to persuade his fellow citizens to care about the condition of their souls (29b,
d; 30a–b). In fact, the god has commanded him to philosophize "from
oracles, and from dreams, and in every way in which any other divine
allotment [*moira*] ever ordered a human being to do anything whatsoever" (33c). Furthermore, he has been sent by the god as a gift to the

city (30e–31a). But does Socrates really serve the god, or does he serve himself? It is noteworthy that, once Chaerephon receives the word of the god at Delphi, it is Socrates who does all the talking – asking and answering questions, as he says, "on behalf of the oracle." What is more, some of what he says later in the *Apology* might seem to cast doubt on his piety, and even to imply that "the god" is in the last analysis indistinguishable from Socrates himself.

At one point, Socrates appears to suggest that what he says about the god is a story he puts forth because it may be somewhat more persuasive than the truth, which is simply that he judges the philosophical life to be the best one available to him. The passage is worth quoting in full:

Perhaps, then, someone might say: 'By being silent and keeping quiet, Socrates, won't you be able to live in exile?' To persuade some of you about this is of all things the most difficult. For if I say that this would be to disobey the god, and on account of this it is impossible to keep quiet, you will not be persuaded by me on the ground that I am speaking ironically. But if in turn I say that this happens to be the greatest good for a human being – to make speeches every day concerning virtue and the other things about which you hear me talking, and to examine myself and others – and that the unexamined life is not livable [*ou biōtos*] for a human being, you will be persuaded by me still less if I say these things. Yet this is how things stand, as I assert, gentlemen, but to persuade you is not easy. (37e–38a)

This quotation calls to mind an earlier passage in which Socrates seems to identify the god with himself by replacing "himself" with "the god" in what looks at first like a chiastic (a : b :: b : a) construction:

This is how it stands, Athenian gentlemen, in truth. Wherever one should station *himself*, believing that it is best, or should be stationed by *a ruler*, it is necessary, as it seems, to remain there and run the risk.... I therefore would have done terrible deeds, Athenian gentlemen, if when *the rulers* whom you chose to rule stationed me [in battle] ... I stood fast ... but when *the god* stationed me ... I should have deserted my station. (28d–29a, emphases added)

How are we to understand these passages? Do they furnish evidence that Socrates philosophizes not because he has been commanded to do so by the god, but because he independently judges the philosophical life to be best?

The impulse to draw the latter conclusion is understandable, because both passages contain complex statements affirming two things that seem on the surface to be incompatible: (1) Socrates has been ordered to philosophize, or stationed at his philosophical "post," by the god, and (2) Socrates philosophizes because he believes that only an examined life is genuinely human. Yet in both passages, Socrates nevertheless asks us to hold these two propositions together, and to forbear from rejecting one in favor of the other. In the first passage, the phrase "this is how things stand" (*ta de echei men houtōs*) could be taken to apply only to the clause that concludes "the unexamined life is not livable for a human being," and thus only to the second explanation of Socrates' activity. It is grammatically no less plausible, however, to read it as affirming the truth of everything he says beginning with "For if I say that this would be to disobey the god...," and thus of *both* explanations (1) and (2). The latter reading is if anything more likely to be correct, because in the second passage (28d–29a) the almost identical phrase "this is how it stands" (*houtō gar echei*) introduces the claim that Socrates has been stationed both by himself and by the god. Both passages, in other words, seem at least telegraphically to convey the "whole truth" that Socrates had promised to tell the jury. The whole truth, however, is complex, ambiguous, and therefore difficult to understand. What might it mean to say that Socrates has stationed himself, *and* that the god has stationed Socrates?

The latter question is complicated by the fact that all this talk of stationing and being stationed does not seem to shed light directly on the origins of Socratic philosophizing. Socrates makes it clear that he stations himself at his philosophical post because he believes that it is best to do what he does. More specifically, he says that making speeches about virtue and examining himself and others is the greatest good, and that the unexamined life is not livable for a human being. Yet these judgments are not what motivated his philosophical quest in the first place. They are offered rather as reflections on the quest from the viewpoint of one who is already in the midst of it. Similarly, the claim that the god has stationed him at his post does not explain why Socrates *began* to examine himself and others. As we have seen, the latter claim expresses a conclusion at which Socrates arrived only after having initiated his philosophical quest.

Why, then, did Socrates begin to philosophize? The answer is already at hand, at least in a general sense. Socrates' brief autobiographical sketch in the *Apology* makes it clear that his examination of himself and others grew out of his reflection on the oracle. The oracle challenged what he thought he already knew about himself and about wisdom. Socrates wanted to understand what the god meant when he said that no one was wiser than he. He began to inquire into the meaning of the oracle, and he persisted in the face of growing hostility, because he judged that the most important thing in his life was to find the answers to two questions that the oracle had intertwined: "Who is Socrates?" and "What is wisdom?" Socrates' philosophical quest, in other words, was originally motivated by his desire for wisdom in the fullest sense – wisdom that includes self-knowledge. This desire for wisdom, which has precedence over any other desires he may have had, also precedes Socrates' awareness of any obligation to the god.

The result at which we have arrived seems to be something like a tautology: at the beginning of Socratic philosophizing we find *philosophia*, the love of wisdom. Were this the end of the story, we would be entitled to conclude that, for all of Socrates' talk about the necessity of obeying the god, the only voice that calls him to philosophize is his own. But this is not the end of the story, for it is *the oracle* that arouses, focuses, and validates his desire for wisdom. What is more, the oracle can do so only because Socrates *already* acknowledges the god's authority as a speaker of truth. "Surely he [the god] is not saying something false," Socrates reasons, "for that is not sanctioned for him." Socrates would not have bothered to inquire into the meaning of the oracle had he not presupposed that the god knew what he was talking about. The decision to philosophize is thus in no way an "existential" one, in the sense that it is not made spontaneously and independently of any support in a world that may ultimately prove to be meaningless. On the contrary, Socrates is confident that the philosophical quest is meaningful because he is confident that there is some truth to be uncovered. His confidence, moreover, is not rooted in any sort of independent understanding, but rather in his trust that the god knows what he himself does not.

This is a striking point that can hardly be overemphasized. The ultimate warrant for Socratic philosophizing is the authority of the god, which Socrates accepts on faith and without argument. What is more, Socratic philosophizing does not independently determine its own fundamental orientation. Rather, the very questions that guide the philosophic quest derive from the oracle, or from what is given to Socrates by the god. In one sense, then, Socrates questions the oracle, but in a deeper sense he does not. In particular, he is willing to accept, on the authority of the oracle alone, that the quest for wisdom is a sensible and significant enterprise.

We asked earlier whether the god is more than a mere occasion for Socrates to learn the truth on his own. The present reflections imply that he is. In the first place, no human being could have given him the direction that the god provided. Socrates heeds the oracle because he believes it is the word of the god: if a human being had declared that no one was wiser than he, it is doubtful that he would have taken this assertion much to heart. Without the riddle posed by the oracle, moreover, Socrates would not have been prompted to ask the right questions, nor could he have been confident that there was any truth to be arrived at by asking these questions. In this sense, the god is unforgettable, and the fact that Socrates has learned from the god has more than historical interest. On the other hand, it would be too much to claim that the god's relationship with Socrates must be understood as an instance of what Climacus calls "the moment." The god does not provide Socrates with the condition for understanding the truth, as he already possesses this condition. Had this not been the case, he would not have been able to formulate the questions that allowed him to unlock the oracle's meaning.

If Socrates can hope to awaken his fellow citizens, it is only because he himself has been awakened by the voice of the god. What is more, Socrates continues to be guided by a kind of orienting divination throughout his philosophical career. In the *Apology*, he tells the jury that a "voice" that is "divine and daimonic" sometimes speaks to him, turning him away from what he is about to do (31c-d). Later, he characterizes this voice as a "sign of the god" and a "divination" (40a-b). Just as in the case of the oracle, Socrates seems to accept the direction of this voice without question.

The upshot of the preceding reflections is that Socratic philosophizing essentially involves a kind of faith. But the nature of this faith is not yet clear. What sense can we make of Socrates' reliance upon divination and prophecy? Why is he willing to acknowledge the authority of certain divine voices? And how can such faith go hand-in-hand with the critical, rational inquiry that is the hallmark of Socratic philosophizing?

SOCRATES' EROS

To answer these questions, we must return to the erotic desire for wisdom that, along with the oracle from Delphi, lies at the roots of Socratic philosophizing. This is because Socrates' philosophic eros is internally inseparable from that which is divine. It is not merely a register of his individual particularity, like an appetite, drive, or impulse. Rather, like enthusiasm – the experience of being *entheos*, inspired by a god – it comes to him from without just as much as it springs from within.

It may be difficult for contemporary readers to take the latter possibility seriously. The legacy of modern philosophy, and especially that of post-Kantian philosophy from Hegel, Marx, Nietzsche, and Heidegger through the twentieth-century French existentialists and postmodernists, has accustomed us to thinking of ourselves not as souls but as "subjects" and of philosophical desire as an "expression" or "projection" of subjectivity. For the subject in its various guises, the world is an arena of self-assertion, a domain of making and doing in which even philosophy is a productive or poetic project.

This modern notion of projective subjectivity is not foreign to Socrates or to the ancients in general. But it is reflected in only one element of the soul: that of *thumos* or spiritedness, which manifests itself not only in aggression, competition, and the like, but also, as Plato's *Timaeus* makes clear, in the drive to render the phenomena intelligible and to impose order upon them.[8] For Socrates, however, philosophy is not essentially an expression of the thumotic will to order. It is rather the love of wisdom, and it is possible because the self is a soul, not a subject. The human soul is receptive as well as projective; it is of all things unique in that it is uniquely open to the whole of things.[9] Conceived simply as projective subjectivity, the self cannot open itself to something outside of and beyond itself, to something that transcends it. It has no room for what Socrates calls eros, the philosophical desire that both nourishes, and is nourished by, the original experience of receptivity or openness.

These remarks about the erotic soul will be fleshed out in the following section. What concerns us now is the way in which Socrates' story about the oracle sheds light on the relationship between eros and openness. Socrates' philosophical labors are a response to the perplexity he experiences as a result of reflecting seriously on the meaning of the oracle. In Plato's *Theaetetus*, Socrates states that philosophy begins in wonder (155d). The *Apology* amplifies this point, in that it dramatically illustrates the natural progression from the soul's experience of openness, to perplexity or wonder, to the philosophical quest for wisdom. In the *Apology*, Socrates indicates that the openness of his soul to the word of the god invigorates and expands his eros for wisdom. This eros is energized by contact between the soul and something greater, to whose mystery the soul already aspires just insofar as it is by nature erotic. What is manifested in eros is thus both the soul and that which, in its transcendence, the soul experiences as divine.

The foregoing description of Socrates' experience borrows language that he employs in other Platonic dialogues, for neither the word "eros" nor any of its cognates appears in the *Apology*. This otherwise remarkable fact is easily explained by the requirements of prudence. In the near aftermath of the Peloponnesian War, the Athenians would inevitably have

[8] See Howland 2002a.
[9] The best discussion of this is Strauss 1988; see esp. 38–9.

associated eros with the lust for power and glory that had recently led
them to the brink of annihilation and that was especially exemplified
by Socrates' tyrannically inclined companions Alcibiades and Critias.[10]
Had Socrates explicitly connected his philosophical activity with eros in
the politically charged context of a public trial, he would have virtually
guaranteed a guilty verdict. Indeed, Plato situates the fullest discussions
of eros in private homes (*Republic* and *Symposium*) and outside the walls
of Athens (*Phaedrus*): while Socrates aims to rehabilitate eros by showing
that it is properly directed toward transcendent beings, this crucial pedagogical task can be safely undertaken only in venues that lie beyond the
public eye.

One of the characters in Jorge Luis Borges's story "The Garden of
Forking Paths" observes that in a riddle whose solution is chess, the only
prohibited word is "the word *chess*."[11] This thought might help us to
understand the absence of any explicit reference to eros in the *Apology*.
The dialogue is pervaded by references to the daimonic, the class of entities within which Socrates elsewhere locates eros – entities that are neither simply divine nor simply human, but somehow both simultaneously.
The daimonic is thematically introduced in the charges against Socrates,
which state that he worships "new and strange *daimōnia*" (24b, 26b).
Socrates accordingly dwells on the subject of daimonia or "daimonic
things" during his argument with Meletus. He refutes Meletus's accusation that he does not believe in gods by pointing out that one who
believes in daimonia must believe in daimons, which are either gods or
the offspring of gods and human beings (27b–e). Immediately after making this point, he compares his disregard of death to the attitude of the
demigods who fought at Troy, including in particular Achilles, the son of a
mortal male and an immortal female (28b–d). It is in this context that he

---

[10] The infrequent uses of eros and its cognates in Thucydides' history of the Peloponnesian
War bring home the association of eros with political sickness. At 2.43.1, Pericles encourages the citizens to "realize the power of Athens" and to become lovers (*erastai*) of the
city; in this, at least, the Athenians follow his advice. At 3.45.5, in the context of the
Mytilenean debates, the Athenian Diodotus finds it necessary to speak of the dangers
inherent in the "lust for all" (*erōs epi panti*). In the course of debating the proposed expedition to Sicily, the Athenian general Nicias warns his fellow citizens against being "sick
with eros [*duserōtas*] for things that lie far away" (6.13.1). His admonition is to no avail:
Thucydides reports that, after having been encouraged by Alcibiades and by Nicias's own
description of the great force that would be required for the expedition, "a passionate
desire [*erōs*] for the enterprise fell upon everyone alike" (6.24.3). On Alcibiades' ambi-
tious nature see Thucydides 6.15; on his plans for the Sicilian expedition, 6.90; on the
tyrannical tendencies of Critias and Alcibiades see Xenophon, *Memorabilia* 1.2.12 ff.
[11] Borges 1964, 27.

speaks of stationing himself and being stationed by the god (28d–29a). Finally, as we have already noted, Socrates refers to his *daimonion*, his daimonic "sign" or "voice," more than once in the course of the dialogue (31c–d, 40a–b).

Taken together, these passages reflect the same ambiguity we have already noted in examining Socrates' relationship to the god. On the one hand, Socrates identifies his daimonion with the god, inasmuch as the daimonic sign or voice is a "sign of the god" (40b). On the other, he suggests that he himself, like Achilles, may be daimonic – or at the very least that he alone has ears for the god, insofar as the voice of the daimonion comes to him privately. While it would be unsafe to conclude that the god or the daimonion to whom he refers in this context is Apollo, Socrates nevertheless delivers oracles near the end of his defense speech (39c). In this, he resembles the priestess of Apollo as well the god Dionysus, who was immortal even though he had a mortal mother.[12]

Perhaps the least one could say in an attempt to summarize these bewildering observations is that the daimonic, the region in between the divine and the human that somehow incorporates both, pervades Socrates' defense speech. This is also the intermediate region of eros, and herein lies the key to understanding what Socrates calls the "whole truth" about his philosophical activity. On the basis of what Socrates says elsewhere in the Platonic corpus, it is evident that his love of wisdom is nothing other than eros, and that eros is neither simply human nor simply divine, but intermediate or daimonic. The question whether Socrates stations himself at his philosophical post or is stationed by the god is therefore misleading. Because eros is daimonic, and because eros makes him receptive to the word of the god, both claims are simultaneously true, although neither is in itself the whole truth. Viewed in this light, the ambiguity of the *Apology* about the origins of Socratic philosophizing arises in large measure from the ambiguity of eros. What, then, is eros?

EROS AND THE SOUL

Socrates discusses eros in a number of dialogues, including the *Republic*, *Symposium*, and *Phaedrus*. Although the emphases and details of these discussions differ according to context, they all have several things in common. While erotic desire manifests itself in sexual impulses, eros is not a mere appetite and cannot be relegated to the lower parts of the

---

[12] See Euripides' *Bacchae*, lines 1330–43.

human soul: it extends throughout the soul in such a way that reason, too, has an erotic component. Socrates regularly depicts eros as aiming beyond the sphere of becoming in which human life unfolds, and at the transcendent realm of being that he associates with divinity. Eros thus draws the soul upward toward the only thing that is naturally suited to satisfy its longing and make it whole. Finally, eros is associated with what one might call philosophical prophecy – a certain foreknowledge of the nature of the soul and the beings that is the mirror image of the process of recollection Climacus regards as the centerpiece of Socrates' thought.

In the *Republic*, Socrates introduces the philosopher in a striking manner. He begins not by speaking (as one might have expected) about the philosopher's intellect, but about the nature of his passion. The philosopher's desire for wisdom, he tells his young companion Glaucon, is akin to Glaucon's erotic love of boys. Just as Glaucon loves boys of every sort, provided that they are in the bloom of youth, the philosopher does not love "one part and not another" of wisdom, but "all of it" (474d–75b). As "lovers of the sight of truth," philosophers are more than willing "to taste every kind of study," and are indeed "insatiable" in their desire to learn (475c–d). The object of this insatiable desire is the domain of being – that which neither comes to be nor passes away, but is always. For the philosopher, knowledge of what is nourishes and completes the soul. Socrates makes extraordinary use of the imagery of love and pregnancy in order to express this point:

> It is the nature of one who is really a lover of learning to strive for what is, and he would not linger by each of the many things that are opined to be, but would go forward and would not lose the keenness of his passionate love [*erōs*] or desist from it until he should touch the nature itself of each thing that is with the part of the soul that is suited to lay hold of such a thing, and it is the part akin to it that is suited. Having drawn near it and coupled with that which truly is, and having begotten intelligence and truth, he would know and truly live and would be nourished and thus cease from labor pains, but not before. (490a–b)

The soul is erotically drawn to "that which truly is" as its natural end and complement. The soul's encounter with being leads to pregnancy, and issues, after a period of labor, in the virtue of intelligence (*nous*) and in truth, which together make it possible both to know what truly is and to live in harmony with this knowledge.

Perhaps because of the soul's kinship with what is, the philosopher is also prophetic, in the sense that he is prescient about the ultimate objects of his desire as well as the true nature of the soul's longing. In fact, Socrates' description of the culmination of philosophic eros is itself

prophetic, as he claims to have only an opinion – and not actual knowledge – of the highest object of wisdom, the Good (506e). The Good,
according to Socrates, is what every soul pursues. It is also divine, as is
suggested by the fact that Socrates chooses the sun (Helios in Greek
mythology) as its image, and mentions more than once that the sun is
the god that presides over the visible domain of becoming (508a). Yet
"while divining that that which it pursues and for the sake of which it does
everything is some one thing," the soul "is at a loss about it and unable
to grasp just what it is." Without knowledge of the Good, Socrates adds,
"I divine that no one no one will adequately know" the just and noble
things. "You divine beautifully," Glaucon responds (505d–06a).[13]

In the *Symposium*, the comic poet Aristophanes also emphasizes the
incomplete yet somehow prophetic understanding that accompanies
eros. The soul of one in love, he claims, "is not able to say, but divines and
speaks oracles about what it wants" (192d). Like Aristophanes, Socrates
understands eros as a desire for that which the soul lacks and of which
it stands in need (200a–b). But he, too, finds it difficult to determine
exactly what the soul wants. Having been unable to discover the activity
or purpose of eros on his own (206b, cf. 207c), Socrates seeks instruction
from a priestess named Diotima. Diotima explains the prophetic character of eros in terms of its daimonic nature. Eros is neither a god nor a
mortal, but is a "great daimon" (*daimōn megas*). Daimons, moreover, are
messengers and interpreters that make it possible for gods and human
beings to communicate. Being in the middle, they are thus a kind of bond
for the whole, "so that the all itself is bound together with itself" (202e).
Eros is intermediate in another sense as well: it is neither wise, like the
gods, nor utterly ignorant, but is instead a lover of wisdom (*philosophos*:
204b).

In spite of their agreement that eros is prophetic, Aristophanes and
Diotima present very different pictures of its nature and significance. In
Aristophanes' mythical account (189d–93d), eros is a desire to rejoin
with one's other half. Long ago we were circular beings with four arms,
two legs, and two heads, but the gods split us in two as punishment for
our hybristic attempt to overthrow them. Reunion with our other halves
would allow us to regain the strength and vigor we enjoyed as circle-
people. Since our original desire was to conquer the gods, we may infer
that we are fundamentally thumotic rather than erotic. Indeed, eros
comes into existence only after we have been severed from our other

---

[13] In each case, the word "to divine" translates a form of the verb *manteuesthai*. Cf. 523a.

halves, and thus only as a consequence of the divine attempt to regulate our otherwise unconstrained aggression (191a). The gods, we may note, are in Aristophanes' view no less thumotic than we are: they choose to weaken us rather than to destroy us altogether because they do not wish to lose our worship (190c).

For Diotima, on the other hand, we are fundamentally erotic beings. Whereas in the *Republic* Socrates maintains that the highest object of eros is the Good, Diotima teaches that the highest object of eros is the Beautiful. It is true that when Socrates cannot explain the love of beautiful things, she allows him to substitute "good things" (*ta agatha*) for "beautiful things" (*ta kala*: 204d–e).[14] Yet this is clearly an accommodation to Socrates, who at one point interrupts Diotima's account of eros to ask about its usefulness for human beings (204c–d). Put another way, Socrates initially approaches eros as a potential subject of technical mastery. But because eros is a religious mystery, it cannot be grasped in a scientific or technical manner. This is the context in which we must understand the criticism implicit in Diotima's remark that "even you, Socrates, might perhaps be initiated into these erotic matters [*tauta . . . ta erōtika*]" (209e–10a). It is noteworthy that Diotima of Mantinea – whose name means something like "Zeus-Honored of Divinersville" – is a prophetess who used her skill to help delay the onset of the plague in Athens (201d). In spite of Socrates' claim to have precise or scientific knowledge (*epistasthai*) of "nothing other than the erotic things [*ta erōtika*]" (177e), eros seems to be a subject more suited to prophetic inspiration than to rigorous philosophical definition or technical control.[15] This must be kept in mind when we consider Climacus's discussion in Chapter Three of the paradoxes of love and understanding.[16]

Diotima goes on to instruct Socrates that eros is directed not at oneself but at the good: it is a desire to possess the good forever (205e–206a). It is in terms of this desire that she explains our erotic attraction to beautiful bodies and souls. Eros, which is itself in between ugliness and beauty, is attracted to beauty because "all human beings are pregnant both in body and in soul, and when we reach a certain age, our nature desires to give birth" (206c). Beauty, in turn, releases us from our labor pains, and it is through reproduction that we may attain a share of immortality and

---

[14] The Greek language also suggests a connection between beauty and goodness, as both nobility and beauty are signified by the adjective *kalos*.
[15] Cf. the decisive failure of the rulers of the city in speech in the *Republic* to regulate sexual intercourse by technical means (545d–47a).
[16] See ch. 5.

thus may hope to possess the good (as well as happiness that comes from possessing the good) forever. Those who are more pregnant in body than in soul seek immortality through physical reproduction; those who are more pregnant in soul than in body seek to give birth to wisdom and virtue. One of this sort naturally seeks the company of another who is beautiful and noble in soul as well as body. In the presence of such a person he find himself "full of speeches about virtue," and in keeping company with and trying to educate the other (here one is reminded of Socrates) he gives birth to "that with which he has long been pregnant" (209b–c). His eros, however, is ultimately not directed at other persons. It is rather a longing for the divine form or idea of beauty, the Beautiful itself. The highest mysteries of eros are accordingly revealed in a vision of the Beautiful that results in the birth of true virtue in the soul of the lover of wisdom (208e–12b).

In sum, Diotima teaches that the erotic, philosophical quest moves from the evanescent beauty that is immanent in bodies and souls to the unchanging, transcendent being of the Beautiful. Diotima's description of the culmination of this quest bears a close resemblance to Socrates' description of the same in the passage quoted above from the *Republic*. The basic structure of this quest is furthermore reaffirmed in the *Phaedrus*, in which Socrates presents eros as the power that enables philosophic recollection.

The *Phaedrus*, like the *Symposium*, is a dialogue about eros. In the first part of the dialogue, Socrates delivers a speech to his young companion Phaedrus that condemns erotic passion and praises the sobriety of the lover who lacks passion. He is about to leave when he has a change of heart. His daimonion, he explains, has come to him, and forbidden him to leave until he purifies himself of the offense he has committed against that which is divine – for eros is either "a god or something divine" (242b–c, e). He is able to understand his error because he is a "seer"; indeed, "the soul is somehow prophetic" (242c). Prophecy, in turn, is a kind of heaven-sent or divine madness that is closely connected with both eros and philosophy. In a playful etymology, Socrates derives the so-called "mantic art" (*mantikē*) from what men of old named the "manic art" (*manikē*: 244c–d). He then goes on to deliver a palinode, or song of recantation, in praise of the madness of love (244a–57b). In this palinode, most of which consists in a great myth, he explains that eros – awakened by the sight of earthly beauty, and reminded of the "true beauty" that we once knew – carries our souls upward in an effort to glimpse, and be nourished by the vision of, the domain of being above and beyond the cosmos that we saw before becoming incarnate (246d–47d, 249d). Philosophy is thus the endeavor to recollect transcendent being and truth under the guidance of divine erotic madness, an endeavor that is possible only because the truth is in some form already present in our souls.

The picture of eros that is presented in the Platonic dialogues fills out the Socratic account of learning by illuminating the psychological and metaphysical assumptions that underlie philosophical recollection and prophecy. The daimonic nature of eros explains how it is that, to borrow Climacus's words, self-knowledge can be God-knowledge: erotic ascent is made possible by the immanence in the soul, and in human experience generally, of that which is transcendent. Yet there is also a divine otherness that is beyond the reach of eros, for the oracle of the god in the *Apology* gives voice to a fundamental truth that is not accessible through philosophical recollection or prophecy. What Socrates learns from the god guarantees that the quest for wisdom and self-knowledge is meaningful in the first place. Because eros is daimonic, however, it is difficult to determine the boundary between the truth that is accessible within us and the truth that is not. Socrates' daimonion speaks within him, yet in the *Apology* Socrates refers to his daimonion as a sign of the god. Where does daimonic eros end and the god begin? Perhaps it is less important to arrive at a definite answer to this question than it is to acknowledge that eros and the god are distinct, and that only the god can disclose certain truths.

Our investigation of the significance of the god in the *Apology* and of the erotic nature of philosophy has helped to establish that Climacus's philosophical hypothesis, at least as initially elaborated, fails to capture certain essential dimensions of Socrates' philosophic enterprise. In particular, it has shown that this enterprise depends on something akin to the faith that is required for learning in accordance with the religious hypothesis. Climacus writes that "the condition for understanding the truth is like being able to ask about it – the condition and the question contain the conditioned and the answer" (14). Socrates is always able to ask about the truth, yet the questions that guide him, as well as his confidence that these questions have answers, spring from his faith in the authority of the god at Delphi. This faith is expressed in the metaphors of philosophical prophecy and recollection, which presuppose the immanence of truth in our souls. For never yet having fully grasped the transcendent truth at which recollection aims, Socrates can have no certainty that the truth is indeed prophetically or recollectively accessible.

That Socrates never actually completes his philosophical quest has another important implication. In setting forth the philosophical hypothesis in Chapter One, Climacus indicates that temporality or life in time is philosophically insignificant but religiously crucial. The moment at which one awakens to the truth is "hidden in the eternal" on the philosophical hypothesis, but it is utterly unforgettable on the religious hypothesis (13). In the former case, the eternal truth is always accessible to us; in the latter, we are rescued from untruth by divine revelation, which occurs at a particular time (or times). Climacus accordingly presents Socratic philosophizing as a flight from temporality to eternity, an impression that might seem to be reinforced by the Platonic texts we have just examined. Yet Socrates is always en route to wisdom, which is to say that he is essentially an erotic being. Driven by eros, and with an eye toward a truth that is always beyond his grasp, he lives in dialogue with others and in engagement with the life of his community. The picture of the philosopher as one who has "no leisure to look down toward the affairs of human beings" because he is absorbed in the contemplation of that which truly is (*Republic* 500b–c) is thus a caricature. Unlike Archimedes, Socrates is not guilty of *apragmosunē*. And even if the philosopher did manage to ascend to the sunlit uplands of truth, Socrates suggests in his famous cave image, he would nevertheless return to the subterranean region of life in time (*Republic* 516e).[17]

Socrates' faith in the god and in the possibility of philosophy calls into question the total opposition between the philosophical and the religious hypotheses that seemed to be implied by the first chapter of *Fragments*. Perhaps this helps us to understand how Climacus might imagine that Socrates could judge the adequacy of the religious hypothesis. Indeed, even Climacus's account of the alternative to Socratic philosophizing seems indebted to Socrates: his repeated assertion that he has "plagiarized" the god in developing the religious hypothesis (21–2, 35–6) echoes Socrates' claim that his defense speech belongs not to him but to the god (*Apology* 20e). Yet as Climacus observes in The Moral, the religious hypothesis "indisputably goes beyond the Socratic" (111), and it does so in at least two fundamental respects. First, the condition for understanding is on the Socratic view not given by the god, because it is always in our possession. The god turns Socrates' soul toward the truth,

---

[17] In *Postscript,* Climacus explicitly acknowledges that Socrates was not a "speculative philosopher" but rather "an existing thinker who understood existing as the essential" (n. on 206–7). For further discussion see ch. 10.

but it does not give him eyes, so to speak, with which to see it (cf. *Republic* 518b–d). This is affirmed by the Socratic teaching that the soul is essentially erotic, for eros, as we have seen, *is* the condition for understanding. Indeed, it is eros – as Climacus will confirm when he speaks about this "paradoxical passion" – that makes Socrates receptive to the word of the god in the first place. Second, because the word of the god in the Socratic context is literally not much more than a word (even including the "oracles," "dreams," and other communications Socrates mentions at *Apology* 33c), Socrates *must* employ his understanding in order to grasp its significance. On the religious hypothesis, however, the interpretive relation is reversed. The god speaks extensively in and through scripture, which we are meant to embrace as the only adequate interpretation of our human situation – including in particular our incapacity to understand ourselves independently of the god's words and deeds. This is perhaps the most fundamental difference between Socratic philosophizing and religious faith.

In the second chapter of *Fragments*, Climacus tries to clarify the claim of the religious hypothesis that the god is moved by love to give us the condition for understanding. Our Platonic interlude has prepared us to formulate some new questions as we approach this chapter. How does the god's love for us differ from eros? What does the god require from us in return? To what extent can philosophical eros guide us in attempting to respond the god's love? Let us now return to *Fragments* with these questions in mind.

4

Climacus's Poetical Venture

In Chapter Two of *Fragments*, entitled "The God as Teacher and Savior (A Poetical Venture)," Climacus asks how and why the god of the religious hypothesis attempts to teach the truth. This poses a special challenge, because "no human situation can provide a valid analogy" to the god's love for the learner or the difficulties he confronts in attempting to reform him. Climacus nonetheless fashions a poem in order to "suggest" such an analogy (26). If this endeavor is even potentially worthwhile, it must be possible for the imagination, at least in some small measure, to bridge the gap that separates us from the god. This does not mean, however, that Climacus is the author of his "poetical venture" any more than he is the author of the religious hypothesis itself. On the contrary, he insists that no human being could have invented his poem. In that case, it must have originated with the god.

As in Chapter One, in which the philosophical hypothesis provides a backdrop for the development of the religious hypothesis, Climacus prepares us for his poem by examining Socrates' pedagogy. In doing so, he notes a major difference between Socrates and the god with respect to teaching and learning: whereas Socrates needs others in order to understand himself, the god is moved to seek out the learner not by need, but by love. It is in pursuing the implications of this insight that Climacus arrives at the necessity of the incarnation of God as proclaimed by Christianity (although he does not utter the name of Christianity until the book's final pages).

The contrast between the Socratic and religious models is not, however, as great as it might initially seem to be. In certain important respects,

Socrates' comportment as a teacher anticipates the conduct of the god, and thus helps to establish some of the terms of Climacus's suggested analogy. Climacus's poetical venture is also in its own way no less prophetic than the mythical or poetic speeches in the *Symposium* and *Phaedrus* in which Socrates envisions the erotic ascent of the soul to truth and being. Climacus takes his bearings by the claim of the New Testament that God is moved by love to become incarnate as a human being, and it is his reliance on scripture that leads him to disclaim authorship of his poem. Yet he goes beyond scripture not only in laying bare the logic of what is revealed therein, but also in attempting to imagine the inner experience of the god in relation to the learner.[1] Because this act of imagination is in the service of a hypothesis, and because it is intelligible even to readers who may not accept the assumptions of this hypothesis, it exemplifies the power even of one whose mind is not informed by religious faith to achieve a certain understanding of the god. Finally, Climacus's disclaimer of authorship is also reminiscent of Socrates, who in the *Symposium* and *Phaedrus* attributes one of his inspired speeches about eros to a priestess and the other to the prompting of his daimonion.

These points of resemblance notwithstanding, the underlying opposition between the poetic discourses of Climacus and Socrates is readily apparent from their content. Climacus once again makes it clear that the religious hypothesis involves a fundamental reversal of philosophical assumptions. Socrates tells us that the learner ascends to the truth through his love of wisdom, whereas in his poem Climacus hypothesizes that the truth descends into human life through the god's love for us – a crucial difference that is dictated by the religious presupposition that the learner is initially untruth. Yet the second chapter of *Fragments* ultimately strengthens the thoughtful reader's conviction that to describe Socrates' condition simply as untruth is inadequate and misleading. In continuing to examine the implications of the religious hypothesis and the philosophical practices of Socrates and Climacus, we will have more than one occasion to acknowledge that the erotic love of wisdom has a certain daimonic capability of anticipating the nature even of that which the understanding cannot fully grasp.

---

[1] While they are too numerous to note here, Climacus's frequent allusions to the New Testament over the course of his poem are tracked by the Hongs in *Philosophical Fragments/Johannes Climacus*. See esp. the notes on 284–6 and 295–6.

SOCRATES AS TEACHER, THE GOD AS LOVER

In reflecting on the models of intellectual activity Climacus presents in the Preface of *Fragments*, I suggested that it is Socrates who in Climacus's view provides the prototype for the middle ground between the apolitical abstraction of Archimedes and the unphilosophical clownishness of Diogenes – that he exemplifies, in other words, a way of minding one's own business as a philosopher that does not also ignore one's business as a human being and citizen. The latter suggestion has now been confirmed by our examination of certain Platonic dialogues. While Socrates' depiction of the erotic, philosophic quest in the *Republic* might create the impression that the philosopher can gain wisdom without the help of others, this impression is dispelled when Socrates makes it clear that philosophic eros is awakened by the intimation of beauty in the soul of another and nourished by dialogue (*Symposium* 209b–c; *Phaedrus* 252c–53c). Socrates' defense speech in the *Apology* furthermore establishes that his philosophical quest coincides with his activity as a teacher. The oracle poses a riddle that moves Socrates to ask who he is and what wisdom is, and Socrates inquires into these matters by interrogating and engaging in dialogue with individual Athenians. Socrates minds his own business in questing for the truth, but he tends to the business of the city by provoking his fellow citizens to reflect on virtue.

In sum, philosophy and politics, inquiry and pedagogy, are ultimately inseparable for Socrates.[2] Climacus shows his appreciation of this point when he begins Chapter Two by reflecting briefly on Socrates' teaching. Socrates, he explains, "felt a call and a prompting" to teach – a phrase that nicely reflects the daimonically ambiguous origins of his philosophizing. Yet Climacus is silent in this context about the role of the god: Socrates was influenced by "circumstances," so that the occasion for him to become a teacher was provided by "life and its situations." His relation to others was furthermore "reciprocal," in that he owed others no less than they owe him: "the pupil is the occasion for the teacher to understand himself; the teacher is the occasion for the pupil to understand himself" (23–4). Socrates' appreciation of this fact led him to rebuff those who, in their infatuation and gratitude, occasionally wish to idolize him. He "disciplin[ed] ... himself with the same divine jealousy with

---

[2] This is one of the main themes of Plato's *Theaetetus*, which is dramatically situated on the eve of Socrates' public trial (cf. Howland 1998, 53–75).

which he disciplined others and in which he loved the divine," making it clear that he is merely human, that he is as dependent on others as they are on him, but that the proper object of love can only be the truth. In doing so, Socrates demonstrated rare integrity and loyalty – cheating no one, "not even the one who in being cheated would stake his eternal happiness," and seducing no one, "not even the person who employs all of the arts of seduction to be seduced" (23–4; cf. *Symposium* 218c–19d).

Unlike Socrates, the god of the religious hypothesis "needs no pupil in order to understand himself." Nor can the god's appearance as a teacher be explained as the result of his being acted upon by an occasion. Climacus supposes that the god must move himself, and yet "continue to be what Aristotle says of him, *akinētos panta kinei* [unmoved, he moves all]" (24). As an "unmoved mover," Aristotle's god causes motion in the manner of a final cause that is an object of desire or thought, that is, "by being loved" (*hōs erōmenon: Metaphysics* 1072b, 3–4). This is precisely how the Beautiful and the Good act upon the soul in Socrates' erotic account of learning.

The god of the religious hypothesis enjoys the attractive power that Aristotle attributes to the highest deity and Socrates to the divine sphere of being and truth. Yet we already know that the god does not initially exercise this attractive power in relation to the learner: the learner is at the outset untruth, and thus "polemical against" both the truth and the teacher of the truth. If the god is beloved, he is only potentially so. What is more, the god – like Socrates, but unlike the eternally unchanging beings toward which his love is directed – is a lover. The god loves the learner, and indeed *must* love the learner if the learner is to come to love the truth. The god's love, moreover, cannot be explained Socratically. For Socrates, love implies a need for that which one lacks (*Symposium* 200a–b), but the god, as Climacus notes, is not in need of the learner (or of anything else). Furthermore, love desires what is good and beautiful, yet the learner who is loved by the god is in the first place not even a learner: he is untruth, and that through sin. As such, the learner is neither good nor beautiful. How, then, can one explain the god's love?

According to Climacus, the god is moved by a love that is not explicable in terms of need, "for love does not have the satisfaction of need outside itself but within" (24). Without the god's love, the learner could not hope to understand the truth; yet this also does not explain his love. On the contrary, the god's love explains his teaching: it is just *because* the god loves the learner that he wishes to disclose the truth. The god's love for the learner is freely chosen, like the matrimonial love between a man and a woman.[3] But it is also unconditional, like that of a parent for a child. Such love is not "reasonable" in that it cannot be satisfactorily explained in terms of other factors such as the goodness or beauty of the beloved. It is rather the reason for, and explanation of, all that follows.

Out of love for the learner, the god resolves "from eternity" to make his appearance in time. This resolution "does not have an equal reciprocal relation to the occasion" as in the Socratic case, for the god needs no one else in order to understand himself (25). Given that this concurs with Diotima's teaching that the gods are not philosophers because they are already wise (*Symposium* 204a), we may ask in passing what moves the god at Delphi to help Socrates – assuming that we are correct in seeing *that* god, too, as more than "circumstance" or "occasion" for Socrates' self-understanding. The question is a potentially illuminating one in the present context because Climacus's answer does not readily apply to the Socratic situation. One might suppose that the god at Delphi is moved by love, but for Socrates love seems to be inseparable from need. If the Delphic god needs human beings, it is perhaps because he longs to be worshiped. This at any rate accords with the "pagan" view of the gods that is expressed by Aristophanes in the *Symposium* (190c). We shall soon have occasion to ask whether it is reasonable to attribute this pagan view to Socrates as well.

The love of the god, when "fulfilled in time," is the moment – the paradoxical coming-into-existence of the eternal. The moment would not occur, or would not have occurred, had the eternal, transcendent truth already been immanent in existence as per the Socratic notion – or rather, had this immanence not been obscured by the learner's sin in such a way that it was no longer accessible. It is worth reminding ourselves that the moment is not to be understood as a single and specific historical event, for the love of the god is fulfilled only when the eternal has come into existence *for the learner*. The goal of the god's love is to "win" the learner: "for only in love is the different made equal, and only in equality or in unity is there understanding" (25). The learner is won when he accepts the god's love and loves the god in return. This reciprocal relationship of love, which in the religious context replaces the reciprocal relationship of need in which Socrates stands to the learner, makes possible the equality of the learner with the god that is a precondition for understanding the god's instruction about the truth. (On the philosophical hypothesis, there

---

[3] The matrimonial images employed by Climacus and Silentio (discussed later in this chapter) are presumably meant to emphasize this freedom on the part of both God and man.

is of course no need for the equalizing relationship of love: the learner and the teacher are already equal in the most fundamental sense, for the truth is latent in both of their souls.)

The god seeks to communicate the truth to the learner, but encounters great difficulty in making himself understood. It is possible to approach this difficulty, if not fully to understand it, by analogy with the human experience of a certain situation of romantic or erotic love (even though the love of the god for the learner is by no means the same as the passion that human lovers might feel for each other). The god loves the learner, and so wants the learner to understand the truth. But the learner, who is untruth, will not understand the truth if he cannot understand the teacher. This means that the god himself seeks to be understood by his beloved – as lovers naturally do. Understanding presupposes equality, but whereas the teacher and the learner are on the Socratic hypothesis absolutely equal with respect to their ability to know the truth, the relationship between the god and the learner is radically unequal. This might not in itself pose a problem for the god, except that, as a lover, he also naturally seeks to preserve his beloved. How can the god make the learner equal to himself, and thus make himself understood, without "destroy[ing] that which is different"? The extent of this problem is such as to make the god's love "basically unhappy." This unhappiness "is the result not of the lovers' being unable to have each other but of their being unable to understand each other" – a sorrow that is "infinitely deeper" than that other unhappiness because it "wounds for eternity" (25–6).

Climacus's poetical venture is designed to illuminate the sorrow that the god experiences as a result of the learner's misunderstanding. Climacus turns to poetry in reflecting on the contact between God and man for the same reason that Socrates turns to myth in reflecting on eros: these are mysteries to which philosophical analysis cannot by itself do justice. In Climacus's hands, the poem or parable is a means of philosophical exploration: like a Platonic myth or a well-crafted novel, it opens up an imaginative space within which certain truths may become perceptible to the mind.[4] The difficulty of this venture is suggested by the fact that, as the superior person, only the god understands the learner's misunderstanding. Because "no human situation can provide a valid analogy," Climacus can only "suggest" one, "in order to awaken the mind to an understanding of the divine" (26).

---

[4] Howland 2005 explores this philosophical use of narrative (*muthos*, as opposed to *logos* or argument).

THE KING AND THE MAIDEN

Climacus's parable begins as follows. A king loved a maiden "of lowly station in life" and wanted to marry her. Because the king was powerful and feared by all, no one opposed him. "So let the harp be tuned . . . for erotic love is jubilant when it unites equal and equal and is triumphant when it makes equal in erotic love that which was unequal." But then a concern "awakened in the king's soul." The king said nothing about this concern, which could only have occurred to one who "thinks royally"; he did not wish to invite the reply that he had done the maiden a favor for which she could never repay him, as this would only have deepened his worry. The king's private sorrow was his doubt whether the girl would be made happy by the marriage, "would acquire the bold confidence never to remember what the king only wished to forget – that he was the king and she had been a lowly maiden." For if this recollection "took her mind away from the king, lured it into the inclosing reserve of secret sorrow . . . what would be the gloriousness of erotic love then!" In that case, "she would indeed have been happier if she had remained in obscurity, loved by one in a position of equality, contented in the humble hut, but boldly confident in her love and cheerful early and late." "Even if the girl were satisfied to become nothing," Climacus adds, "that could not satisfy the king." Because he loved her, and because inequality is the failure of love, "it would be far harder for him to become her benefactor than to lose her." The king's secret sorrow is complete if we assume only one more thing: an intellectual difference that makes it impossible for the girl to understand his concern (26–7).

In order to appreciate the implications of Climacus's parable, we must attend to the difference between the king and the god. The king approaches the maiden as a lover, not a teacher. The poem, however, is meant to illuminate the situation of the god as a teacher as well as a lover. This suggests that, in misunderstanding the king, the maiden would fail to grasp something like what the learner needs to understand in order to be taught by the god. The elevation of the maiden to the side of the king at court is analogous to the rebirth of the learner at the hands of the god. The king wants the formerly lowly maiden to forget that she once was nothing in comparison with him, and to be "boldly confident" in her love for him. He wants to teach the maiden is that she no less worthy of love and royal splendor than the king himself. So, too, the god wants the learner to forget that in his condition of untruth he was like one who had not even been born (cf. 19), and to enjoy the confidence that comes from knowing that he is equal to the god and no less worthy of love. Only then will the learner be able to understand the god, and only then will the god's love be happy. Does this not mean, however, that the learner must forget the moment when he was reborn and the eternal came into existence? Given that the moment, unlike the Socratic occasion, has "such decisive significance that for no moment will I be able to forget it" (13), it would seem that the learner must continue to misunderstand the god and that the god's love must remain unfulfilled. For how could he remember the moment while forgetting that he once was nothing?

Although "a depth of sorrow" slumbers in the "unhappy erotic love" that is sketched in the poem, Climacus notes that only the god can truly experience this kind of unhappiness. "A human being will not suffer this [unhappiness], for we shall refer him to Socrates" – who teaches that all human beings are equal in the most fundamental sense – "or to that which in a still more beautiful sense is capable of making unequals equal" (27–8). What "that" is, Climacus does not say, but one suspects that he is thinking of death. If the inevitability of death makes humans equal, however, death must by the same token be an impediment to the equality of the learner with the god. In that case, the love that unites the learner with the god must overcome death – because love moves the god to die, or because it makes the learner deathless, or for both reasons. While Climacus does not explicitly reflect on death in this connection, his parable brings out the inner, erotic logic of the story about the god that is told in the New Testament.

If the god cannot bring about equality with the learner through love, "the instruction becomes meaningless, for they are unable to understand each other." We might think that the god is indifferent to this fact, since he does not need the learner, "but we forget – or rather, alas, we demon-strate – how far we are from understanding him; we forget that he does indeed love the learner." Indeed, Climacus adds, "human language is so self-loving that it has no intimation of such a sorrow [as the god's]" (28). In the previous chapter, Climacus stated that he who loses the condition for understanding the truth does so by forgetting that God is (17). Here, Climacus claims that we have forgotten that the god loves us. Neither Socrates nor any other human teacher, we may note, can help us to rec-ollect these things. Philosophy is by itself incapable of reminding us that there is a god who loves us, for this is not something that one can discover on one's own. It is of course easy to recognize one's own love for another, just as it is easy for Socrates to become conscious of his eros for the truth. But without action on the part of the god, we cannot know even that he exists, much less that he loves us.[5] It is thus not surprising that, on the philosophical hypothesis, the truth to which the soul aspires is nonliving being – for what other kind of truth could reason alone disclose? On the religious hypothesis, however, the truth, or at least a key part of it, is that the god is and the god loves us. Climacus has indeed gone beyond Socrates.

AGNES AND THE MERMAN

In *Fear and Trembling*, which was published in 1843, the year before the appearance of *Fragments*, Johannes de Silentio relates a parable that anticipates and complements that of the king and the maiden. The tale of Agnes and the merman originates in a Danish legend about a seducer who "breaks" an "innocent flower" (94; cf. 352 n. 25). Silentio's version of the legend gives the merman a conscience, so that it is he who is broken and not Agnes. While one could offer a full interpretation of this important section of *Fear and Trembling* only within the context of an analysis of the book as a whole, a brief examination of it will help to bring into sharper relief both the problem Climacus is attempting to illuminate and the limits of the parable with which he tries to do so.

Silentio's merman is a seducer in whom Agnes "found what she was seeking . . . as she stared down to the bottom of the sea." Like the king and the maiden, Agnes and the merman come from different worlds – they literally live in separate elements – but only in Silentio's parable do these worlds actually meet: the merman embraces Agnes and she throws her arms around his neck, "trusting with all her soul." The merman is prepared "to dive out into the sea and plunge down with his booty" when Agnes looks at him once more, "not fearfully, not despairingly, not proud of her good luck, not intoxicated with desire, but in absolute faith and in absolute humility . . . and with this look she entrusts her whole destiny to him in absolute confidence." The effect on the merman is profound:

The sea no longer roars, its wild voice is stilled; nature's passion, which is the merman' strength, forsakes him, and there is a deadly calm – and Agnes is still looking at him this way. Then the merman breaks down. He cannot withstand the power of innocence, his natural element is disloyal to him, and he cannot seduce Agnes. He takes her home again, he explains that he only wanted to show her how beautiful the sea is when it is calm, and Agnes believes him. Then he returns alone, and the sea is wild, but not as wild as the merman's despair. He can seduce

5 Cf. ch. 5, 116–19.

Agnes, he can seduce a hundred Agneses, he can make any girl infatuated – but Agnes has won, and the merman has lost her. Only as booty can she be his; he cannot give himself faithfully to any girl, because he is indeed only a merman. (94–5)

Silentio's parable, like Climacus's, is about unhappy love in the most profound sense: one party is unable to make himself understood by, or to disclose himself to, the other. Both parables are told from the viewpoint of the male, but in the case of the king and the maiden the male is the lover while in that of Agnes and the merman he is the beloved. The king's love is therefore properly compared with that of Agnes, and the merman's situation with that of the maiden. What might such a comparison disclose?

Agnes (in Danish, *Agnete*) – whose name reminds one of Agnus, the lamb of God, and whose free and unconditional love for the merman is meant to recall Christ's love for fallen man – "trust[s] with all her soul" and looks at the merman "in absolute faith." The significance of this becomes clear when we reflect that the Greek word for faith in the New Testament, *pistis*, is in extrareligious contexts the word for trust. Religious faith, in other words, is not primarily a matter of belief in the truth of certain dogmas. On the contrary, such beliefs are properly rooted in the trust one has in the person of God. To call a steed "trusty" or a friend "faithful" is to assert that he or she can be counted on and will not let one down. So powerful is this trust that it can sometimes overcome the most serious reasonable doubts, as when a beloved father, having asked his daughter to do something that seems foolish to her, overcomes her objections by saying: "Just trust me, you must do it."

This personal relationship of trust seems to explain the faith Abraham shows in God when he obeys God's seemingly absurd command to take Isaac up Mount Moriah in order to sacrifice him. But whereas Abraham was familiar with God and knew him to be trustworthy in advance of receiving this command, Agnes has faith in the merman even though she is entirely unfamiliar with him. Agnes is indeed Christlike: she feels no fear, despair, pride, or intoxicating desire in relation to the merman, and her trust, humility, and confidence are absolute.[6] It is therefore no surprise that, in comparison with Agnes, both the king and the merman fall short in faith.

---

[6] Cf. Silentio's admission that he has "changed Agnes a little" by making her entirely innocent, although "generally it is pure nonsense ... to imagine a seduction in which the girl is utterly, utterly, utterly innocent" (95).

To return to Climacus's parable, note that we see the maiden only through the eyes of the king. The king's worry is that the maiden will lack the confidence to love him as an equal, but perhaps he is mistaken. Indeed, the only reason the parable gives us to suppose that she might lack the necessary confidence is one that Socrates would regard as irrelevant: she happens to be a maiden of lowly station and he happens to be a king. Unlike the merman, whose "being a merman signif[ies] a human preexistence, in consequence of which his life was entrapped" (96), there is no suggestion that the maiden's lowly status is in any way her fault. Climacus's parable, in other words, does not explicitly reflect the phenomena of sin and guilt that play such a large part in Silentio's adaptation of the legend of Agnes and the merman, which adaptation Silentio describes as "a sketch along the lines of the demonic" (94).[7] Climacus's parable is accordingly incomplete precisely to the extent that the situation of the learner cannot be fully appreciated without considering the effects of sin and guilt. By the same token, the fact that the king seems oblivious to these phenomena underscores the limited extent of even his understanding – a royal understanding that Climacus supposes is far superior to that of the maiden.

The king claims to regard the difference between himself and the maiden as inessential, yet he supposes that the maiden will be unable to see the matter as he does. In a word, he lacks faith in her. Is his lack of faith in the maiden a sign of his lack of faith in himself? That is, does the king secretly despair of the power of his *own* love?

This question is prompted by a further reflection on the parable of Agnes and the merman. The merman is oblivious to the potential power of Agnes's love, and this obliviousness is intertwined with his lack of faith in himself. The merman, as we have seen, "breaks down"; he "is saved by Agnes; the seducer is crushed, he has submitted to the power of innocence, he can never seduce again" (96). In short, Agnes causes the merman to repent of his demonic nature. Repentance is possible only because he is more than a beastly seducer; he is also human, and this combination of the demonic and the human is visible in his amphibian body, which is half fish and half man. In one sense, then, the merman is saved by repentance, but in another sense he is lost. For he is henceforth

---

7 This notion of the demonic, which appears elsewhere in Kierkegaard's pseudonymous writings, should not be confused with Socrates' daimonion. "One who is demonic experiences the same attraction and repulsion from the good as do others from a prospective evil action" (Watkin 2001, 63).

paralyzed or suspended between his beastly and human natures, his past and his future: he cannot give himself faithfully to Agnes "because he is indeed only a merman" (95). This phrase is ambiguous: does it mean that the merman is incapable of loving Agnes faithfully because of who he is, or because of who he *thinks* he is? In any case, the merman has repented and the seducer is crushed, which is to say that he is not – and can never again be – "only a merman." So why does he continue to regard himself as one?

Silentio writes that "immediately two forces struggle over him [the merman]: repentance, Agnes and repentance. If repentance alone gets him, then he is hidden; if Agnes and repentance get him, then he is disclosed" (96). The question, then, is whether the merman will communicate his repentance to Agnes. To do so would be to lay bare his whole sordid story. Now, one might assume the merman fears that Agnes would no longer love him if she knew the truth. But this does not concern him in the least. In fact, he would welcome such a result, for he knows that Agnes loves him and he supposes that "if he could tear this love away from Agnes, then in a way she would be saved." But saved from what? The answer must be: from him, for he is "only a merman," a vile seducer, and as such is unworthy of her love. And if the merman does not confide in Agnes, it is only because he "is too sensible to reckon that a frank confession would arouse her loathing" (96).

The merman, in other words, has repented, but repentance alone cannot remove his burden of guilt. He consequently believes that he deserves to be loathed, not loved. In the merman's eyes, a frank confession could only mislead Agnes, because the very nobility of this gesture would obscure the fact that he is a rapacious seducer. In sum, the merman has no faith in his ability to be anything other than just a merman – no faith, in other words, in his ability to love faithfully – nor is he capable of imagining that Agnes's absolute and unconditional love might help him to do so. Yet according to Silentio the merman has *already* been saved from his demonic nature by Agnes's love, and could be saved by it in another sense if only he became disclosed (99). For then he truly could give himself faithfully to Agnes, and their love would no longer be unhappy.

The predicament of the merman as displayed in Silentio's parable is relevant to Climacus's purpose in *Fragments* because it helps us to grasp the full extent of the problem that the god confronts in trying to win the love of the learner who has become untruth through sin. It is also worth noting that Agnes and the merman are initially even farther apart than the king and the maiden, for just as the merman's demonic nature puts him beneath the maiden (at least given what we know of her from the parable), Agnes's capacity for absolutely faithful and humble love places her higher than the king. Agnes's complete innocence in relation to the merman makes her superior to any actual girl (cf. 95), but her superiority lies precisely in her ability to annul the difference between herself and the merman. On the other hand, the king – to whom Climacus incidentally attributes a reputation for wrath (26, 27) – is all too human. Climacus later suggests that his love is too weak, or perhaps one should say too proud, to allow him genuinely to descend to the level of the maiden (31–2) – an act that would presumably require, among other things, abdicating his throne. Yet Climacus nevertheless likens the king to the god. His reason is not hard to discern: whereas Agnes in her simplicity and innocence feels no sorrow in relation to her beloved, the god does. We may infer that the god combines the faithfulness and humility of Agnes with the reflectiveness of the king, for the king's sorrow is born of reflection.

THE POET'S TASK

We return now to *Fragments*. Up to this point, Climacus has sketched the problem that the god confronts in trying to win the learner. He now invites the poet to find a solution to this problem, or to find "a point of unity where there is in truth love's understanding" (28). As Climacus is himself a poet, he puts his own hand to the task he has described. Like Socrates, who claimed to know only the erotic things, he would seem to have some expertise in the affairs of love.

The first solution Climacus considers is that "the unity is brought about by an ascent." In other words, "the god would draw the learner up toward himself, exalt him, divert him with joy lasting a thousand years." Yet the "noble" king, being "something of a connoisseur of human nature," rejected this approach, because he saw that by this means the girl would be "essentially deceived." This deception is especially terrible because the one who is deceived "does not even suspect it," for the learner "would perhaps be very much inclined to consider himself blissfully happy" were he to be exalted by the god (29).

What is the nature of the learner's deception? The learner would inevitably experience ascent to the god as a kind of lucky hit, as though he had "score[d] a great success because the god's eye fell upon him" (29). The happiness of the learner would thus be based on his adoration of the god, not on his love of the god as an equal. The learner would

persist in regarding himself as an inferior person (albeit one who has
been marvelously favored by fortune), and in this he would be deceived.
As Climacus puts the point, the god takes joy in adorning the lily, but
it "would be a tragic delusion on the part of the lily if, in observing the
costume, it considered itself to be the beloved because of the costume"
(29–30; cf. Matthew 6:28–30).

Climacus goes on to say that, were he to accept the adoration of the
learner, the god would cause the learner to "forget himself" (29). This
remark is puzzling, since the god does want the learner to forget that
he was once even more lowly than the lowliest maiden. In Chapter One,
moreover, Climacus stated that the learner *must* "forget himself" in order
to be delivered by the god from the self-imprisonment of sin (19). How
is this self-forgetfulness consistent with self-recollection?

An answer is suggested by the observation that the god and Socrates
share similar concerns about the learner. Just as the god refuses to be
adored by his beloved, Socrates refuses any attempt on the part of young
men infatuated by philosophy to glorify or idolize him. He understands
that to allow others to idolize him would be to suggest that the truth was in
him and not in them, and so to cheat them of their prospects for achieving eternal happiness through philosophy. In a word, Socrates – who, as
Climacus will later remind us, is also "a connoisseur of human nature"
(37) – is concerned lest the learner forget himself. This is precisely the
concern of the god. If the god wants the learner to forget that he once
was as nothing, it must be in order that he can recollect who he truly is.
Although this recollection is not philosophical in that it requires the aid
of the god, it is in another respect analogous to the Socratic case. Being
unable to forget that one is nothing more than untruth would be like forgetting that the truth is immanent in one's soul: in either case, learning
(whether conceived religiously or philosophically) becomes impossible.
But according to the religious hypothesis, the learner was not always
untruth: he became untruth when he lost the condition for learning the
truth – a condition that is essential to his being. In the eyes of the loving
god, the learner is such as he was created, not such as he has become
through sin. To remember who he truly is, the learner must be able to
forget what the king "only wished to forget" (27) and what the god has
in effect already forgotten. If he cannot do this, he will be unable to
understand the instruction of the god and so will remain untruth.

"There was a people," Climacus writes of the Jews, "who had a good
understanding of the divine; this people believed that to see the god
was death" (cf. Exodus 33:20). This remark applies to the sorrowful

contradiction that confronts the god: "not to disclose itself is the death of love; to disclose itself is the death of the beloved." Yet because "the human mind so often aspires to might and power...as if achieving it would transfigure everything," the learner longs precisely for the god to disclose himself. Part of the god's secret sorrow is therefore "to have to deny the learner that to which he aspires with his whole soul and to have to deny it precisely because he is the beloved" (30).

The god must refrain from revealing himself in all of his glory: if this did not literally kill the learner, it would at least render him unable to be reborn in the truth. Yet he cannot refrain from self-disclosure altogether, for this would result in the death of love. The god must therefore find some way to disclose himself while at the same time not disclosing himself. While this sounds deeply paradoxical, an analogue to what the god must do is provided by the irony of Socrates.

Climacus implicitly adverts to Socrates' irony when he notes that the unity of the god and the learner must be brought about otherwise than by ascent. "Here we are once again mindful of Socrates," he writes, "for what else was his ignorance but the unitive expression of love for the learner." "But, as we have seen," he adds, "this unity was also the truth" (30). The "ignorance" that Climacus has in mind is in the first place the assumed ignorance by which Socrates regularly concealed his own mind and thereby forced his interlocutor to think for himself. But Climacus is aware that Socrates' ignorance was not simply feigned. He remarks that the unity established by his assumed ignorance was *also* the truth, because the Socratic learner and teacher are equal in their access to the truth. So, too, Socrates' claim of ignorance, even if superficially false (because he "knew," if only in a prophetic and imprecise manner, much more than he let on), was true in the deeper sense that he was not a wise man but only a lover of wisdom. This doubleness, wherein Socrates simultaneously revealed and concealed his own mind, is already familiar to us from the *Apology*, where it was necessary in order to convey the unity of immanence and transcendence in eros. The name for this manner of self-disclosure, as well as for the ambiguity of identity that is thereby disclosed, is Socratic irony.[8]

---

[8] See Vlastos 1991, 31 on the "peculiarly Socratic" phenomenon of complex irony: "In 'complex' irony what is said both is and isn't what is meant: its surface content is meant to be true in one sense, false in another." Schaerer 1941 describes irony of the Socratic sort as "a deceit that betrays itself" and that "depends on a duality at the heart of the real." The practitioners of irony, he adds, are "always elsewhere and always present, like Socrates" (185).

The god requires something analogous to Socratic irony because his love must somehow find a way in between the horns of a difficult dilemma. Unlike Socrates' love for the learner, a love rooted in his desire to gain access through dialogue to the truth that is immanent in every human soul, the god's love is not only "assisting" but genuinely "procreative" (30). Climacus goes on to point out that this is not the sort of procreative love of which Socrates speaks in the *Symposium* – a love that expresses "the relation of the autodidact to the beautiful," whereby the lover, "ignoring dispersed beauty, envisions beauty-in-and-by-itself and now gives birth to many beautiful and glorious discourses and thoughts" (31). Whereas Socratic love brings forth that which was already present in the soul of the learner, "to beget is reserved for the god." In allowing him to make the transition from "not to be" to "to be," the god "gives birth to the learner"; the learner therefore owes the god "everything." But the god does not simply want to lay claim to everything, and in any case could not directly do so without contradiction; otherwise the learner would misunderstand the god, would remain untruth, and would indeed owe the god nothing. At the same time, however, the god wants the learner fully to understand his situation:

[T]hat which makes understanding so difficult is precisely this: that he [the learner] becomes nothing and yet is not annihilated; that he owes him [the god] everything and yet becomes boldly confident; that he understands the truth, but the truth makes him free; that he grasps the guilt of untruth, and then again bold confidence triumphs in the truth. (30–1)

How is this understanding to be achieved?

If the god cannot bring about unity with the learner by an ascent, he must, Climacus maintains, attempt to do so by a descent. The god will come down to the learner, and "will appear . . . as the equal of the lowliest of persons." Since the lowliest is one who must serve others, the god will appear to his beloved in the form of a servant. This is a form that does not announce his godhood. Yet Climacus insists that the form of a servant is "not something put on like the king's plebian cloak . . . [and] the light Socratic summer cloak, which, although woven from nothing, yet is concealing and revealing." Whereas Socrates' character as a lover of the learner is "assumed" and thus "still a kind of deceit," servitude is the god's "true form," and is such through "the omnipotence of resolving love" (31–2).

It is not yet clear where the analogy to Socratic irony breaks down. That servitude is the god's true form cannot mean that it is the *whole* truth about the god. The descent of the god introduces doubleness, and therewith irony. There is the god, and there is the god who has descended, and the task for faith is to hold these two – the lowly servant and the almighty god – together in their identity. At first sight, this seems to be structurally the same task as the one that confronts those who seek to understand Socrates. Socrates' expresses his love in the form of ignorance, but his appearance is not the whole truth: Socrates is and is not just what he seems to be. The god expresses his love in the form of the servant, but the god's appearance is also not the whole truth: he, too, is and is not just what he seems to be. This is obvious from the fact that those who take him to be just what meets the eye – a servant and nothing more – have not grasped that this servant, unlike any other servant, is the god.

There remains, however, a fundamental difference between the Socratic case and that of the god. According to Climacus, the god's servitude is his true form because he really *is* "absolutely the equal of the lowliest of human beings," who as such "must suffer all things, [and] endure all things" (32–3). At the same time, the god is also absolutely the god, and so is as unequal to the learner as truth is to untruth. Socrates, on the other hand, is neither absolutely equal nor absolutely unequal to the learner. He is not equal to the learner because he is in certain respects superior to other men. As Climacus frequently reminds us, he is a teacher of rare integrity and loyalty, and his passion for the truth is unparalleled. His assumed ignorance thus resembles the plebian cloak of a king, "which just by flapping open would betray the king" (32). Yet he is not unequal to the learner in that, although both have access to the truth, neither is wise. If Socrates is not a plebian just to the extent that he is a king, he is also not a king just to the extent that he is a plebian.[9]

The limits of the Socratic analogy can now be expressed in terms of the difference between the irony of Socrates and that of the god. Socrates is and is not A and also is and is not B, whereas the god is absolutely A and also is absolutely B. In both cases, irony means that one must think A and B together. Yet thinking faces a different kind of challenge in each instance. The Socratic case is intelligible because it involves no fundamental contradiction: Socrates can ambiguously be both A and B because he is neither exactly one nor the other. The god, however, is fully and completely A (the infinite and eternal god) while being fully and

---

9 Because of his ignorance Socrates is not even fit to be a philosopher-king, such as is meant to rule the city in speech of Plato's *Republic*: the philosopher-kings must know the being of the Beautiful/Noble, the Just, and the Good (*Republic* 484c–d).

completely *B* (the finite and time-bound servant). The understanding is thus confronted with what Climacus will go on to call the "absolute paradox" – a paradox that cannot be comprehended by reason and so must be grasped by faith.

The god, as we have seen, cannot make himself understood by bringing the learner up to himself. Descent to the learner is the only alternative. What is more, this descent must take the form of incarnation: any other sort of revelation would maintain the inequality between the god and the learner that love seeks to overcome. This does not mean, however, that descent will bring about the unity with the learner that the god desires. In order to understand the god's instruction, the learner is required to accept that one who is "like unto the lowliest" is in fact the god, that the god made himself such through his omnipotent love for the learner, and that the god deserves to be loved in return. But the recognition that the god *deserves* to be loved is only the beginning of understanding, for the fullest response to the god would be to love as one is loved – freely and unconditionally. Only then would there be genuine equality between the god and the learner.

There is, however, a critical obstacle to the god's attempt to win the learner's love: because the god's existence as a lowly servant surpasses understanding, the learner is apt to take offense at the notion of the incarnation (32). Climacus will later speak at length about the nature of this offense (49–54). Here we need only note that it springs from philosophical pride – the presupposition (or rather, presumption) that the truth must in principle be fully comprehensible to reason – and that there is nothing the god could have done in order to avoid the circumstances that give rise to offense. For one who lacks the condition for understanding the truth is apt to have serious difficulty embracing it.

The god's existence is thus one of sorrow, because his love is bound to be largely unrequited. There is, however, no other way for the god to fulfill his work as a teacher. For love, Climacus maintains,

any other revelation would be a deception, because it would first have had to accomplish a change in the learner (love, however, does not change the beloved but changes itself) and conceal from him that this was needed, or in superficiality it would have had to remain ignorant that the whole understanding between them [i.e., the god and the learner] was a delusion (this is the untruth of paganism). (33)

The first alternative operates outside the framework of love, for love does not change the learner. Nor does love tolerate deception, as it longs for mutual understanding. But without love, what would move the god to reveal himself? The pagan answer is need or desire, and specifically the desire to be worshiped. Yet we have already seen that, in glorifying himself before the learner, the god would undermine the learner's confidence and cause him to forget himself. Pagan revelation (the second alternative in the passage quoted above) is thus a "delusion," in that it leaves the learner in untruth. For Climacus, however, it is an open question whether the learner is capable of loving "him who humbled himself in equality with you," and indeed of loving any god but "the omnipotent one who performs miracles" (33).[10]

It is easier to worship the god than to love him, because love requires courage. The god's concern is that we "sit with him as his equal," yet this is a terrifying prospect for the learner – so much so that it would be "less terrifying to fall upon one's face while the mountains tremble at the god's voice" (34–5). What makes it terrifying is the learner's sense of his own unworthiness. The learner, we recall, must come to understand that in his condition of untruth he was nothing, that he was so through his own fault, and that he owes the god everything (30–1). Under the circumstances, he is bound – like the merman in relation to Agnes – to experience "the anxieties of guilt." While these anxieties might be assuaged by the act of worship, they can only be exacerbated by the invitation to sit with the god as an equal. The learner cannot contain his knowledge of the god as simultaneously his savior and his equal any more than a clay pot can contain a sprouting oak seed. When the god "plants himself in the frailty of a human being," the human being must therefore become "a new person and a new vessel" (34). The learner will never come to love the god with bold confidence unless he is able to abandon his initial understanding of his intrinsic worthlessness in relation to the god. This is in itself a deeply frightening prospect, even though he may come to recognize that the weakness of his understanding is the ultimate source of his terror.

At the conclusion of his "poem," Climacus imagines that someone might accuse him of "composing the shabbiest plagiarism ever to appear." He does not dispute this description. Indeed, he readily admits to having "robbed the deity," who must be the true author of his poem (35–6).

---

[10] Cf. the doubts of Ivan Karamazov's Grand Inquisitor in bk. 5, ch. 5 of Fyodor Dostoyevsky's *The Brothers Karamazov*.

But it is in his view quite remarkable that no human being could have imagined what he has just related to his readers:

Presumably it could occur to a human being to poetize himself in the likeness of the god or the god in the likeness of himself, but not to poetize that the god poetized himself in the likeness of a human being, for if the god gave no indication, how could it occur to a man that the blessed god could need him? (36)

In Climacus's view, the notion that the blessed god could need a human being is "so bad a thought that it could not arise in him," even though, when the god has confided it to him, he finds it to be "the most wondrously beautiful thought." The poem fills one with wonder; indeed, it "was so different from every human poem that it was no poem at all, but *the wonder*" (36, emphasis in original).

Two things are noteworthy about Climacus's remarks at the end of Chapter Two. First, his claim that no human being could have invented the poem he has just related is no more convincing than the similar claim at the end of Chapter One. It is true that philosophical inquiry could never by itself disclose God's love for human beings. But has God in fact revealed His love, or are the scriptures that report His love a human invention? Because it is clear that there is no demonstration that can decide this question, Climacus must know that he has not shown that "the deity" is the true author of his poem. Thoughtful readers – at least those who are not already Christians – must therefore continue to regard the philosophical and religious accounts of learning as equally compelling hypotheses.[11] We may now add, however, that the ambiguity pertaining to the origin of Climacus's poem is identical to the ambiguity associated with Socratic philosophizing owing to its erotic character. Socrates, we recall, claimed both to have been stationed at his philosophical post by the god and to have stationed himself. To the extent that the passion of faith proves to be analogous to the daimonic passion of philosophical eros, its work, too, might be neither simply human nor simply divine, but somehow both simultaneously.

Second, it is strange that Climacus chooses to speak in the present context of the god's need and not the god's love. As we have seen, Climacus

---

[11] Evans 1992 notes that "only the believer will be inclined to accept the claim of Climacus that the hypothesis he has spun out is of divine origin. The unbeliever will reject this notion in rejecting the 'proof,' and properly so" (42). Yet he also observes that Climacus's talk of "the wonder" is meant to rekindle a sense of "the strangeness of the Christian story" in "a culture where familiarity with the Christian message has brought with it dullness if not contempt" (55).

challenges the Socratic view that love is rooted in need. He explains that the god "needs no pupil in order to understand himself," and that, there being "no need that moves him" to make his appearance, he must be moved by love for the learner (24). Yet in the passage quoted above, Climacus states that the god does need the learner. In doing so, he brings to mind the Socratic view of the gods – a view that is captured neither by classical paganism nor by the religious hypothesis. For it *did* occur to Socrates that the god needs him, and not simply, as Aristophanes supposes, in order that he might be worshiped.

In the *Apology*, Socrates claims to serve the god by exemplifying the relative worthlessness of human wisdom and by acting as a philosophical gadfly to awaken his fellow Athenians (23a–b, 30e–31a). In Plato's *Euthyphro*, which is dramatically situated on the eve of his public trial, Socrates elicits from his interlocutor the view that that the gods require our "service" in order to bring to completion some "noble work" (13d–e). When Euthyphro fails to specify what this joint work is, Socrates tells him that he gave up just when they were on the verge of understanding the nature of piety (14b-c). This amounts to a strong suggestion that, in Socrates' view, the gods need our assistance in order to accomplish something that they cannot accomplish on their own. In that case, philanthropy and need are inseparable: the gods care for us as coworkers whose help they need to achieve some good.

If the gods need our help in this way, there must be something that we can do together with them that they cannot do alone. On the philosophical hypothesis, there is one thing that no one – not even a god – can do for anyone else: no one can make another person understand the truth, for learning takes place only through the independent effort of the learner. Perhaps, then, our joint work with the gods consists in our learning the truth, or at least requires that we learn the truth as a precondition for further service. In either case, piety requires us to philosophize. This conclusion can be reached in another way: philosophical inquiry is necessary in order to disclose how we are to serve the gods as coworkers.[12]

Socrates' understanding of piety may shed some light on Climacus's remark that the god needs us. According to Climacus, the god loves us, but not because he needs us. Were his love at bottom a desire for something that he lacks (as per the Socratic explanation of eros), it would cease when his need is fulfilled. The god's love, however, is an end in itself;

---

[12] For a similar line of reflection see Vlastos 1991, 174–6.

in Climacus's words, "love does not have the satisfaction of need outside itself but within" (24). But this means that the god's philanthropy is not entirely free from need. Given that the god loves us and wants us to learn the truth, there is indeed something that he needs from us: he needs to be understood, for if he is not his love will be unhappy.[13] As in the Socratic case, however, he cannot make us understand him. He cannot even prevent us from taking offense at the fact that he is so hard to understand. The god can prepare the way for understanding ever so carefully, but if we are somehow actually to come to know him, we must do so through our own effort.

Because Socrates recognizes that the god needs him, he must have come to this insight either on his own or in response to some indication on the part of the god (such as the oracle that Chaerephon received at Delphi). In the former case, Socrates' prophetic imagination is able to accomplish what Climacus said could not be accomplished by a human being. In the latter, Socratic philosophizing is once again shown to be dependent on his faith in the meaningfulness of divine action. In either case, Socrates, guided by eros, grasps that the god needs us to make an effort to understand him. That such an effort need not be entirely futile even on the religious hypothesis is indicated by the partial, if paradoxical, success of Climacus's poetical venture, which has at least managed to help us understand the sorrow that the god experiences because he cannot be understood.

The preceding reflections suggest a certain convergence of the paths of philosophy and religion. They lend credence to Merold Westphal's claim that "it is not reason as such that is opposed to faith but modes of human reason that have forgotten their limits as human and have lapsed into self-deification."[14] But they also highlight the essential difference that continues to divide the aforementioned paths, for on the religious hypothesis the appearance of the god poses an absolute paradox that philosophy cannot fathom. Socratic philosophizing, it seems, can go only so far in understanding the god. Yet Socrates is at least not the sort to take offense at the god, for otherwise Climacus could never have imagined presenting *Fragments* to him for his inspection.

Why is this? Does Socrates not stake his life on the assumptions of the philosophical hypothesis? Climacus's introduction of the problem of offense makes it still more difficult to understand his gesture of homage

---

[13] Mulhall 1999 also notes the god's neediness and links it to his love (11–12).
[14] Westphal 1998, 112.

to Socrates in The Moral. While it is still too early to explore the full implications of this paradoxical gesture, Climacus seems to see something in the nature of Socratic philosophizing that allows it to appreciate its own limitations, and to do so in such a way as to open the philosopher's mind to the potential truth of the religious hypothesis.

The foregoing suggestion will be confirmed in the next chapter of *Fragments*, in which Climacus discusses paradox in connection with what he calls "the passion of thought" – a passion with which he is intimately familiar by virtue of his own disposition. It is in reflecting on thought's passionate attraction to paradox, a subject he views through the lens of Plato's portrayal of Socrates, that Climacus provides his deepest insights into the nature and significance of philosophical eros. With this interpretation of eros, he arrives at the heart of the question of the relationship between philosophy and faith.

5

The Paradox and the Passion of Thought

From what we have seen so far, it would be fair to say that *Fragments* is driven by paradox. It begins with what appears to be a total opposition between the philosophical and religious hypotheses. Climacus paints in black and white with no shades of gray. If the truth can be learned, we can either learn it on our own or we cannot; there is logically no other possibility, nor can both claims be true at the same time. Either the religious hypothesis is true, or it is an illusion; either the philosopher has access to the truth, or he is simply untruth. There seems to be no middle ground, nor any ground outside of philosophy and religion besides the skepticism that insists that the truth cannot be learned at all. To borrow the Hegelian terminology that Climacus draws on in Chapter Three, the difference between philosophy and religion cannot be mediated.

Yet *Fragments* concludes with the suggestion that the proper judge of Climacus and his thought is Socrates, the philosopher. What is more, Socrates is hard to pin down in *Fragments*, just as he is in the pages of Plato.[1] Socrates' relationship with "the god" fits neither of the two hypotheses. The same is true of Climacus's own thinking: although faith is absurd from the standpoint of philosophy and philosophy is untruth from the standpoint of faith, Climacus somehow manages to illuminate the implications of both.

Climacus's use of paradox in *Fragments* is dialectical, in that it reflects his practice of introducing into the inquiry elements that force the reader to revise earlier assumptions and inferences. Chapter Three, "The Absolute Paradox (A Metaphysical Caprice)," is no exception. In Chapter Two,

---

[1] For further discussion of Socrates' elusive and ambiguous character, see Howland 1993.

Climacus offers a poetic analogy "in order to awaken the mind to an understanding of the divine" (26), and in particular to suggest the difficulty the god experiences in getting the learner to understand him. In Chapter Three, however, he suggests that this analogy cannot have helped to illuminate the god's situation: the god is absolutely different from us, and absolute difference can in no way be grasped by human understanding alone or by any of the tools available to it, including analogy (which presupposes some degree of similarity in its terms). The god nevertheless wants to "annul" this absolute difference by making himself absolutely equal to the learner, for only in this way, as Climacus's poetical venture has (paradoxically!) helped to establish, can he become the learner's teacher. That the absolutely different can become absolutely equal is yet another paradox. Indeed, the unity of absolute difference and absolute equality is the "absolute paradox" – absolute because, unlike relative paradoxes that can be mastered by concentrated reflection, it poses a question that the understanding cannot answer.

In spite of these baffling twists of thought, Chapter Three promises to shed light on Climacus's practice as an author and a thinker, for its leading theme is the relationship between paradox and philosophical inquiry. In this chapter, it quickly becomes apparent that Climacus's use of paradox is designed both to ward off those readers who are deficient in philosophical eros and to entice and provoke those who are not. He lays his cards on the table almost immediately: "the thinker without the paradox," he writes, "is like the lover without passion: a mediocre fellow" (37). Any thinker who aspires to something more than mediocrity must have a sense of paradox, and of the wonder that paradox naturally elicits. What is more, philosophy is not a cool intellectual exercise: as Climacus shows by his own example, it is fundamentally a passionate or erotic activity. Yet the thinker with a passion for paradox is like a moth drawn to flame, in that this passion, by "want[ing] to discover something that thought itself cannot think," thereby "will[s] its own downfall" (37). And this unknown and philosophically unknowable "something" – this thing that thought cannot think – turns out to be nothing other than the god.

Climacus's interpretation of the passion of thought is rooted in his understanding of that most passionate of all thinkers, Socrates. His interpretation is a kind of internal critique of Socratic philosophizing: he shows that philosophical eros ultimately leads one to encounter absolute difference, and therewith to discover the limits of philosophizing. The Moral furthermore implies that this critique – which is made possible by Climacus's Socratic ability, already evidenced in *Johannes Climacus,* to enter into a way of thinking and try to make it one's own – is one to which Socrates might be expected to be open, presumably because it simply renders explicit what is already implicit in philosophical eros.[2] For the first time, Climacus thus seems seriously to take sides with respect to the contest between philosophic reason and religious faith. The Socratic attempt to recollect that which truly is and to achieve full self-knowledge cannot be completed, and the failure of this attempt implies that if we are to know the truth it must be revealed to us. The most sustained and concerted effort to learn the truth philosophically thus prepares the way for religious faith. It is our task in this chapter to try to understand why this should be so.

SOCRATES AND SELF-KNOWLEDGE

Climacus's reflections in Chapter Three focus on the theme of self-knowledge. This is appropriate because self-knowledge is central to Socrates' erotic, philosophical quest. Self-knowledge implies knowledge of that which truly is – for how can I be said to know myself if I do not know the beings to which I aspire, and the knowledge of which constitutes the soul's proper nourishment? A certain degree of self-knowledge is furthermore required simply in order to philosophize. If I am to seek wisdom on my own, I must be confident that I am in fact capable of calling the truth to mind and distinguishing it from that which is false.

Climacus begins the chapter by considering the figure of Socrates as he is presented in the *Phaedrus*, the Platonic dialogue that provides the fullest account of eros.[3] The starting-point for his reflections is *Phaedrus* 230a, in which Socrates claims not to know whether he is, in Climacus's paraphrase, "a more curious monster than Typhon or a friendlier and simpler being, by nature sharing something divine" (37). Typhon, a dragon with

---

[2] Even the most thoughtful studies of *Fragments* have failed to do justice to the erotic nature of Socratic philosophizing. Evans 1992 makes much of reason's essentially "imperialistic" character, as expressed in a desire to "master" and "domesticate" that which it seeks to understand. This leads Evans to conclude that reason requires a revelation to discern its sinfulness. Reason "cannot on its own produce" the collision with that which is absolutely different (78); "imperialistic reason" must be "given a hard knock," but "this hard knock . . . must be imparted by revelation" (76). While Evans is right to remind us that the desire for mastery is evident in all spheres of thought, it is subordinate to eros in the paradigmatic case of Socrates. This is why Climacus suggests that, in comparison with Socrates, most thinkers are "lovers without passion."

[3] Like Chapter One, Chapter Three begins with Socrates and thus represents "a kind of starting-over" (Evans 1992, 58). The theme of eros, however, was absent in Climacus's earlier exposition of the Socratic or philosophical hypothesis.

a hundred heads and multiple animal voices, fought Zeus for the rule of gods and men and was the last obstacle to the cosmic imposition of Olympian order (Hesiod, *Theogony* 820–80). Socrates' uncertainty about whether his nature shares in the divine or is monstrously opposed to it brings to mind the predicament of Silentio's merman. As we shall see, Socrates manifests both Typhonic and divine qualities in the course of the *Phaedrus*. And while the merman is at least partly saved by Agnes's love, Socrates makes it clear that he is rescued from depravity by his daimonion and the divine madness of eros.

The context of Socrates' remark about Typhon is as follows. Phaedrus has just asked Socrates whether he believes the myth about the rape of Oreithuia by Boreas. Socrates responds by noting that he could, in a "clever or quibbling manner" (*sophidzomenos*, a word related to the term "sophist"), explain the myth as the poetic embellishment of Oreithuia's having been blown from the rocks by a gust of wind. These sorts of explanations, however, are the work of "an excessively clever and laborious and not very fortunate man," for there is no end of such myths. For his part, Socrates has no time for demythologizing: "I am not yet able, in accordance with the Delphic inscription, to know myself; so it seems ridiculous to me, while I am ignorant of this, to inquire into things that do not belong to me" (229c–30a).

Climacus's citation of the *Phaedrus* is highly suggestive. In the passage to which he calls our attention, Socrates presents his philosophizing as adherence to the words carved in the temple of the god at Delphi. This coheres with the *Apology*, especially inasmuch as the injunction to seek self-knowledge is consistent with Socrates' interpretation of the oracle. Climacus thus once again emphasizes the centrality of the god to Socrates' philosophical quest. Furthermore, Socrates resists the scientific explanation of myths insofar as it involves the reduction of divine beings (like Boreas, the north wind) to natural phenomena. He is too busy minding his own business – the business imposed on all human beings by the command of the god to "Know Thyself" – to meddle in affairs that he cannot hope to understand if he does not even understand himself. Nor is he interested in acquiring knowledge that seems irrelevant to his life. Socrates' clear grasp of his primary philosophical task, and of the vast extent of his ignorance, goes a long way toward explaining why he might not be inclined to take offense at the god of the religious hypothesis.

For Climacus, it is well worth noting that Socrates, a "connoisseur of human nature" who "did his very best . . . to know himself" and who "has been eulogized for centuries as the person who certainly knew man best," did not really know who he was. "This seems to be a paradox," he writes.

"But one must not think ill of the paradox, for the paradox is the passion [*Lidenskab*] of thought, and the thinker without the paradox is like the lover without passion: a mediocre fellow" (37). The lover without passion, we recall, is a key figure in the *Phaedrus*: it is by praising such a lover that Socrates offends against eros, and it is to atone for this offense that he offers his palinode to divine erotic madness (242b–d, 244a–57b).

Socrates would certainly agree that the thinker without passion is mediocre, for philosophy, as the love of wisdom, is essentially erotic. Yet Socrates suggests that the passion of thought is beauty or goodness, not paradox. In the *Phaedrus* and *Symposium*, he teaches that philosophical eros is awakened by the vision of beauty and aspires to the Beautiful itself; in the *Republic*, he explains that every soul longs for and pursues the Good. Socrates nevertheless anticipates Climacus's claim about paradox in the *Republic*, where he notes that the activity of the intellect is provoked by the strange impression that a thing is somehow simultaneously its opposite. The soul that undergoes such an experience "would be compelled to be at a loss and to inquire, by setting in motion the intelligence within it" (524e). Thinking, in other words, is questioning, and as such is summoned and awakened by that which is fundamentally questionable – or, as Climacus puts it, by paradox.

While the relationship between beauty, goodness, and paradox in Socrates' thought is the subject for another inquiry, these are evidently three basic ways in which the beings that philosophy seeks to know manifest themselves.[4] In the Platonic dialogues, however, Socrates supposes that philosophy culminates, at least in principle, in the knowledge of the Beautiful (or the Good) and the achievement of wisdom, and thus in the *resolution* of paradox. Socrates' vision of this erotic culmination of thought is of course prophetic and poetic; he is in practice always still en route to wisdom, and thus never actually free from paradox or from the questions it provokes. Climacus departs from Socrates, however, precisely insofar as he reverses his prophetic vision of the end of philosophy. In Climacus's view, Socrates' uncertainty about who he is shows that philosophical eros or passion leads not to answers, but to ever greater questions, to the point where thought encounters a paradox that admits no resolution.

"The ultimate potentiation [*Potens*] of every passion," Climacus writes, "is always to will its own downfall, and so it is also the ultimate passion of the understanding to will the collision, although in one way or another the collision must become its downfall" (37). Passion wills its own downfall

---

4 On the unity of the Beautiful and the Good in Socratic thought, however, see ch. 3, 74 with n. 14.

because it is not its own end. Unlike the love of the god, which "does not have the satisfaction of need outside itself but within" (24), passion is a longing for something beyond itself. This longing ceases when passion acquires its object; since passion wills this acquisition, it also wills its own cessation. The passion of the understanding, provoked by paradox, thus wills its own downfall in the sense that it longs to put an end to questioning by achieving a knowledge of the truth that is no longer questionable.

So far, so good. But Climacus says that the passion of the understanding ultimately wills "the collision" – which presumably means the collision with paradox – and to *collide with* paradox is by no means the same thing as to *understand* it. What is more, the collision becomes the downfall of the passion of the understanding "in one way or another," and thus not necessarily in the way the understanding had hoped. In the case of a satisfied passion, downfall is a consequence of success; a passion that is blocked at every turn, however, would experience downfall in the sense of frustration and failure. It is also worth noting that the Danish, like the Hongs' English translation, is ambiguous as to whether the downfall that results from the collision is that of the passion or of the understanding itself. This is appropriate if downfall in this context implies some sort of failure, but not otherwise, for the understanding whose passion is satisfied does not itself cease from understanding and thus experiences no downfall.

In sum, Climacus suggests that the passion of the understanding, provoked by paradox, wills something that turns out to produce a result opposite to the one it was longing for. This is itself paradoxical. Indeed, it is what Climacus immediately goes on to call "the ultimate paradox of thought," namely, "to want to discover something that thought itself cannot think" (37). But in what sense does thought will the collision with the unthinkable? The answer must be that, unbeknownst to itself, the path of questioning that it follows in its desire to understand leads inevitably to that which cannot be thought. This is certainly not what the understanding had envisioned at the outset of its philosophical journey, but it is nevertheless what transpires as a result of its eagerness to inquire more and more deeply into the nature of things.[5]

---

5 Mulhall observes that Climacus "reiterates the famous opening declaration of the first *Critique* [of Immanuel Kant], that it is the fate of human reason to set itself questions that it is capable neither of answering nor dismissing" (Mulhall 1999, 15; cf. Kant 1965, 7 with Rudd 1993, 61). On the Kantian background of *Fragments*, see Green 1994 and cf. Green 1992.

Climacus's reflections about the passion of the understanding must be seen against the backdrop of Hegel. The experience of thought that Climacus has just sketched is dialectical in the sense specified earlier: the attempt to think something through leads to results that are not only unexpected, but often contrary to one's initial assumptions and intentions. Hegel fully appreciates the dialectical character of thought, yet he attempts to show that wisdom is nevertheless philosophically attainable. His *Phenomenology of Spirit* presents the dialectical process as one of *Aufhebung*, whereby earlier stages of thought are both transcended and preserved by being grasped in successively broader and richer contexts.[6] Once thought becomes sufficiently self-conscious of its own dialectical development, it abandons the nondialectical standpoint of the understanding (*Verstand*) and adopts that of speculative reason (*Vernunft*), which alone is capable of "mediating," or reconciling in a higher unity, the oppositions and contradictions that have repeatedly frustrated the understanding. For Hegel, the conclusion of this process is "absolute knowing" and the unfolding of the system in the *Encyclopedia of the Philosophical Sciences*, to which the *Phenomenology* provides a kind of philosophical ladder.[7] Hegel thus claims to arrive at the end of philosophy – the ultimate resolution of dialectical tension and paradox that Socrates, for his part, could only envision as a distant possibility. For Climacus, however, the experience of the understanding (in Danish, *Forstand*) results not in absolute knowing but in a collision with absolute paradox, or with that which is altogether unintelligible to thought. Put another way, Climacus denies the claims of *Vernunft*: he rejects the notion that there is a kind of philosophical thinking that is capable of resolving the dialectical contradictions inevitably uncovered (or produced) by the activity of the understanding.[8]

If Climacus is correct, why has the unavoidable downfall of thought in its collision with the unthinkable escaped the notice of Hegel and his philosophical heirs? Climacus's answer is that the speculative philosophers, like most people, are not genuinely passionate thinkers. The passion of thought "is fundamentally present everywhere in thought,"

---

[6] See the account of the meaning of the verb *aufheben* at Hegel 1969, 107.

[7] See ch. 1, 10–11.

[8] I agree with Evans 1992, 188 n. 7 that Climacus's use of the term *Forstand* should not be taken to support Hegel's distinction between *Verstand* and *Vernunft*. In other words, Climacus does not imply that the limits of thinking he points out in this chapter apply only to the understanding and not to reason.

he writes, but "because of habit we do not discover this." To illustrate, he offers the analogy of walking:

[W]alking, so the natural scientists inform us, is a continuous falling, but a good steady citizen who walks to his office mornings and home at midday probably considers this an exaggeration, because his progress, after all, is a matter of mediation – how could it occur to him that he is continually falling, he who unswervingly follows his nose. (37)

This analogy is unusually provocative. Walking cannot be accomplished if standing does not give way to falling. Walking is thus neither standing still nor falling, but somehow both together. How is one to comprehend this unity? To the "good steady citizen," the opposition between standing and falling is mediated by being grasped within the larger context of his existence, which has acquired form and solidity from well-established habit. His walking is clearly more like standing still than falling, for its inevitable and completely predictable result is to be at the office in the morning and at home at midday. When the good steady citizen walks, he "unswervingly follows his nose," which is to say that he always has in view nothing other than himself – a self that is everywhere reflected in the familiarity of his surroundings.

"We," Climacus claims – in what may be an ironic echo of the philosophical "we" who look on, with Hegel, at the drama that is played out in the *Phenomenology of Spirit*[9] – do not discover the passion of thought "because of habit." In thinking, we resemble the citizen who walks between office and home according to his daily routine. Like him, we follow well-worn paths, only to arrive at destinations with which we are already familiar. We "follow our noses," which is to say that we are open to, and so can discover, nothing other than ourselves. Our thinking looks to us like motion, but this is an illusion. Like Plato's Meno, whose name means "staying" or "tarrying" and who doubts the very possibility of learning, we are really standing still.

Climacus's sweeping "we" amounts to a cleverly constructed challenge to the reader to distinguish himself from the good steady citizens of the domain of thought – including, no doubt, the great middle class of philosophy professors.[10] Like lovers without passion, these thinkers

9 See, for example, Hegel's use of "we" in §92 and §93 in the first chapter of the *Phenomenology* (Hegel 1977, 59).
10 Cf. this statement in Kierkegaard's journals: "Take the paradox away from a thinker – and you have a professor. A professor has at his disposal a whole line of thinkers from Greece to modern times; it appears as if the professor stood above all of them. Well,

are "mediocre." To think, Climacus implies, is to give oneself over to the vertiginous experience of falling: just as lovers fall in love, genuine thinkers fall in thinking. This is perhaps what Socrates sought to convey when, in the *Phaedrus*, he associated philosophy with erotic madness.

To understand the passion of thought, we must consider a thinker who gives himself over to falling because thinking is his love. Socrates fits the bill perfectly, for his philosophical ardor leads him to welcome even, and perhaps especially, those inquiries in which he is bound to lose his footing. As he says to one of his interlocutors, "thousands of Heracleses and Theseuses, mighty in speaking, have before now met and thrashed me roundly, but I nonetheless do not stand aside and withdraw – it's to that extent that a dreadful love [*erōs*] of exercise in matters of this kind has slipped into me."[11] Because he is passionate about learning the truth, Socrates has no fear of falling. Hence he is brutally honest about his ignorance.

In Climacus's view, Socrates' most noteworthy admission of ignorance concerns his lack of self-knowledge. As he observes in the very first sentence of the chapter, Socrates – "the person who certainly knew man best" – did not even know himself. Was he "more inflamed with violence than Typhon," or did he partake by nature in something "divine and un-Typhonic" (*Phaedrus* 230a)?

Although Climacus cites Socrates' question about his nature as if it were his last word on the subject of self-knowledge, in the context of the *Phaedrus* it actually serves as a preface to the dramatic action of the dialogue. This fact suggests a rather different interpretation of Socrates' question than the one Climacus advances. In the *Phaedrus*, Socrates' initial uncertainty about himself is reflected in what follows: he gives a speech condemning erotic passion and then recants it almost immediately. In condemning eros, Socrates speaks in the voice of what has aptly been termed a "concealed lover" – the suitor of a beautiful youth, who attempts to win over the object of his longing by pretending *not* to be in love with him.[12] Socrates' recantation is motivated by his daimonion, which forbids him to leave until he has purified himself of his offense against eros (242b–43a). Graced now by the heaven-sent madness of eros itself, Socrates goes on to speak prophetically about the soul's true nature. In

---

many thanks – he is, of course, the infinitely inferior." JP 3566, 3.636 (X.1 A 609), cited in *Philosophical Fragments/Johannes Climacus*, 287 n. 3.
[11] *Theaetetus* 169b–c, translation of Benardete 1984.
[12] Griswold 1986, 57–69.

the great myth of the palinode, he depicts the soul's erotic awakening and its struggle to return to the transcendent being and truth of which it was once vouchsafed a direct vision. The drama of the *Phaedrus* thus seems to answer Socrates' question: there *is* something gentle and divine in his nature, and it makes him who he is. Socrates learns that he is not (simply) a monster, because his soul is essentially erotic. In the end, Socrates does know what a human being is: it is an embodied soul that longs to ascend to, and be nourished by, the truth, and that has some fair hope of doing so.

We need not speculate about how Climacus might respond to the fore-going reading of the *Phaedrus*, for his response can be inferred from what he goes on to say. Socrates does indeed know himself to be an essentially philosophical being, one who is by his very nature passionately disposed to learn. But in reflecting on *how* he is able to learn – how he knows what he knows, and what it is that guides him toward the truth – he inevitably comes face-to-face with something utterly unfamiliar, something that he cannot fathom. This enigmatic and unknowable other disturbs his self-knowledge, for it is indispensable to who he is and yet is impenetrable to his understanding.

SOCRATES AND THE COLLISION

"In order to get started," Climacus is willing to concede that we know what a human being is. "In this we do indeed have the criterion of truth," he adds, "which all Greek philosophy *sought*, or *doubted*, or *postulated*, or *brought to fruition*" (38, emphases in original). The "criterion of truth," a phrase used frequently by the Stoics and Skeptics (both of which schools traced their philosophical lineage back to Socrates), refers to the means by which we are able to know whatever it is we can know. Without some criterion of truth, philosophy would fall prey to skepticism at the very outset, for it would then be impossible to explain how we can acquire knowledge. For Socrates, "the single individual is for himself the measure [of truth]" – a claim that rests upon "the Socratic theory of recollection and of every human being as universal man" (38). In other words, reason is universal, and it is the criterion of truth – but only insofar as the single individual uses it to think for himself.

"We know, then, what man is, and this wisdom . . . can continually become richer and more meaningful," Climacus writes. "But then the understanding stands still, as did Socrates, for now the understanding's paradoxical passion that wills the collision awakens and, without really understanding itself, wills its own downfall."[13] "It is the same with the paradox of erotic love," he continues. "A person lives undisturbed in himself, and then awakens the paradox of self-love as love for another, for one missing" (38–9).

Climacus's analogy between love and knowledge is rich with implications. At some point, self-love turns into love for another. This involves a transformation in the character as well as the object of love. Whereas "self-love" implies selfishness and pride, the love for another of which Climacus speaks is erotic and therefore neither selfish nor proud, for "erotic love is jubilant when it unites equal and equal and is triumphant when it makes equal in erotic love that which was unequal" (27). If self-knowledge is like self-love, then self-knowledge, too, ultimately turns into the humble knowledge of another, of something that is missing.

The transformation of self-love into love for another parallels the transformation of thumos or spiritedness into philosophical eros that Socrates hopes to accomplish in the case of honor-loving young men such as Glaucon, whom Socrates describes as "always most courageous in everything" (*Republic* 357a). As Aristotle observes, men seek honor because they wish to be assured of their own worth (*Nicomachean Ethics* 1095b26–29). But the love of self that is at the root of thumos can be turned outward toward wisdom if the opinion of one's own excellence or virtue (*aretē*) is successfully called into question, and if the Socratic question "What *is* virtue?" becomes paramount in one's mind. However, Climacus's understanding of erotic love differs from that of Socrates in one crucial respect: whereas for Socrates the ultimate objects of eros are non-living beings, Climacus makes it clear that erotic love can find satisfaction only in the love of another person. If the path of eros is a fruitful one, it must therefore lead to a being that is capable of returning one's love.

Climacus's religious "romanticization" of Socratic eros has implications for the analogy between erotic love and the knowledge of another. In particular, it suggests that, just as romantic love longs for reciprocation, the self that knows longs to be known in return. Like self-love, self-knowledge has in view only itself; like romantic love, however, knowledge of the other seeks to unite the self and the other in a relationship of equality. And if this relationship is truly to be one of equality, it would seem that the missing other must be equal to the self in its capacity to know as well as to be known.

---

[13] When deeply absorbed in thought, Socrates was in the habit of standing still for long periods of time; cf. *Symposium* 175a, 220c–d.

In sum, the paradoxes of love and knowledge that Climacus has identified are meant to suggest that philosophical passion culminates, not in
the achievement of wisdom, but in an experience that intimates the existence of the god as a lover and teacher. Climacus's observations about
love and knowledge nonetheless build upon Socratic insights. Socrates
teaches that we are essentially erotic beings, beings characterized by a
profound longing for what we lack. This means that self-love is ultimately
a form of self-deception. Self-love may cause us to deny our essential
neediness, and, like the concealed lover of the *Phaedrus*, to try to hide
our love for another from ourselves as well as others. Yet just as erotic
love motivates the concealed lover's condemnation of eros, erotic love
lies at the bottom of every instance of self-love. Genuinely erotic love is
furthermore unselfish. In his recantation of the speech of the concealed
lover, Socrates makes it clear that eros, properly understood, loves what
is best for the soul of the beloved as well as for one's own soul, and seeks
to draw both "to a well-ordered way of life, and to philosophy" (*Phaedrus*
256a).

It is also important to reiterate that the drama of the *Phaedrus* frames
in a Socratic context what would later be understood as the problem
of sin, and speaks to this problem in a way that qualifies the hypothesis
of philosophical recollection. When Socrates delivers the speech of the
concealed lover, he does not merely "forget" the truth about eros. Rather,
his speech is a willful and Typhonic (or demonic) assertion of self-love
that obscures or suppresses this divine truth. This offense or *hamartēma*
(242c) – a synonym of *hamartia*, the word Aristotle uses in his *Poetics* for
the failure of moral vision on which tragic drama turns – is the pagan
equivalent of the admittedly much stronger Christian conception of sin
as the perversity of the will that refuses to choose the good that it knows.[14]
But Socrates shows that eros, or at least *his* eros, is capable of overcoming
the self-love that lies at the root both of his offense and of sin as it is
understood on the hypothesis of faith. While forgetfulness is thus not a
purely intellectual phenomenon, the example of Socrates shows that the
fall from truth that results from self-love, unlike the fall involved in the
Christian conception of sin, can in principle (if not always in practice)
be overcome by eros.[15]

---

[14] The *locus classicus* for this conception of sin is Augustine's discussion of the pear-stealing
episode at *Confessions* 2.4–10.
[15] This is noted by F. C. Baur, whose monograph on Socrates and Jesus, *Das Christliche des
Platonismus*, Kierkegaard read prior to writing *Fragments*. Possen (in press) observes that

Finally, Socrates teaches that the self that does not acknowledge its erotic nature cannot come to know itself. In the *Symposium,* as we have seen, Aristophanes tells a myth that presents eros as the longing for one's missing half. One implication of Aristophanes' speech is that we must look beyond ourselves in order to know ourselves. This point is reflected in the great myths Socrates tells in the *Symposium* and *Phaedrus,* which teach that the soul's erotic openness is rooted in its incompleteness, and that we consequently cannot know ourselves without knowing other souls, the cosmos in which we live, and the beings to which we aspire.

For his part, Climacus embraces Socrates' insight that self-knowledge involves knowledge of the mysterious world that lies beyond the boundaries of what one initially takes to be one's self. To the extent that Socrates does not yet know that mysterious world, he does not have self-knowledge. Yet the myths he weaves in the *Symposium* and *Phaedrus* express the beautiful hope that, by means of philosophy, he may someday achieve at least a measure of such knowledge. Climacus insists, however, that this hope is groundless: the unknown other must remain unknown to the philosophical intellect.

Socrates' uncertainty about who he is, Climacus claims, is an effect of this strange and unknowable other:

Just as the lover is changed by this paradox of love . . . so also that intimated paradox of the understanding reacts upon a person in such a way that he who believed he knew himself now no longer is sure whether he perhaps is a more curiously complex animal than Typhon or whether he has in his being a gentler and diviner part . . . (39)

On Climacus's reading, Socrates is no more sure of himself at the end of the *Phaedrus* than he is at the beginning. Philosophical eros, Climacus maintains, cannot deliver us from uncertainty about who we are. On the contrary, such uncertainty is in his view the inevitable *result* of philosophical passion. Why might he think so?

As we have noted, Socrates has a change of heart in the *Phaedrus.* This change of heart is brought about by his daimonion, which forbids him to leave before he has made amends to eros. It is the daimonion, in other words, that is in this instance Socrates' "criterion of truth," for it alerts

"for Baur . . . when Socrates asks whether he might not be more monstrous than Typhon, he is already in the act of discovering his own entanglement in sin." Possen's article leads one to ask whether *Fragments* was intended to be a kind of mirror-image of Baur's monograph, which starts by emphasizing the similarity between Socratic philosophizing and Christianity and ends by emphasizing their difference.

him to his mistake and tells him what he must do in order to correct it. This is not altogether surprising, for Socrates observes in the course of his defense speech that his daimonion is accustomed to intervene "even in very small matters" to prevent him from going wrong (*Apology* 40a). But as we saw in studying the *Apology*, the identity of the daimonion is no less uncertain than that of the god who prompts Socrates' philosophical quest as a whole. Does Socrates know what the daimonion and the god *are* – these things that speak to him and guide him in the most important matters? If not, can he really be said to know himself?

From what Climacus goes on to say in the immediate sequel, it is clear that these questions point us in the right direction.

[W]hat is this unknown against which the understanding in its paradoxical passion collides and which even disturbs man and his self-knowledge? It is the unknown. But it is not a human being, insofar as he knows man, or anything else that he knows. Therefore, let us call this unknown *the god*. It is only a name we give to it. (39, emphasis in original)

In this passage, Climacus strikingly identifies the god of whom Socrates speaks with the god of the religious hypothesis. What is more, he manages at the same time to explain the vagueness of Socrates' mode of expression. For Socrates, "the god" is a name for the unknown – just as it is for those of Climacus's readers who, being untruth, nevertheless hope to understand something of the hypothesis of religious faith. That it is in another sense not *only* a name, in spite of what Climacus says, will become clear in due course; in this, as in other matters, Socrates proves to be prophetic. What deserves emphasis here, however, is not the name itself, but rather the fact that Socrates' philosophical eros led him to understand that there was *something* – he knew not what – that had to be named. For it is Socrates' "paradoxical passion" that opens his soul to the god and draws him toward its mysteries.[16]

As Climacus observes near the beginning of *Fragments*, Socrates initially supposes that self-knowledge is God-knowledge, which is to say, first, that we genuinely are (or can become) *selves* – independent beings, responsible for our own actions and thoughts – and second, that we may discover the truth within ourselves. The Socratic, philosophical project thus essentially aims to achieve selfhood in the highest and fullest sense, including full self-knowledge. The god, however, is the reef on which this project comes to grief. As we have seen, the god incites and guides Socrates'

[16] See ch. 3, 68–9.

philosophical quest.[17] Insofar as this quest is essential to his identity, it would not be too much to say that the god makes him who he is. Viewed in this light, "the god" may be understood as the name Socrates gives to the missing part of himself – the unknown other into which the passions of love and understanding ultimately collide, and without which the self would be less than whole. Socrates' acknowledgement of this unknown other is an admission that the self is both incomplete and mysteriously elusive, an insight that may be telegraphically expressed in the counterthesis that God-knowledge is necessary for self-knowledge. And insofar as Socrates, in seeking to know himself, turns his thought toward this enigmatic other that is at the same time not an other, he truly does will the collision with paradox.

EXCURSUS ON DEMONSTRATING THE EXISTENCE OF GOD

At this point, Climacus launches into a digression on the impossibility of furnishing a philosophical proof of the existence of God. It is true that such a proof would be irrelevant to understanding the absolute paradox, but showing that it cannot be achieved is perhaps the best way to drive home this fact. One of the primary aims of the digression is also to defend Socrates, who does not bother with such proofs but instead "constantly presupposes that the god exists" (44).

"It hardly occurs to the understanding," Climacus asserts, "to want to demonstrate that this unknown (the god) exists." In this context, "the understanding" must refer to the passionate understanding of the likes of Socrates, for many other philosophers have attempted just such a demonstration. Climacus's argument is simple. If the god does not exist, the demonstration will be impossible. "But if he does exist, then it is foolishness to want to demonstrate it": in beginning the demonstration, I would presuppose the god's existence "not as doubtful . . . but as decided, because otherwise I would not begin, easily perceiving that the whole thing would be impossible if he did not exist" (39).

At first blush, Climacus's argument seems quite unsatisfactory. To take another example, it would be strange to maintain that it hardly occurs to the understanding to prove that the solution to a given mathematical problem is this-and-such, because I would not attempt such a demonstration if I had not already decided the question. To be sure, few would undertake a mathematical proof without reason to believe that it might

---

[17] See ch. 3, 66–8.

succeed. But the purpose of the proof is to establish the truth of a given hypothesis – a hypothesis that must otherwise appear at least somewhat doubtful even to the one undertaking the demonstration.

Yet there is a crucial difference between a mathematical proof and a demonstration of the existence of God: the former is concerned not with existence, but with conceptual relations. The mathematician might say: "I plan to show that there exists a solution to this problem," but what this actually means is: "I plan to show that this hypothesis (which obviously exists) is in fact the solution we are seeking." Mathematical proofs make perfect sense, because they attempt only to show that a is b – not to establish that b exists. A demonstration, as Climacus observes, can only "develop the definition of a concept." One could therefore reasonably seek to demonstrate that "the unknown, which exists, is the god," but to want to demonstrate that the god exists is another matter. For any attempt to demonstrate that something exists "becomes something entirely different, becomes an expanded concluding development of what I conclude from having presupposed that the object of investigation exists" (40).[18]

Those who attempt to demonstrate God's existence sometimes try to do so on the basis of works that, so it is argued, could only have been performed by God. Climacus notes that such a demonstration could not succeed in the case of any other individual. I could never show in such a manner that Napoleon exists; I could only "demonstrate (purely ideally) that such works are the works of a great general etc." "However," he continues, "between the god and his works there is an absolute relation. God is not a name but a concept, and perhaps because of that his *essentia involvit existentiam* [essence involves existence]" (41). Can we not then infer God's existence from God's works?

Climacus's response to this question is incisive:

> But, then, what are the god's works? The works from which I want to demonstrate his existence do not immediately and directly exist, not at all. Or are the wisdom in nature and the goodness or wisdom in Governance right in front of our noses? Do we not encounter the most terrible spiritual trials here, and is it ever possible to be finished with all these trials?. . . [E]ven if I began, I would never finish and also would be obliged continually to live *in suspenso* lest something so terrible happen that my fragment of demonstration would be ruined. (42)

The reader who pauses to reflect on the theological crises of the past century – crises that were in no small measure precipitated by terrible

---

[18] Here Climacus echoes the Kantian argument that existence is not a predicate (Green 1994, 179–83; cf. Kant 1965, 500–7).

events such as the Holocaust, and that shook the faith of many Christian as well as Jewish thinkers – must regard Climacus's remarks as prophetic. Climacus nicely underscores the pointlessness of attempts to rest religious faith on the foundation of experience. Such attempts put the cart before the horse: faith provides a framework within which to make sense of experiences, including suffering and death, that would otherwise seem to be meaningless. "Wisdom in nature" and "the goodness and wisdom in Governance" are thus articles of faith, not conclusions from our observation of the way of the world. To try to derive faith from the good order of the world is therefore to overlook precisely those features of our experience that drive so many human beings to seek refuge in God.

Insofar as the existence of the god is to be demonstrated from his works, Climacus concludes, it must be demonstrated "from the works regarded ideally – that is, as they do not appear directly and immediately." In that case, however, I "only develop the ideality I have presupposed." In other words, I actually begin with an idea or concept of my own making, which I then proceed to analyze. What else is that, Climacus asks, but "presupposing that the god exists and actually beginning with trust in him?" (42).

Finally, Climacus observes that in any demonstration the existence of the god emerges "by a leap." "Is it not here as it is with the Cartesian dolls? As soon as I let go of the doll, it stands on its head." So, too, the existence of the god emerges from the demonstration only when I "let go" of it (42–3). By analogy with the cleverly weighted Cartesian dolls (a reference that puts one in mind of the circular argument by which Descartes purports to prove God's existence in Book Three of the *Meditations*), the demonstration, once it is complete, "stands on its head" of is own accord. In other words, it establishes the existence of the god only insofar as it involves a movement made independently of rational inference. The existence of the god is thus the consequence, not of a valid chain of reasoning, but of a leap from the premises of the demonstration to its putative conclusion.[19]

We are now prepared to appreciate the merits of Socrates' conduct. Socrates, Climacus observes, reverses the efforts of natural theology to demonstrate the existence of the god on the basis of his works. For his

---

[19] Evans 1992 suggests that this "leap," which involves "letting go" of the proof, amounts to "remov[ing] myself from the indifferent standpoint of the disinterested speculator and tak[ing] up once more the standpoint of the concretely interested person, replete with interests and passions" (71).

part, Socrates "constantly presupposes that the god exists, and on this presupposition he seeks to infuse nature with the idea of fitness and purposiveness." Why does he proceed in this manner? Climacus answers as follows:

> He presumably would have explained that he lacked the kind of courage needed to dare to embark on such a voyage of [philosophical] discovery without having behind him the assurance that the god exists. At the god's request, he casts out his net, so to speak, to catch the idea of fitness and purposiveness, for nature itself comes up with many terrifying devices and many subterfuges in order to disturb. (44)

Socrates wisely foregoes any attempt to place religious faith on a foundation of philosophical demonstration. Instead, he assumes what he must assume if he hopes to make sense of the world philosophically. He "presupposes that the god exists." What this means is suggested by his practice of referring to the unknown as "the god": he presupposes that the unknown, which he already knows to exist, is the god – a being whose works are by definition characterized by fitness and purposiveness.

In the end, then, "the god" is for Socrates both a mere name and more than a name. It is only a name in the sense that Socrates is well aware that he does not know what this unknown is. But it is also more than a name, because "the god" signifies a being of a definite sort – one whose very nature serves to guarantee the meaningfulness of Socrates' philosophical quest.

Climacus's excursus on demonstrating the existence of God (or the god) sheds light on the limits of philosophical demonstration as such. Demonstration is an excellent means of establishing conceptual relations. Because it is restricted to the sphere of concepts, however, it is not possible by its means of demonstration to derive the existence of God from a concept of God or His works. According to Climacus, Socrates reverses the intended movement of demonstration: beginning with the existence of the unknown, he attaches to it his concept of the god. But it deserves repeating that he does not pretend to have arrived at the god by means of demonstration: that the unknown is the god is, for him, nothing more than a presupposition, albeit a necessary one.

ABSOLUTE DIFFERENCE AND SIN

For reasons we shall soon consider, Climacus maintains that Socrates is right to regard the unknown as the god. That Socrates does so is perhaps the most important evidence one could find of the prophetic character of philosophical eros, the "paradoxical passion" of the understanding. In the final pages of Chapter Three, however, Climacus argues that the unknown god is "the absolutely different" and that the absolute difference between the god and human beings is nothing other than the difference between truth and untruth that results from sin. Because the unknown is the absolutely different, Socrates can know nothing about the god. He can, of course, attend to communications that he attributes to the god, but he can only guess what the unknown itself must be. In the face of his ignorance, in other words, he finds it necessary consciously to produce a concept of the god – and it is to his everlasting credit that he acknowledges this necessity.

"The paradoxical passion of the understanding," Climacus writes, "is, then, continually colliding with this unknown." The understanding cannot get beyond the unknown, yet it "cannot stop reaching it and being engaged with it." The understanding perceives the unknown as a "frontier." "But a frontier is expressly the passion's torment, even though it is also its incentive." Yet the understanding "can go no further," because the unknown is "the absolutely different" (44).

The absolutely different is, as such, absolutely different from the understanding and all that it knows. What can the understanding grasp about such a thing?

> Defined as the absolutely different, it [the unknown] seems to be at the point of being disclosed, but not so, because the understanding cannot even think the absolutely different; it cannot absolutely negate itself but uses itself for that purpose and consequently thinks the difference in itself, which it thinks by itself. It cannot absolutely transcend itself and therefore thinks as above itself only the sublimity that it thinks by itself. (45)

The understanding cannot think the absolutely different because any difference it can cognize is only relative. In the first place, it cannot think anything that is absolutely different from that with which it is already familiar, because all objects that fall under the purview of the understanding are at least to some degree similar. Even if the only thing that any given objects have in common is the sheer fact of being numerically distinct items, this point of comparison constitutes a shared horizon against the backdrop of which their differences may come to light. Nor can the understanding cognize that which is absolutely different from *itself*, for it cannot absolutely "negate" or "transcend" itself. Insofar as it thinks at all, it is still the understanding that does the thinking; hence whatever it thinks must be brought within the boundaries of its own capabilities.

It follows that whenever the understanding attempts to grasp absolute difference "it is basically an arbitrariness." As a consequence, the understanding invests the unknown god with an intelligible form of its own invention: "at the very bottom of devoutness there madly lurks the capricious arbitrariness that knows it itself has produced the god." It is this "capricious arbitrariness" that even Socrates, for all his passion, cannot overcome. Yet here, too, Socrates' passion is his saving grace. Owing to his knowledge of ignorance, he is under no illusions about his capacity to fathom the unknown: "whatever I do not know, I do not even suppose I know" (*Apology* 21d). Hence, he is intentionally vague in speaking about "the god" or "the gods" (he uses both terms interchangeably when he discusses divine matters in the *Republic*, precisely because, as he remarks at 382d, "we don't know where the truth about ancient things lies"). In a word, Socrates is fully aware of what Climacus calls "the self-ironizing of the understanding" – a kind of self-deception that in Climacus's view especially afflicts paganism, and according to which "the understanding that... does not know itself... quite consistently confuses itself with the difference" (45).[20]

In order to illustrate the problem of self-ironizing, Climacus asks us to consider what the understanding, left to its own devices, can make of the incarnation of the god. He asks us to imagine that "there exists... a certain person who looks just like any other human being, grows up as do other human beings, marries, has a job," and so on. "This human being," he adds, "is also the god." But how do I know this? According to Climacus, I cannot know it by means of the understanding alone, "for in that case I would have to know the god and the difference, and I do not know the difference inasmuch as the understanding has made it like unto that from which it differs." The god has thus (inadvertently, to be sure) "become the most terrible deceiver through the understanding's deception of itself" (45–6).

When Climacus raises the question of how the understanding can recognize the incarnate god, it becomes apparent that the whole discussion

---

[20] It once again follows that Socrates' conception of the god is in important respects not a pagan one. Cf. ch. 4, 83 and 98–9. Climacus is of course especially concerned with the "paganism" of those theologies that fail to recognize Christ's challenge to the understanding, and so "present him as one more religious teacher among many – even if he is absolutely the greatest and profoundest teacher and the best man who ever lived" (Roberts 1986, 26).

of absolute difference must be understood within the context of his reflections, in the previous two chapters, on the god as teacher. Incarnation, we recall, is the solution hit upon by the god in response to the difficulty of making himself understood by the learner without destroying the learner's ability to love the god as an equal. Yet it is now more unclear than ever how we can hope to understand anything at all about the god. In thinking about the relationship between the god and the learner, Climacus takes his bearings by our experience of human love, and specifically by the analogy of the king and the maiden – even though he warns us that "no human situation can provide a valid analogy" (26). We are now in a position to appreciate the force of this caveat, for we have learned what it means to say that the difference between the learner and the god is absolute. Climacus's poetic analogy is supposed to help us grasp the god's unhappy love for the learner and the necessity of incarnation. But it would seem that it cannot actually teach us *anything* about the god, because *a* is analogous to *b* only insofar as *a* and *b* resemble each other in some respect. What, then, is the point of the poem?

While this question is a difficult one, Climacus's use of analogy seems to be a tacit indication that we are to take his talk of absolute difference with a grain of salt.[21] As we have already seen, the god is not *simply* the absolutely different, for by virtue of incarnation he is *also* "absolutely the equal of the lowliest of human beings" (32–3). While this unity of absolute equality and absolute difference (the absolute paradox) is not itself intelligible to the understanding, it does open up a space in which analogy can function: insofar as the god is the equal of the lowliest of human beings, his situation must resemble many human situations in many respects. Furthermore, Climacus claims that his poem might at least help "to awaken the mind to an understanding of the divine" (26). If the mind can be "awakened" to such an understanding – a Socratic turn of phrase – it is presumably because, at least when it is animated by genuine philosophical passion, it can have some awareness even of that which ultimately lies beyond its ken.

To continue: we have seen that the self-ironizing of the understanding is a consequence of its absolute difference from the god. Climacus now asks whether the understanding is capable even of acknowledging that the god *is* absolutely different. "In defining the unknown as the different," he writes, "the understanding ultimately goes astray and confuses

[21] The same is true with respect to Climacus's analogous assertion that one who is untruth is completely "excluded from the truth" (14). Cf. Rudd 2000/2002, 2.264–5.

the difference with likeness" (46). In other words, the absolute difference that characterizes the unknown god is utterly unlike anything that
the understanding has in mind when it employs the concept of "difference." In employing this concept, it thus reduces the unknown god
to something with which it is already familiar. But this is exactly what
Climacus himself has just done: his definition of the god as the absolutely
different is an instance of the self-ironizing of the understanding. The
reader's recognition of this fact is perhaps meant to underscore the basic
point toward which Climacus is in the process of turning our attention,
namely, that it is hopeless to suppose we can relate positively to the god
through the medium of understanding as long as we do not acknowledge
the reality of sin and undergo the existential transformation of rebirth
in faith.[22]

In order "truly to know something about the unknown (the god),"
Climacus continues, a human being "must first come to know that it
is different from him, absolutely different from him." As we have just
seen, however, "the understanding cannot come to know this by itself"; it
follows that, "if it is going to come to know this, it must come to know this
from the god" (46). But even if a human being did come to know this
from the god, he could not directly understand it, for in the absence of
the condition for understanding he is simply not equipped to do so. Nor,
we may add, could a human being come to know anything at all from
the god as long as the god remains absolutely different, for under such
circumstances communication is by definition impossible.

"Just to come to know that the god is the different," Climacus concludes, "man needs the god and then comes to know that the god is absolutely different from him." This is indeed "a paradox": the god cannot
communicate the fact of his absolute difference from man without revelation, but the revealed god is no longer absolutely different. However –
and this point cannot be overemphasized – our inability to understand
absolute difference does not mean that we cannot understand the god *as*
god, for the difference between man and god is not *essentially* absolute:

[I]f the god is to be absolutely different from a human being, this can have its
basis not in that which man owes to the god (for to that extent they are akin)

---

[22] Mulhall claims that Climacus intentionally "develops his idea in a way that is gradually
but increasingly distorted by the perversity of the understanding" so as to "inoculate" his
readers against this perversity. In his view, Climacus employs indirect communication
in *Fragments* in order to "overcom[e] our resistance to thinking of ourselves as radically
sinful creatures" (Mulhall 1999, 27, 32).

but in that which he owes to himself or in that which he himself has committed. What, then, is the difference? Indeed, what else but sin, since the difference, the absolute difference, must have been caused by the individual himself.
(46–7)

In this passage, Climacus illuminates the problem of absolute difference
by connecting it with his earlier discussion of untruth and sin in Chapter One. The absolute difference, which no act of understanding can
bridge, is nothing other than the difference between truth and untruth.
Untruth lacks the condition for understanding the truth. Truth is therefore unintelligible to untruth, just as absolute difference is unintelligible
to the understanding. But because the god would not have created us
without the condition for understanding the truth, and because it could
not have been lost by accident (it being, as Climacus says, an "essential
condition" [15]), we must have lost it through our own fault. Hence it is
sin that has deprived us of this condition. The god is thus not essentially
unknown and unknowable to human beings: he becomes such through
sin, which produces the absolute difference insofar as it alters the sinner's
nature.

Climacus is now in a position to explain the confusion experienced by
Socrates, "the connoisseur of human nature [who] became almost bewil-
dered about himself when he came up against the different." In a word,
Socrates lacked "the consciousness of sin" (47). Whether this is completely fair is open to debate, for we have seen that Socrates *is* conscious
of the self-love that lies at the root of sin. For his part, however, Climacus takes his bearings by "the Socratic principle that all sin is ignorance"
(note on 50), a principle that seems to confirm Socrates' obliviousness
to the perversity of the will that is central to the religious understanding
of sin.

The consciousness of sin, Climacus continues, was something that
Socrates "could no more teach to any other person than any other person could teach it to him" – for if one cannot discover on one's own that
one is untruth, how could one discover the sin by which one has become
untruth? Only the god could teach the consciousness of sin, "if he wanted
to be teacher." But "as we have composed the story," Climacus writes, the
god did want this; he therefore "wanted to be on the basis of equality
with the single individual so that he could completely understand him."
In becoming incarnate, the god accordingly manifests himself as absolute
paradox in two ways: "negatively, by bringing into prominence the absolute difference of sin and, positively, by wanting to annul this absolute
difference in the absolute equality" (47).

Socrates, however, knew nothing of the incarnate god. Hence, he could only continue to regard the god, in all humility, as the unknown other that lies beyond the frontier of understanding. Climacus has a simple explanation for why Socrates was in the habit of speaking so vaguely about "the god": he did not know who or what he was referring to. But because the god remained unknown, Socrates also had to remain unknown to himself. For he, too, divined that self-knowledge, like self-love, relates essentially to an other – a missing other that is integral to the being of the self, even though, as it turns out, it eludes every attempt to pin it down philosophically.

Climacus concludes his discussion of the absolute paradox by underscoring the limitations of philosophical understanding. The understanding "certainly cannot think it [the paradox], cannot hit upon it on its own." And if the paradox is proclaimed, "the understanding cannot understand it and merely detects that it will likely be its downfall" (47). Baldly stated in this way, however, these conclusions do not do justice to what has been accomplished in Chapter Three of *Fragments*. For Climacus insists from the beginning that philosophy is essentially an erotic activity, and he goes on to show that a deeply passionate understanding – the kind of understanding that is above all exemplified by Socrates – is capable of far more than one might have initially supposed.

Perhaps because it is by nature attracted to paradox, the passion of thought has a prophetic grasp even of that which lies beyond the limits of thought. By faithfully following his eros for wisdom, Socrates *does* manage to hit upon the paradox. His eros opens him up to the mysterious voice of the unknown other, and in so doing teaches him to recognize the ultimate limits of his philosophical quest. Socrates is well aware of his ignorance, including what he does not know about himself. Yet "the god" is for Socrates more than a name: to speak of the god is to acknowledge the divinity of that which thought cannot penetrate. Finally, in guiding Socrates' philosophical quest, the unknown god even provides him with something like the consciousness of sin (a consciousness Climacus claims he lacks): in the *Phaedrus*, Socrates' daimonion warns him that the speech of the concealed lover commits an offense against eros, which is "a god, or something divine" (242e).

To be sure, Socrates does not understand sin, or the god, or the paradox as these concepts have been explicated in accordance with the religious hypothesis. Yet it is remarkable that his experience of philosophical eros has given him a powerful intimation of all of these things. According to the hypothesis of religious faith, Socrates lacks the condition for under-standing. The very intensity of his passion of thought nevertheless seems to prepare him for what follows from this hypothesis, including the ulti-mate failure of the philosophical quest, the unintelligibility of the self to reason alone, and the necessary role of the god as teacher.

A clarification is in order. That eros opens Socrates up to the absolute paradox does not mean that the paradox becomes accessible by means of philosophical recollection. We may note in this connection a prob-lem raised by Climacus's assertion in Chapter One that on the religious hypothesis the teacher is the occasion of the learner's "recollecting that he is untruth." The learner, in other words, must discover his untruth by himself – this being "the one and only analogy to the Socratic" (14). As Ettore Rocca has recently observed, to understand that one is untruth implies that one understands what untruth *is*; to understand this, how-ever, it would seem to be necessary to understand what *the truth* is. But on the religious hypothesis the latter understanding requires the condition, which can be provided only by the god in the moment. Hence, the recol-lection of one's situation as untruth would seem to be impossible on the religious hypothesis.[23] Socrates avoids this problem, however, because his eros makes possible a kind of recollection other than the sort in terms of which the philosophical hypothesis is framed. What Climacus intends to remind Socrates of, and what eros allows him to "recollect," is noth-ing other than the essential dependence of his philosophical enterprise on the unknown and unknowable god. To recognize this dependence, however, is to acknowledge the *impossibility* of learning the truth simply by means of philosophical recollection. We see once again that the sharp distinction between philosophy and faith Climacus draws at the outset of his study breaks down when it applies to Socrates, and that it does so on account of his relationship to the god.

While philosophy falls silent in the face of the absolute paradox, the understanding and the paradox can under certain conditions neverthe-less achieve what Climacus calls a "mutual understanding." Just as the understanding, in its paradoxical passion, wills its own downfall, so, too, the paradox wills the downfall of the understanding. "Thus the two have a mutual understanding, but this understanding is present only in the moment of passion." To illustrate, Climacus once again turns to erotic love, "even though it is an imperfect metaphor": "Self-love lies at the basis of love [*Kjærlighed*], but at its peak its paradoxical passion wills its own

[23] Rocca 2004, 32–3.

downfall. Erotic love [*Elskov*] also wills this, and therefore the two forces
are in mutual understanding in the moment of passion, and this passion
is precisely erotic love" (47–8).[24] Like self-love, the understanding initially "follows its nose," discovering everywhere only itself (37). This is,
and remains, the condition of the speculative philosophers in particular.
But if the understanding is genuinely passionate, as was Socrates', and if
its passion, inflamed and nourished by paradox, is allowed to grow and
flourish, it is ultimately opened up to a paradox that is absolute. This is
the peak of philosophical eros and the downfall of the understanding,
which Climacus analogizes as the downfall of self-love – and so of selfishness and pride – in erotic love. In this ultimate moment of passion, the
understanding gives up its proud claims and hopes: it cannot learn the
truth on its own. This is also a moment of mutual understanding. The
absolute paradox (the god as encountered by one who is in the condition
of untruth) mirrors the passion of the understanding in willing its downfall, for just as the god cannot be united with the learner in the equality
of erotic love as long as the learner is gripped by self-love, so, too, the
god cannot teach as long as the learner thinks no teacher is required.

It is crucial to observe, however, that self-love "is not annihilated" in
the moment of passion, but is rather "taken captive" by erotic love (48).
Self-love is both transcended and preserved (or in Hegelian terms, *aufgehoben*) in erotic love, for the self can know itself, and can be wholly a
self, only through the love of another. So, too, the analogy of self-love
and erotic love suggests that the understanding that meets the paradox
in mutual understanding is *aufgehoben* in a higher passion, and thus, in
the last analysis, experiences "downfall" as the *satisfaction* of its longing
for wisdom rather than as failure and frustration. Or rather, it experiences the frustration only of its former longing to understand by means
of reason alone – the longing it felt when it manifested the narrowness
of unenlightened self-love.

Climacus has no name as yet for the passion in which the understanding and the paradox achieve mutual understanding. He will later divulge
that the name of this passion is "faith." An initial speculation that was
prompted by Climacus's name has thus been partially confirmed: in the
case of Socrates, at least, philosophy – or more precisely, philosophical eros – is a preparation for faith, if not quite a ladder by which one
may ascend to it. For even though Socrates experienced the peak of

---

[24] *Kjærlighed* is "love" or "affection," without the suggestion of an erotic dimension that is
implied by *Elskov*.

paradoxical passion, he did not enjoy the relationship of equality with the god that Climacus associates with faith, as the paradox did not respond in kind. In brief, Socrates was not a Christian, nor could he have been; hence, the god remained unknown to him.

While the exact nature of the relationship between Socrates' philosophical passion and Christian faith is of the utmost interest, it cannot be explicated prior to our examination of Climacus's final treatment of the matter in *Postscript*.[25]

Before further exploring the nature of faith, Climacus pauses to consider the phenomenon of offense at the paradox. Why, he asks, is the understanding inclined to take offense, and what is the significance of this response to the paradox? It is to these questions that we now turn.

[25] As we shall see, however, Climacus never fully clarifies this issue (see ch. 10 and Epilogue).

6

Self-Love and Offense

One of the stylistic peculiarities of *Fragments* is the habit Climacus develops of concluding each chapter by responding to the objections of an imagined interlocutor. Chapter Three is no exception. Having explained that the relationship between the understanding and the unknown god is one of absolute difference, Climacus supposes that someone might take offense at this notion. Such a person might accuse him of being a "capricemonger," who has presented his readers with "a caprice" that is "ludicrous" and "so unreasonable that I would have to lock everything out of my consciousness in order to think of it" (46).

In responding to this accusation, Climacus puts his finger on the origins of the feeling of offense that it so strongly expresses. Locking everything out of one's consciousness, he observes, "is exactly what you have to do, but then is it justifiable to want to keep all the presuppositions *you* have in your consciousness and still presume to think about your consciousness without any presuppositions?" (46, emphasis in original). When the objector envisions locking everything out of his consciousness, he finds it "unreasonable" to do so. But his judgment is at bottom nothing more than an expression of his desire to keep hold of everything that is *in* his consciousness, and in particular to cling to his "presuppositions." He is, in other words, deeply prejudiced in favor of his own understanding, and this prejudice causes him to meet any challenge to his understanding – particularly the suggestion that his condition is one of untruth – with hostility.

Climacus's brief retort to his imagined interlocutor merely hints at what he goes on to say about offense in the short "Appendix" to Chapter Three, the title of which is "Offense at the Paradox (An Acoustical

Illusion)." Although the Appendix is Climacus's only extended discussion in *Fragments* of the problem of offense (a problem specifically associated with the teaching of Jesus: cf. Mark 6:3), the topic initially surfaces when he speaks of the necessity for the god to descend to the learner by means of incarnation (32). Seen from the perspective of the philosophical hypothesis, offense at the claim that the god has become man is a justifiable response to the absurdity of the identity of absolute difference with absolute equality. Seen from that of the religious hypothesis, however, offense is a natural consequence of the self-love to which Climacus likens the initial condition of the understanding. For what could be more offensive to one's pride than being told that one is untruth? Yet in Climacus's view offense at the paradox is also a manifestation of the moment, and as such provides evidence for the truth of the hypothesis. The investigation of offense thus forms an integral part of Climacus's development of the religious hypothesis. In particular, it provides an opportunity to hold up a mirror to philosophically inclined souls – a mirror that might help to soften their presumed hostility toward faith, especially insofar as it discloses that such hostility is an effect of the paradox itself.

SPIRITEDNESS AND SUFFERING

As long as the understanding and the paradox "meet in the mutual understanding of their difference," Climacus writes, the encounter is a "happy one, like erotic love's understanding." It is "happy in the passion to which we have as yet given no name," the passion that Climacus will later identify as faith. But "if the encounter is not in mutual understanding," the relation is unhappy. In that case, the understanding's unhappy love "resembles . . . the unhappy love rooted in misunderstood self-love" (misunderstood, because enlightened self-love allows itself to be "taken captive," as Climacus so aptly puts it, by erotic love). This unhappy love Climacus terms "offense" (49).

Like the unhappy love that is rooted in misunderstood self-love, offense "is always a suffering." By this, Climacus means not only that offense involves pain, but, more important, that it is essentially passive rather than active.[1] The offended understanding is indignant. Hence, it wears its pain like a badge of honor: it is "incapable of tearing itself

---

[1] The term the Hongs translate as "suffering" (*lidende*) "is not the common Danish noun for painful suffering (*lidelse*), but an adjective formed from the verb *at lide* (to let or allow) that emphasizes passivity" (Evans 1992, 83).

loose from the cross to which it is nailed." It is thus active just to the extent that "it cannot altogether allow itself to be annihilated" (50). The active dimension of offense, as Climacus observes, is indicated by the fact that we say – in Danish as well as English – "to *take* offense" (note on 50). To take offense is to assert oneself, to stand up in defense of one's wounded pride. But offense is nonetheless fundamentally a mode of suffering or passivity, because it is always a reaction to something that has been done *to* one. Offense "has struggled with the stronger" and has been broken, so that its "posture of vigor has a physical analogy to that of someone with a broken back, which does indeed give a singular kind of suppleness" (50).

The foregoing reflections suggest a question about the essential nature of the understanding. Because erotic love, unlike misunderstood self-love, does not take offense at the paradox, the offended understanding must be moved to defend its wounded pride not by eros but by thumos. This is confirmed by Socrates' observation that thumos is essentially defensive and reactive. "Haven't you noticed," he asks Glaucon, "how unbeatable and invincible spiritedness [*thumos*] is, which, when it is present, makes every soul fearless and unconquerable in the face of everything?" (*Republic* 375b). We have already noted that thumos manifests itself not only in aggression and competition, but also in the will to impose order on phenomena and to render them intelligible.[2] To what extent, then, is the understanding in general motivated by thumos rather than eros? Stated more precisely, to what extent does the work of understanding involve a combative closing of ranks in the face of the unknown, a movement that is precisely the opposite of the erotic opening of the soul exemplified by Socrates?

We do well to recall in this connection that, according to the speech of Aristophanes in the *Symposium*, human beings are fundamentally thumotic. Aristophanes teaches that eros, the self's love for its other half, is merely an unintended consequence of thumos – a natural response to the near-fatal wound inflicted upon our ancestors when the gods split them in two as punishment for their hubristic violence (191a–b). The issues raised by the reaction of the philosophical understanding to the absolute paradox are thus the same ones that are at stake in the debate between Socrates and Aristophanes in the *Symposium*. Is the philosophical enterprise at bottom erotic, or thumotic? Is it characterized more by the openness of eros, or the defensiveness of thumos – more by love, or by pride?

---

[2] See ch. 3, 69.

These are large questions that are most meaningfully posed by the would-be philosopher to himself. If we may judge by the examples of Socrates and Climacus, however, the genuine philosopher is an erotic thinker. Few people, on the other hand – including those who call themselves thinkers – are genuine philosophers. The phenomenon of offense against the paradox is accordingly echoed in the Platonic dialogues in the widespread phenomenon of offense against *Socrates*. As Socrates observes in the *Apology*, his practice of demonstrating that others do not know what they think they know commonly results in his being hated (21e). What is more, this hatred is especially evident among those with intellectual aspirations, including sophists and their students. It springs from the wounding of the interlocutor's pride by the experience of perplexity, not before the absolute paradox, but before some relative (but nonetheless seemingly intractable) paradox that he has been forced by Socrates to confront.[3] In many cases, wounded pride causes the interlocutor to accuse Socrates of engaging in philosophical discussion only in order to satisfy his own pride by vanquishing opponents in argument.[4] On rare occasions, however, thumos manages to make common cause with philosophical eros by driving the interlocutor to try to defeat his perplexity.[5]

Let us leave Plato to one side and return to Climacus's characterization of offense. Because offense is suffering, Climacus observes, the understanding does not originate offense. Had it done so, it would also have had to originate the paradox. Of course, this is precisely what the understanding claims to have done.[6] According to Climacus, however, the truth is exactly the opposite: "Although the offense . . . sounds from somewhere else – indeed, from the opposite corner – nevertheless it is the paradox that resounds *in it*, and this indeed is an acoustical illusion" (emphasis added). The paradox resounds in offense, because offense is suffering; in offense, in other words, the understanding does not act but is instead acted upon. Like one "caricaturing another . . . [who] only copies the other in the wrong way," the one offended "does not speak

---

[3] This can be seen clearly in the revealing remarks of Meno, a student of Gorgias, at *Meno* 80a–b. Beneath wounded pride, there may also be fear in confronting the difficulty of the task of learning. Cf. the discussion of the terror and struggle involved in faith in ch. 9.

[4] See for example Plato's *Protagoras* 360e and *Gorgias* 461b–c, and cf. Alcibiades' claim that Socrates is guilty of *huperēphania*, arrogant disdain for others (*Symposium* 219c).

[5] Thus the general Laches, annoyed by his inability to define courage, asserts that he is compelled by "a certain love of victory" to continue the inquiry (Plato, *Laches* 194a).

[6] Consider, for example, Ludwig Feuerbach's assertion in *The Essence of Christianity* (1841) that God is a product of the human imagination – the illusory objectification or externalization of the being of man.

according to his own nature but according to the nature of the paradox" (50–1).

Climacus's reflections on offense are intended to reveal the derivative and dependent character of the understanding, and thus the hollowness of its pride. In its expressions of offense, the understanding is, so to speak, a puppet of the paradox. It has no authority, because it is not the author of its own utterances. What it attributes to itself should properly be attributed to the paradox.

If Climacus is correct, the paradox is visible in offense as in a distorted mirror. Because offense at the paradox is precisely what one should expect if, in fact, the condition of the learner is untruth, it can be regarded as "an indirect testing of the correctness of the paradox." Offense is also a negative register of the moment: it "*comes into existence* with the paradox, and if it *comes into existence*, here again we have the moment" (emphases in original). It is "through the moment," Climacus observes, that "the learner becomes untruth." He means by this not that the learner was previously something other than untruth, but that the moment provokes him either to express his untruth in offense or to discover his untruth for himself. In the latter case, "the person who knew himself becomes confused about himself and instead of self-knowledge he acquires the consciousness of sin etc." (51).

Socrates, as we have seen, experiences just such confusion about himself. Yet Climacus associates the "Socratic point of view" not with discovery but with offense, because Socrates' orienting hypothesis that we possess the condition for understanding the truth cannot, after all, explain his confusion (51–2). According to the philosophical hypothesis, the moment does not exist: "the learner himself is the truth, and the moment of occasion is merely a jest." It follows that "the moment of decision [about embracing the god in faith] is *foolishness*, for if the decision is posited then . . . the learner becomes untruth, but precisely this makes a beginning in the moment unnecessary" (52, emphasis in original).[7]

Offense "remains outside the paradox, and the basis for this is: *quia absurdum* [because it is absurd]." The offended understanding is proud to observe that offense "retains probability," while the paradox is admittedly "the most improbable." Yet in declaring the absurdity of the paradox, "the

---

7 The Hongs (*Philosophical Fragments/Johannes Climacus*, 294 n. 10) note that Climacus echoes 1 Corinthians 1:22–3, where Paul writes: "[T]he Greeks seek after wisdom: but we preach Jesus Christ crucified, unto the Jews a stumbling-block [*skandalon*], and unto the Greeks foolishness." *Skandalon*, Climacus observes, could also be translated "affront" or "offense" (n. to 50).

understanding merely parrots the paradox," for "the paradox is indeed the paradox, *quia absurdum.*" So, too, when the understanding "flaunts its magnificence in comparison with the paradox," the paradox willingly "hands over all the splendor to the understanding, even the glittering vices." The paradox even allows the understanding "to have pity on the paradox and assist it to an explanation . . . for is that not what philosophers are for – to make supernatural things ordinary and trivial?"[8] (Yet we recall that Socrates refuses to do just this when he is asked about the myth of Oreithuia and Boreas in the *Phaedrus*. Once again, the philosopher *par excellence* seems to transcend the limitations of his class or kind.) In sum, "everything it [the understanding] says about the paradox it has learned from the paradox, even though, making use of an acoustical illusion, it insists that it itself has originated the paradox" (52–3).[9]

At the conclusion of his discussion of offense, Climacus once again gives voice to what "someone may be saying" in criticism of his exposition. As in the first two chapters of *Fragments*, an imaginary critic charges Climacus with plagiarism: "all the phrases you put in the mouth of the paradox do not belong to you at all." "How could they belong to me," Climacus retorts, "since they do indeed belong to the paradox?" He is furthermore happy to admit this, adding that "I could not recognize myself" in writing them down. But his critic means something else, namely, that he has borrowed from such authors as Tertullian, Hamann, and Shakespeare.[10] "As you see," he tells Climacus, "I do know my business and know how to catch you with the stolen goods" (53).

In thinking about Climacus's ongoing relationship with this indignant and rather self-satisfied critic, it dawns on one that he has all along been mimicking the paradox's relation to the understanding in such a way

---

[8] As Nielsen notes, the understanding's desire to "domesticate" the paradox, and so to "de-intensify" the paradox's "offensively personal" imputation that one is fundamentally in error, is especially evident in attempts (including those of Kant as well as Hegel) to present the essence of Christianity in ethical or philosophical terms (Nielsen 1983, 91, 96, 121). Cf. Thulstrup's survey of German philosophical theology in his introduction to Kierkegaard 1962, xlvi–lx.

[9] The question remains whether the paradox, which strikes the understanding as absurd, actually involves a formal, logical contradiction. Evans 1992 (96–106; cf. 89–90) and Emmanuel 1996 (39–50) review the scholarly debate on this issue and argue persuasively that the paradox is not logically absurd. In the tradition of Augustine and Aquinas, Climacus holds that the mystery of the incarnation is not irrational but suprarational, "above" reason but not "against" it.

[10] Cf. *Philosophical Fragments/Johannes Climacus*, 294–5, nn. 11, 14–17.

as to underscore the problem of intellectual authorship and authority. The critic charges plagiarism, but he is, after all, a fictional product of Climacus's imagination. He *himself* is a plagiarist, for everything he says in objecting to Climacus is in fact put into his mouth by Climacus. So, too, everything the offended understanding says in objecting to the absolute paradox is borrowed from the paradox itself. What is more, Climacus is quick to admit that "his" words and ideas are not his at all, but those of the paradox or the god. Neither Climacus nor his critic is the real author of his speeches, because neither has the independent authority in the realm of knowledge that the philosophical hypothesis attributes to the understanding. Put another way, neither can truly speak for himself, because in their separation from the paradox there is in neither case a self in the full, Socratic sense – an active, reflective center of intellectual and moral responsibility – to speak for.[11]

Climacus's dramatic use of the theme of plagiarism in some ways anticipates more recent philosophical thinking. In a famous essay on Plato's *Phaedrus* that exemplifies the philosophical principles of deconstructionism, Jacques Derrida argues that the Socratic attempt to achieve self-knowledge through dialogue must fail.[12] Derrida suggests that one is never present to oneself as the author of one's own speeches. Our words are "orphans," and this is as true of the spoken word (when the speaker is allegedly present) as it is of a writing whose author is long gone (cf. *Phaedrus* 275d–e). There is, in other words, no genuinely authorial self to be known – no Socrates, for example, standing beneath or behind his speeches like a father.

Derrida echoes Climacus in arguing that the self is ultimately inaccessible to the philosophical understanding. Yet it is important to observe that Climacus is no deconstructionist. This is because he supposes that there *is* in fact a self to be known, a self that has been lost through sin but that can be recovered with the aid of the god. This is not the fragmented and misunderstood self of untruth, in which condition the relation between the understanding and the paradox is "unhappy," but the self that is united with the paradox "in that happy passion to which we have not as yet given a name" (54). In Chapter Two, Climacus stated that the god wanted to make himself understood by the learner in such a way that he did not "destroy that which is different" (25). The happy passion that is akin to

---

[11] One could take these reflections a step further by observing that Climacus is a product of Kierkegaard's literary imagination. But this would not alter the essential point.
[12] Derrida 1981.

erotic love makes this possible. Moved by passion, "the understanding surrendered itself and the paradox gave itself (*halb zog sie ihn, halb sank er hin* [she half dragged him, he half sank down])" – a mutual accommodation in which "the [absolute] difference is in fact on good terms with the understanding" (54).

The foregoing remarks raise a number of questions. How does the learner come to an understanding with the paradox, and what is the nature of this understanding? How does the god's teaching differ from the truth as the philosophical hypothesis understands it? If, as I have suggested, offense against the absolute paradox is echoed in offense against Socrates and his philosophical paradoxes, does being open to the occasion for learning presented by Socrates also help to prepare one for receiving the condition for learning from the god? These are some of the main questions that Climacus will address in the next chapter of *Fragments*.

7

Faith and the Contemporary Follower

Robert Roberts has observed that the first half of *Fragments* is a kind of ladder whereby Climacus ascends to Christianity "with nothing more substantial to go on than a simple hypothesis and a fancy for inferences."[1] Our reflections on Chapter Three confirm Roberts' observation while suggesting that Climacus's means of ascent is more substantial than he allows: Socratic eros is itself a ladder by which one could climb up to an understanding of the necessity of faith. Having followed the passion of thought to its ultimate destination in paradox, Climacus is prepared to focus more closely on the nature of faith. Faith is accordingly the central theme of the second half of the book.

Climacus divides the topic of faith into three parts. In Chapter Four, "The Situation of the Contemporary Follower," he examines the problem of faith in the context of those followers of the incarnate god who live contemporaneously with him. In Chapter Five, "The Follower at Second Hand," he examines the situation of those who, because they come later, can know of the god only through the report of others. These two chapters are separated by an "Interlude," in which Climacus spells out why it is impossible that the god's incarnation could be an object of philosophical knowledge.

In Chapter Four, Climacus attempts to characterize the life that the god must lead when he descends to the learner. Once again, the figure of Socrates hovers in the background: Climacus's description of the god's life is in certain respects strongly reminiscent of the life of Socrates. In particular, Socrates' extraordinary devotion to the quest for wisdom provides

[1] Roberts 1986, 8.

an analogy to what Climacus calls the "exalted absorption" of the god in his spiritual work (57). This analogy turns out to be crucial to Climacus's enterprise: for reasons we shall consider directly, it must be possible for a human being to live a life no less "in the service of the spirit" than that of the incarnate god.

Socrates' philosophical devotion to the truth nonetheless differs fundamentally from the mutual and faithful devotion that unites the god and the follower, and Climacus's evocation of the spiritual resemblance between Socrates and the god makes it all the more important for him to emphasize this fact. He does so by attempting to show how philosophical and historical knowledge differ from the passion of faith, how the Socratic learner differs from the religious follower, and how the truth as the object of philosophy differs from the god as the object of faith. Climacus reminds us that the god, unlike the truth that philosophy apprehends, sees just as he is seen, and he examines the paradoxical double vision that is required of both the god and the learner in order to apprehend each other through the eyes of faith. Yet here, too, there are provocative Socratic parallels, the exploration of which helps us to appreciate more deeply the religious character of Socrates' philosophical faithfulness as well as the philosophical character of religious faith.

CLIMACUS'S POETICAL VENTURE, CONTINUED

Climacus picks up in Chapter Four where he left off in Chapter Two, namely, with the god's resolution to descend to the learner. "So, then (to continue with our poem)," he writes, "the god has made his appearance as a teacher" (55). His decision to continue his poem reconfirms that, in spite of the absolute difference between the god and the understanding, poetic analogy can in some measure illuminate the god's situation. This conclusion follows also from Climacus's discussion of the absolute paradox: as the unity of absolute difference *and* absolute equality, the paradox implies that the god's life on earth must exemplify a certain sort of human possibility.[2] Climacus will accordingly make it clear that, if the god's speeches and deeds were to express a level of spiritual fidelity and intensity that no human being could possibly realize, he could not hope to achieve absolute equality with the learner.

There is a further point to be made about Climacus's decision to continue his poem. By resuming his poem, which was designed to shed light

---

[2] See ch. 5, 122.

on the situation of the god both as a teacher and as a lover, Climacus is able to keep in the foreground of our attention erotic love and the passion of faith that is analogous to it. Love causes the god himself to descend to the learner, because "to send someone else ... in his place could no more satisfy him than it could satisfy the noble king to send in his place [to the maiden] the most highly trusted person in his kingdom." Yet there is also a pedagogical consideration that obliges the god not to send someone else: if the god did not come himself, "everything would remain Socratic." Even if we could imagine a human being capable of acting as the god's emissary because he had already learned what the god has to teach – which seems impossible, given that the incarnation is necessary in order for the learner to (re)acquire the condition for learning the truth – such a person could at best only assist the learner in thinking for himself. This would be to no avail insofar as the learner is untruth; what is more, "we would not have the moment, and we would fail to obtain the paradox" (55).

So the god himself comes to the learner in the form of a lowly servant. But because the god actually *is* the lowliest of human beings, because he is an "actual body," he "has become captive, so to speak, in his resolution." In other words, he must live and die as a servant; "unlike that noble king, he does not have the possibility of suddenly disclosing that he is, after all, the king" – a possibility that is really "no perfection" in the king, because it "merely manifests his impotence ... that he actually is incapable of becoming what he wanted to become [i.e., the equal of the lowly maiden]." The god is nevertheless presumably "able to send someone in advance who can make the learner aware" (55). The god can send before him a prophet who will awaken the learner to his coming, much as John the Baptist attempted to do for Christ.

The activity of the god's predecessor is limited in scope. "Through a predecessor of this kind," Climacus observes, "a learner can become aware, but no more than that" (56). This bears some resemblance to Climacus's own activity: he, too, attempts to make the learner religiously "aware," or, to use the words with which he introduces his poem about the god, "to awaken the mind to an understanding of the divine" (26). It is true that the prophet precedes the god's appearance on earth, whereas Climacus speaks many centuries after the coming of Christ. But Climacus will try to establish in his discussion of the various followers of the god that even those who come later can by virtue of the moment be genuinely "contemporaneous" with the god, just as in the Socratic view every human being is by virtue of recollection "contemporaneous" with the eternal truth. What is more, the god, like Socrates, comes not to teach the crowd but the individual. Just so, there may well be individuals for whom Climacus serves to announce the god's coming, precisely insofar as it is he who awakens them to the possibility of faith.

Because the god's predecessor "cannot know what the god wants to teach," he can only "make the learner aware" (55). Climacus's explanation of the predecessor's ignorance is worth dwelling on. "The god's presence," he writes, "is not incidental to his teaching but is essential. The presence of the god in human form – indeed, in the lowly form of a servant – *is* precisely the teaching" (55, emphasis added). On the philosophical hypothesis, the learner needs no teacher because he already has the condition for learning the truth. Because there is no teacher, there is no teaching as such. But if there were a teaching, it would convey precisely what the learner strives to learn on his own, namely, the nature of that which truly is. On the religious hypothesis, however, the god is needed to provide the learner with the truth along with condition for understanding it (14). The truth that the god enables the learner to understand would seem to be identical to the teaching of the god. But Climacus now informs us that this teaching is actually nothing other than the presence of the god in human form. What could this mean?

To begin with, the fact of the god's incarnation has profound implications that could in themselves be regarded as his teaching, namely, that the god exists and the god loves man. Climacus's poem must be understood in the light of these implications. The poem may be viewed from two angles, one of which could be considered more philosophical and the other more religious. Climacus attempts philosophically or psychologically to deduce the necessity of the incarnation from the god's love for man, but the poem may also be read backwards, as an explanation of the incarnation for those who already accept it as a fact. Either way the poem underscores the god's love for the learner, the proof of which is furnished by the incarnation – for as we have noted, the existence of a loving god can be established only by the action of the god himself.[3]

On the philosophical hypothesis, all human beings possess the condition for understanding the truth, but few make use of it by undertaking to learn the truth philosophically. It now appears that on the religious hypothesis the situation is roughly reversed: few come to possess the condition, but those who do possess it thereby also understand the truth. It is easy to see why this must be so. The god, we recall, is obliged to descend

---

[3] See ch. 4, 86–7; ch. 5, 116–19.

to the learner in order to give him the condition. As Climacus will soon divulge, this condition is faith. Faith acknowledges the god's incarnation, but the god's incarnation is his teaching. Faith thus seem to be more than a mere condition: to grasp that the god is present in human form is not simply to be able to understand the truth, but *actually* to understand it (or at least its most essential part).

The question remains, however, whether the god also makes it possible for the learner to learn something beyond what can be immediately inferred from his presence. Once the learner has the condition for understanding the truth, he would seem to be such as Socrates assumed him to be all along: he can learn the truth on his own. But does faith also give the learner a field within which to employ his understanding Socratically, and thereby to learn on his own something more than the essential truth entailed by the god's presence? In other words, does Climacus see faith as a precondition for what is in effect Socratic philosophizing, except that it takes place within the context provided by revelation? Climacus does not address this question, perhaps because he does not know the answer.[4] But if the answer is affirmative, it would be possible for the "follower" discussed in this and subsequent chapters also to be a "learner" in the Socratic sense.[5]

The god takes the form of a servant but wishes to be known as the god, for to remain utterly incognito would be "to mock human beings." Hence, he is obliged to "allow something about himself to be understood," even though this cannot help "the person who does not receive the condition" and may indeed "just as well alienate the learner as draw him closer." The

---

4 He does not, after all, claim to be a Christian (*Postscript*, 617). But see the remark later in Chapter Four: "once the condition is given, that which was valid for the Socratic is again valid" (63).

5 Although Climacus does not speak to this issue – perhaps because, in his account, the importance of the incarnation eclipses that of the holy scriptures – the coincidence of following and learning may be found within Christianity (e.g., in the thought of Thomas Aquinas) as well as in other faith traditions. One of the earliest and most attractive models of philosophizing within the bounds of faith is provided in the Jewish tradition by the Talmud, which presupposes the supreme authority of the Word of God as revealed in the Hebrew Bible. The Talmud, whose "ultimate purpose ... is not in any sense utilitarian," and whose "sole aim is to seek out the truth" (Steinsaltz 1989, 2), consists of a series of Socratic, dialectical discussions that attempt to resolve various issues by weaving together the evidence of experience with the teachings of scripture. Many of these issues are never fully resolved in the text, and readers – who traditionally study in the company of others, so that the reflections of the rabbis may be seen from a variety of perspectives – are constantly provoked to think for themselves in attempting to arrive at answers to the questions that have been raised.

god takes the form of a servant, but does not come in order to live in the service of a particular master. His being a servant meant simply that "he was a lowly man who did not set himself off from the human throng either by soft raiment or by any other earthly advantage." "But even though he was a lowly man," Climacus continues, "his concerns were not those that men generally have." He was unconcerned with the goods of the world, and "as unconcerned about his living as the birds of the air." He was not "attracted by things that commonly attract the attention of people," nor enthralled by the love of a woman. He sought only one thing: "the follower's love" (56).

Climacus's description of the god, in which he once again relies heavily on scripture,[6] is "very beautiful" but perhaps implausible. One is accordingly forced to ask whether the god does not "elevate himself above what is ordinarily the condition of human beings" by means of his unusual behavior (56–7). "We are unable to poetize the god otherwise," Climacus notes, "but what does a fiction prove?" "The question is this," he adds: "May a human being express the same thing? – for otherwise the god has not realized the essentially human." Climacus's answer is oddly conditional:

Yes, if he is capable of it, he may also do it. If he can become so absorbed in the service of the spirit that it never occurs to him to provide for food and drink, if he is sure that the lack will not divert him, that the hardship will not disorder his body and make him regret that he did not first of all understand the lessons of childhood before wanting to understand more – yes, then he truly may do it, and his greatness is even more glorious than the quiet assurance of the lily. (57)

If he is capable, he may also do it. But is a human being capable of this? Has anyone ever actually lived this way?

One example comes readily to mind: that of Socrates. Like the god, Socrates was by no means well-born or wealthy. Like the god, he did not set himself off from others, his concerns were not those other men generally have, and he was as carefree about his living as the birds of the air (cf. 57) – so much so that his devotion to philosophy caused him to live "in ten-thousandfold poverty" (*Apology* 23b–c) and ultimately resulted in his execution (and in this, too, he resembles the god). Like the god, Socrates lived with only one thing in mind – his philosophical service to the god at Delphi – and was so absorbed in this service of the spirit that he was virtually immune to hunger, cold, and fatigue (*Symposium* 219e–220d).

---

[6] See ch. 4, n. 1.

A skeptic might assert that Plato's description of Socrates is a poetic fiction. That Climacus did not seem to think so hardly matters, for *he* is undoubtedly a fictional character. (For the same reason, the skeptic would find it irrelevant that Climacus himself, who "dance[s] lightly in the service of thought, as far as possible to the honor of the god ... renouncing domestic bliss and civic esteem" [7], seems to be an example of the sort of person who is wholly absorbed in the service of the spirit.) Perhaps the only satisfactory way to respond to this kind of objection would be to ask whether the objector is willing to acknowledge the essential truth of Plato's depiction of Socrates as an expression of the great spiritual devotion that *some* human being – possibly some other martyr to God or truth – has at one time or another actually attained. If this response is not convincing, there is nothing more to say: only actuality can convincingly establish possibility, and a committed skeptic might nevertheless maintain that certain human achievements are no longer possible.[7]

For his part, Climacus is clearly aware of the parallels between the god and Socrates – so much so that he must ultimately take pains to distinguish the god's conduct from that of the philosopher. "This exalted absorption in his work," he continues, "will already have drawn to the teacher the attention of the crowd, among whom the learner presumably will be found" (cf. *Apology* 23c). "The wise and the learned will no doubt first submit sophistic questions to him ... or put him through an examination" (in Socrates' case, the reverse is true, for he himself sought out the wise and the learned in order to examine *them*). "After that [they will] guarantee him a tenured position and a living" – a little irony on Climacus's part, for of course the god, like Socrates, would presumably never accept money for teaching (cf. *Apology* 19d–e, 33a–b). "So now we have the god walking around in the city in which he made his appearance ... to proclaim his teaching is for him the one and only necessity of his life, is for him his food and drink" (the same is true for Socrates, except that his work is to promote philosophizing and care for the soul; cf. *Apology* 29d–e). "He has no friends and no relatives, but to him the learner is brother and sister" (cf. *Apology* 31b: Socrates neglects his family and goes privately to each of the Athenians "like a father or an older brother, persuading you to care for virtue"). But the learner, Climacus insists, is not

---

[7] It is perhaps worth noting that Kierkegaard speaks as if he has no doubt about the essential truthfulness of Plato's portrait of Socrates: "Socrates is an ideality higher than any poet is able to poetize it," he writes in a journal entry, "and he actually is this; it is his actuality" (JP 4301, 4.222 [XI.1 A 430]). Yet it is difficult to take this claim at face value (see the Epilogue).

the "curious crowd" or any of the "professional teachers" in the crowd. As in the Socratic case, the learner is the *individual* – and not just any individual, but one who, in all humility, is willing to acknowledge his own profound ignorance (57).

It is at this point, however, that the Socratic analogy breaks down. Whereas learning can always take place when all that is required is an occasion to reflect, the individual who is untruth needs more in order to learn from the god. "If the populous or if that professional teacher *learns* something, then in the purely Socratic sense the god is only the occasion" (58, emphasis in original). This is because no learning can occur apart from the condition for understanding the truth, which the god must first give to the learner. The learner, in other words, must first become a *follower*.

FAITH AND THE DECISION OF ETERNITY

The appearance of the god does, of course, occasion many things:

> [I]t is the occasion for much loose and empty talk, perhaps also the occasion for more serious reflection. But for the learner the news of the day is not an occasion for something else, not even the occasion for him in Socratic honesty to immerse himself in himself – no, it is the eternal, the beginning of eternity! The news of the day is the beginning of eternity! (58)

In this passage, Climacus uses the term "learner" in an honorific sense. It designates not simply one whom the god wishes to save from untruth, but one who is actually receptive to the god and his teaching. This learner is struck by the paradox that Climacus calls "the moment": the news (*Nyhed*) is something new or novel, but what is new today is nothing other than that which is always. It is news not in itself, but *for the learner*: in his condition of untruth, he had been separated from the being and truth of eternity by an infinite abyss.

The moment – the unity of eternity and time in the earthly presence of the god, which is also the paradox, or the unity of absolute difference with absolute equality – is "the decision of eternity" (58). And just as Socrates is an occasion for learning only in relation to the individual (who may or may not seize the occasion) so, too, the god is the moment of decision only in relation to the individual (who may or may not seize the moment). On one side, the moment is the decision of the eternal god to enter into time for the sake of the learner; on the other, the moment is the decision of the learner in response to the news of the god's appearance.

What is at stake in the moment of decision? While the answer of Christianity is "eternal salvation," the questions on the title page of *Fragments* speak more Socratically of "an eternal consciousness" as well as "eternal happiness." By introducing the religious hypothesis within the context of Socrates' philosophical concerns, Climacus allows us to see the concept of eternal salvation in a new light. For Socrates, the philosophical project promises to make one enduringly whole and therefore happy. On the Socratic hypothesis, philosophy allows one to transcend time and recover one's "forgotten" being in eternity. This is possible because the eternal truth is immanent in one's consciousness. On the religious hypothesis, too, the self is initially (i.e., in its untruth) separated from its being in eternity, but the eternal truth is not immanent in one's consciousness and is in all other respects completely inaccessible. The self that is untruth is thus utterly time-bound. There can be no question of eternal happiness, for the self that is untruth is entirely evanescent; by the same token, it is but a fragment of a whole (and therefore happy) self. The decision of eternity is thus the decision *to be* as well as *to be whole.*

That the moment is the decision of eternity, Climacus emphasizes, must be taught by the god: "if the god does not provide the condition to understand this, how will it ever occur to the learner?" But the god does provide the condition: otherwise "we come no further but go back to Socrates." More precisely, the moment or the paradox "intends to interest him [the learner] otherwise than merely historically, intends to be the condition for his eternal happiness" (58). The learner, then, must "come to an understanding with this paradox," which is to say that he must accept that it is the decision of eternity – "for we do not say that he is supposed to understand the paradox but is only to understand that this is the paradox" (59). The learner cannot understand the paradox because he is untruth; were he not untruth, the god would not be the absolutely different and there would be no paradox. But how is it possible even for the learner to understand that this *is* the paradox?

Climacus's answer is that the understanding "steps aside" and the paradox "gives itself" to the learner. All of this, moreover, occurs neither through the understanding (which "is discharged," and so has no further role to play in embracing the paradox) nor through the paradox, but in "a third something." This third thing is nothing other than the condition for understanding the truth that, according to the religious hypothesis, the god must give to the learner. It is the "happy passion" akin to erotic love that Climacus first mentions at the end of Chapter Three (48; cf. 49, 54). This passion, we are now told, is faith (*Tro:* 59).

Climacus's account of faith has a number of implications. Let us begin with the most important one. Climacus's poem was designed to illuminate the unhappiness that the god experiences if he is not understood by the learner, an unhappiness akin to that which occurs when lovers are "unable to have each other" (25–26). Faith, on the other hand, is a happy passion because it allows the god to be understood. In faith, the god's love for the learner is answered by the learner's love for the god, for "only in love is the different made equal, and only in equality or unity is there understanding" (25). But if the encounter between the learner and the god is by virtue of faith "a happy one, like erotic love's understanding" (49), then faith must be something in which *both* the god *and* the learner partake. In other words, the god has faith in the learner no less than the learner has faith in the god.

Our previous reflection on the parables of the king and the maiden and Agnes and the merman have prepared us to understand the latter point. The god is no less trusting than Agnes and no less reflective than the king. Put another way, the god's faith in the learner proves that he is able to do something the king could not, namely, to discharge his understanding – for as both parables make clear, the understanding is the source of the most serious doubts about the prospects for love between unequals. And if the learner accomplishes something difficult and wonderful, it is only by virtue of the god's faith that he is able to do so.[8] The wonder is not simply that the learner accepts that which is absolutely paradoxical. In faith, the learner "becomes nothing and yet is not annihilated . . . owes him [the god] everything and yet becomes boldly confident . . . understands the truth, but the truth makes him free" (30–1). The god's faith in the learner is thus faith in the possibility of faith itself – something that "is just as paradoxical as the paradox" and is itself "a wonder" no less wonderful than the paradox. "Everything that is true of the paradox is also true of faith," Climacus observes, for "how else could it [faith] have as its object the paradox and be happy in its relation to it?" (65). Faith begets faith: the god's faith in the learner – without which he would not have undertaken to descend to the learner – makes the learner's faith possible.

What, then, is faith – this thing that lets one embrace the paradox and decide for eternity, and that thereby makes one a follower of the god? Climacus's poem has already given us the answer: it is a passion

---

[8] Cf. Silentio's remark that, if the merman "lets himself be saved by Agnes, then he is the greatest human being I can imagine" (*Fear and Trembling*, 99). But his salvation is nevertheless made possible only by Agnes's faith.

resembling erotic love, and thus also philosophical eros. Beyond this, Climacus will tell us only what faith is not. It is not knowledge, nor, as he goes on to explain, can knowledge substitute for faith or be prerequisite to faith. And it is not an act of will.

In the first place, absolutely exact historical knowledge is unavailable about what must be the most decisive event of the god's life from the point of view of the potential follower, namely, his birth. About this subject, the only human being that "would be completely informed" is "the woman by whom he let himself be born." Furthermore, although it is otherwise easy for the contemporary learner to "become a historical eyewitness" and so acquire detailed historical information, such information "by no means makes the eyewitness a follower" (59). To be a follower is to embrace the paradoxical unity of the historical and the eternal, and historical knowledge alone cannot lead one to do so. Even if one were to learn all there is to know about the life of a certain man, such knowledge could never entail that this man is also the god.

Nor can faith be knowledge – even if it should be as exact as possible – of "the teaching which that teacher [the god] occasionally presented." To focus on such knowledge would be to treat the god as if he were merely a Socratic occasion. It would be to approach this knowledge as though *it* might be the eternal truth, while regarding knowledge about the god as "contingent and historical knowledge" (60). Like historical knowledge about the life of the god, knowledge about his teaching separates the eternal from the historical; what faith grasps, however, is the paradoxical *unity* of the historical and the eternal, the human and the divine, and the finite and the infinite, not in the teaching of the god but in the teacher himself. What is more, because both historical knowledge about the god's life and knowledge of the god's teaching separate the eternal from the historical – because neither, in a word, allows one to understand the essential truth that *this man is the god* – it is no more helpful to combine these kinds of knowledge than it is to pursue either one independently of the other.

One implication of the foregoing is that neither critical philological study of the New Testament nor the most careful historical scholarship about the life of Christ – two intellectual pursuits that flourished in the nineteenth century – can in any way provide support for religious faith. Knowledge cannot replace faith or come to its aid, because the object of faith is a paradox that unites contradictories and thereby surpasses understanding: it is "the eternalizing of the historical and the historicizing of the eternal" (61). It follows from this also that historical ignorance about the god's life or about his occasional teachings cannot impede faith, which is to say that in this respect (as well as in almost all others, as Climacus will later make explicit) the historically contemporary learner has no advantage over the follower at second hand.

Climacus sums up the preceding reflections by observing that all knowledge is "either knowledge of the eternal, which excludes the temporal and the historical as inconsequential" – for example, mathematics and logic – "or it is purely historical knowledge." But "no knowledge has as its object this absurdity that the eternal is the historical." If I comprehend the metaphysics of Spinoza, for example, I consider it from the perspective of eternity, for it concerns the nature of God and its truth or falsity is independent of history. At some other time, I may be "historically occupied" with Spinoza himself. "The follower, however, is in faith related to the teacher in such a way that he is eternally occupied with his historical existence" (62).

What does it mean to be eternally occupied with the teacher's historical existence? On the philosophical hypothesis, "the learner, because he himself is the truth and has the condition, can thrust the teacher away." Indeed, "the Socratic art and heroism" consisted precisely in "assisting people to be able to do this" (62). The Socratic learner owes the teacher nothing, for as Climacus reminds us, Socrates "was not capable of *giving birth*" (61, emphasis in original; cf. 10). On the Socratic hypothesis, the teacher is merely a midwife, and the learner "gives birth" to himself by acquiring on his own the knowledge that makes one wholly and fully a self (cf. 19). But if the teacher provides the learner with the condition for learning the truth, it is the teacher who gives birth to the learner. The learner consequently "owes that teacher *everything*," and "the object of faith becomes not the *teaching* but the *teacher*" (61, 62; emphases in original). Faith must therefore "constantly cling firmly to the teacher," and what it clings to is a contradiction: "[I]n order for the teacher to be able to give the condition, he must be the god, and in order to put the learner in possession of it, he must be man. This contradiction is in turn the object of faith and is the paradox, the moment" (62). Faith is not knowledge, because the paradoxical unity of the eternal and the historical in the teacher cannot be grasped by reason alone.

Nor is faith an act of will. If one lacks the condition for understanding the truth, one cannot come to possess it by willing. As Climacus puts the point, "it is always the case that all human willing is efficacious only within the condition." In other words, I can successfully will only that which I am already able to accomplish, or that for which I *already* possess the condition. Thus, if I possess the condition for understanding the truth and "I have the courage to will it, I will understand the Socratic – that is, understand myself." But "if I do not possess the condition (and we assume this in order not to go back to the Socratic), then all my willing is of no avail" (62–3).

Climacus's reflections on faith help us to appreciate the peculiarity of his remark that the moment is "the decision of eternity" (60). A decision is an informed act of the will that results from deliberation. This certainly applies to the god, who "wills to be the equal of the beloved" through "the omnipotence of resolving love" (32). But it does not apply to the learner. If the faith that allows the learner to embrace the moment is a "decision," it is nevertheless not one that is informed by his knowledge or determined by his will. This is confirmed in *Postscript*, wherein Climacus speaks of "the risk in which passion chooses and in which passion continues upholding its choice" (42). The passion that chooses is, of course, faith. While faith is neither willing nor knowing, it is the nevertheless the precondition of a more expansive kind of willing and knowing for the learner who is reborn: for "once the condition is given, that which was valid for the Socratic is again valid" (63).[9]

SEEING IS NOT BELIEVING, BELIEVING IS NOT SEEING

When it comes to faith, one might imagine that the god's historical contemporaries must have a significant advantage over those who come later precisely because the incarnate god is immediately present to them. Climacus now takes a closer look at the paradoxes associated with "seeing" the god – both literally and through the "eyes" of faith – in order to establish that this is by no means so.

It is natural that the learner who lives after the god has died will "very much envy" the contemporary learner because "the contemporary can go and observe that teacher." To have been able to see the god – this seems like a great boon for faith. But the later learner's envy is misplaced. Suppose that the contemporary "dare[s] to believe his eyes": this does not make him a follower, for "if he believes his eyes, he is in fact deceived, for the god cannot be known directly" (63). What he sees with his eyes is

---

9 Cf. Climacus's later comment that "the relation between one contemporary and another contemporary, provided that both are believers, is altogether Socratic: the one is not indebted to the other for anything, but both are indebted to the god for everything" (65–6).

nothing more than a lowly servant. The servant is indeed the god, but the *divinity* of the servant – hence the god *as such* – is not visible to the naked eye. To become a follower, the contemporary learner must still decide for eternity, and the immediate physical presence of the servant in itself contributes nothing to this decision.

Suppose, then, that the contemporary closes his eyes. But if he does so, Climacus asks, "then what is the advantage of being contemporary?" Suppose further that he tries to envision the god with his eyes closed. In that case, he will fail: "the god . . . cannot be envisioned, and that was the very reason he was in the form of the servant" (63). Because the god is the absolutely different, the learner who attempts to see him in his mind's eye necessarily falls victim to what Climacus has called the self-ironizing of the understanding. In order to make himself understood, the god is accordingly obliged to reveal himself; in order to do so in such a way as to preserve the independence and confidence of the learner (cf. 26–30), he is obliged to take a form in which his divinity is not directly visible.

The same conclusion can be reached from the other direction as well. Suppose that the learner *could* by himself successfully envision the god. In that case, he would need only a Socratic "reminder" in order to do so, for "he himself would possess the condition [for understanding the truth]." The god would be present to the mind of the learner as he is in himself, and the learner would be able, without assistance, to understand the god's teaching – both because "the condition and the question contain the conditioned and the answer" (14), and because the god's presence, as Climacus has said, *is* his teaching. But the god takes the form of the servant precisely because the learner does not possess the condition (63–4).

Finally, it is mistaken to imagine that envisioning the god is somehow a matter of penetrating beneath the "external" form of the servant, as though faith requires something like x-ray vision. A better analogy for faith would be seeing double. The servant form, Climacus reminds us, is "no incognito." It is the god's true form, in which he has by his "omnipotent resolution" become absolutely the equal of the lowliest of human beings (64, cf. 32). The form of the servant, then, is "not inconsequential" for the follower. One who sees this form when faith is absent sees only a servant. One who sees it through the "eyes of faith" that have been "opened" by the god sees both the god who is a servant and a servant who is the god. To see through the eyes of faith is, in other words, to behold the absolute coincidence of the lowly servant with the infinite and eternal god. It is to catch sight of the unity of absolute difference and absolute equality in the paradox. Faith sees double because the paradox is double, and faith is "just as paradoxical as the paradox" (65).

Climacus now encounters a predictable objection from his imaginary interlocutor: how can it be that the god's contemporaries have "no advantage whatsoever from being contemporary," because "it seems natural to regard as blessed the contemporary generation that saw and heard him"? Climacus responds to this objection by asking his interlocutor to imagine that, long ago, there occurred a magnificent imperial wedding "with a festiveness the like of which had never been seen." We who come later would "regard the contemporaries as fortunate – that is, those contemporaries who saw and heard and touched, for otherwise what is the good of being contemporary?" "But now," he adds, "suppose that the magnificence was of a different kind, something not to be seen immediately." In that case, the person who is immediately present at the imperial wedding would not thereby be "contemporary with the magnificence," for while his immediate presence might make it possible for him to see and hear much else, it would not in itself allow him to see and hear anything of the magnificence. Curiously, the immediate or historical contemporary who saw and heard much but lacked that which was needed to see and hear the magnificence would thus be a noncontemporary, while the noncontemporary in the sense of immediacy (i.e., one who comes later) who *is* able see and hear the magnificence would be a contemporary. The real or genuine contemporary – the one who sees and hears the magnificence – is thus not such by way of immediate contemporaneity, but becomes such "by virtue of something else." And since immediate contemporaneity is irrelevant to genuine contemporaneity, it follows that "someone who comes later must be able to be the genuine contemporary" (66–7).

Climacus's analogy is well chosen. It reminds us of the wedding envisioned by the king who had fallen in love with a lowly maiden, and just as there seemed to be nothing in the lowly maiden that merited the attention of a king, there seems to be nothing at all magnificent about a lowly servant. The immediate contemporary does not, simply by virtue of being present when the imperial wedding occurs, possess the condition for seeing and hearing its magnificence. So, too, the condition for seeing and hearing the magnificence of the incarnate god is that one possess the "eyes" and "ears" of faith, without which even the immediate contemporary would be able to declare only that "he was an unimpressive man of humble birth, and only a few individuals believed there was anything extraordinary about him, something I certainly was unable to discover" (67). Through faith (and only through faith), Climacus observes, one knows as one is known (68). Just as faith allows the learner to recognize the divinity of the lowly servant, so it allows the god to discern the worthiness of the learner – for the god sees in the learner what the king sees in the maiden: something more than the lowliness that meets the naked eye.

GODS, PHILOSOPHERS, AND IMPOSTERS

Like the other chapters of *Fragments*, Chapter Four is structured in such a way as to suggest certain potentially illuminating comparisons between faith and philosophy. In the present context, we may note that Climacus's reflections on what makes it possible to recognize the god call to mind a similar problem with regard to the philosopher. Two Platonic dialogues, the *Sophist* and the *Statesman*, are explicitly concerned with distinguishing philosophers from two close look-alikes, sophists (itinerant teachers who in the dialogues are typically characterized as sham-philosophers and bad citizens) and statesmen. At the beginning of the *Sophist*, Socrates compares the difficulty of recognizing the philosopher to the difficulty of recognizing the gods, who sometimes walk among men in the guise of human beings (216a–d).[10] This problem is relevant to his own situation: the *Sophist* and *Statesman* take place concurrently with Socrates' public trial at Athens, in which he is ultimately convicted and sentenced to death – a result that suggests many of his fellow citizens have mistaken him for a sophist.[11] As in the case of the god, immediate contemporaneity seems to confer no special advantage when it comes to discerning who or what the philosopher *is*.

But is the foregoing comparison a meaningful one? Because of the radical dissimilarity of their relationships to the learner, it might appear that the situation of the philosopher bears no essential resemblance to that of the god. On the philosophical hypothesis, after all, the teacher is merely an occasion for the learner to give birth to himself; the learner therefore owes the teacher nothing (19).[12] Even so, it is necessary for the learner to recognize that the teacher *is* an *occasion*, and what is more, an occasion for the kind of reflection that promises to transform one's life. This is something that most of Socrates' contemporaries failed to

---

[10] Cf. Euripides' *Bacchae*, a tragedy that turns on the inability of King Pentheus of Thebes to see that a troublesome stranger is actually the god Dionysus.

[11] For further discussion see Howland 1998.

[12] Yet as Rudd 2000/2002 observes, the latter claim is "somewhat misleading; had I failed to meet this teacher at this time, then I might have gone to the grave without ever coming to recollect the Truth" (2.263).

appreciate. And as in the case of the god, the learner's recognition of what the teacher has to offer answers to the teacher's ability to see human beings not as they are – i.e., ignorant and self-satisfied – but, so to speak, as they once were and might with effort become again.

There is another point of comparison between the philosopher and the god: both can fulfill their pedagogical roles in relation to those who come later (the one serving as an occasion for, and the other giving the condition to, the learner) at least as successfully as they can in relation to their immediate contemporaries. Yet the mechanisms whereby they are able to do so differ from each other in a revealing way. Socrates can arguably serve as an occasion for learning through the medium of the writings of Plato or Climacus just as well as he can by being present to the learner immediately.[13] For that matter, anyone could in principle serve as an occasion for learning no less effectively than Socrates did, since on the philosophical hypothesis no one has more authority in the sphere of teaching and learning than anyone else. In relation to the god, however, Climacus can only prepare the way by attempting to awaken the learner's mind to the divine. The person who receives the condition for understanding the truth must receive it from the god himself; if one could receive the condition at second hand, "the second hand would have to be the god himself" (69).

In the very last pages of Chapter Four, Climacus extends his implicit use of philosophy as a foil for faith. His depiction of the transformation effected in the learner by faith echoes Socrates' understanding of the transformation of the learner at the culmination of the philosophical quest. The learner who receives the condition from the god, and thereby becomes a believer and a follower, is able to "see the glory with the eyes of faith." In receiving the condition he becomes the god's genuine contemporary (even if he came later), and is distinguished from the immediate contemporary in that he "is not an eyewitness... but as a believer he is a contemporary in the *autopsy* [*Autopsi*] of faith" (70, emphasis in original). This is a striking phrase. The Greek word *autopsia* means "seeing with one's own eyes," which implies that faith renews the vision proper to a human being as such – vision that was lost when we blinded ourselves in sin. In giving us back our own eyes and, as Climacus will indicate momentarily, our own ears (for untruth is deafness as well as blindness), faith allows us to recover our original wholeness. Seeing and hearing "the

[13] Perhaps the Platonic representation of Socrates, just *because* it is indirect, is pedagogically even more effective than Socrates was in person. Cf. Howland 2002b.

glory" thus goes hand-in-hand with being wholly ourselves. The structure
is the same as that posited by Socrates on the philosophical hypothesis,
according to which being a self in the fullest sense requires coming to
know that which truly is.

On the philosophical hypothesis, self-knowledge is God-knowledge:
knowing that which truly is and achieving self-knowledge are two faces of
the same coin. Climacus accordingly takes pains to reiterate faith's claim
to making possible genuine self-knowledge. He does so by way of a highly
suggestive image. Anyone who comes after the god and is so "carried away
by his own infatuation" that he wishes to be an immediate contemporary
is "an imposter, recognizable, like the false Smerdis, by having no ears –
namely, the ears of faith" (70). This is a reference to a story in *The History
of Herodotus.* Smerdis was a Magian who usurped the Persian throne
while pretending to be the brother of the Persian emperor Cambyses, a
man whom he closely resembled and who was also named Smerdis. This
false Smerdis, however, was ultimately betrayed by the fact that, unlike
the real Smerdis, he had no ears (Herodotus 3.61, 69). Like the false
Smerdis, Climacus implies, the imposter who longs to be an immediate
contemporary of the god is the look-alike of the genuine man of faith,
except that he is less than whole. In particular, he lacks something that is
essential for self-knowledge as well as knowledge of the god. Rather than
acting as though he were "on the way to the terror of the paradox" – a
phrase wherein Climacus first hints at the difficulty of faith, about which
he will say more later – the imposter "is bounding away like a dancing
teacher in order to reach that imperial wedding on time." In so doing,
he is "running on a wild-goose chase and *misunderstands himself,* like the
bird catcher, for if the bird does not come to him, running after it with a
lime twig is futile" (70–1, emphasis added). The imposter, like the false
Smerdis, wrongly fancies himself as one who belongs in the imperial
court. Yet the wedding he is rushing to attend is not for him. Because
he lacks the *autopsia* of faith, he cannot see with his own eyes; because
his condition is the blindness of untruth, he also has no adequate vision
(*opsis*) of himself (*autos*).

Reflection suggests that there have been, and will continue to be, many
imposters of faith. This thought leads Climacus to suggest that there
may be only one respect in which the immediate contemporary has an
advantage over someone who comes later: the former did not have to
deal with centuries of "loose chatter" about the god. In comparison with
this chatter, the "untrue and confused rumors that the contemporary (in
the sense of immediacy) had to put up with did not make the possibility

of the right relationship [with the god] nearly as difficult" as it is for one who comes later. Far from being "riddled . . . with chatter" and perhaps even "eliminated," as it is in our day, faith in the time of the immediate contemporary "must have appeared in all its originality, by contrast easy to distinguish from everything else" (71).

Climacus's remarks about the problem of chatter allow us to see that one of his primary goals in *Fragments* is to open his readers' ears to the originality of faith by silencing the idle talk that obscures this originality. What is more, it has been clear since the very first words of the book that Climacus is no less concerned with philosophical imposters than he is with imposters of faith. By exposing as "empty talk" all claims to have gone beyond Socrates in the domain of philosophy (11), he is also attempting to silence centuries of philosophical chatter. In a word, Climacus wants us to develop eyes and ears for philosophy "in all its originality" no less than for faith. Only when we have done so will we truly appreciate what philosophy is and what faith is, as well as what is at stake in the decision between them.

The preceding line of thought brings us to a difficult issue. Why were so many of the immediate contemporaries of the god and of Socrates – people for whom no Climacean philosophical excavation was necessary in order to see faith or philosophy in all of their originality – nevertheless unable to understand them? Perhaps some focus can be brought to this question by the observation that Climacus frames his entire investigation in *Fragments* in terms of the relationship of the teacher, not to human beings as such, but to the individual learner. Why, then, were so many would-be learners unprepared to recognize what was being offered to them by Socrates on the one hand and the god on the other?

As we have seen, Socrates was in Climacus's view amply prepared to learn from the divinity he called "the god." He was so by virtue of his philosophical eros, which opened him up to the god as an unknown and ultimately unknowable other. It was eros, in other words, that made him a *learner*. The same is true of Climacus, whose philosophical eros – so evident in *Johannes Climacus* – gives him a well-tuned ear for what Socrates was able to offer his fellow men. This suggests that those contemporaries who failed to seize the occasion for learning presented by Socrates did so because they were for some reason deficient in philosophical eros, which is to say that they were simply not genuine learners.

Is the lack of preparedness to learn in the company of Socrates analogous to the lack of preparedness that prevents the individual from receiving the gift of faith? While it might seem preposterous to assert that philosophical eros is in general prerequisite to faith, Climacus claims in *Postscript* that "every human being is by nature designed to become a thinker."[14] Whether this means that the god expects every human being to relate to him initially as a learner is another matter.[15] Be that as it may, Climacus is concerned in *Fragments* with the case of the learner to whom the god comes as a teacher. If the Socratic case is analogous to this one, the learner who fails to learn from the incarnate god by becoming a follower is only a would-be learner, not a genuine one. This would-be learner understands himself to be engaged in the pursuit of wisdom, but is insufficiently erotic to grasp what the god offers. Climacus's comparison of faith with erotic love is helpful in this connection. The would-be learner's love of wisdom is more like self-love than erotic love, which is to say that he is prevented from opening himself up to the god by his own intellectual pretensions. For the same reason, his response to the absolute paradox, to say nothing of the relative paradoxes with which Socrates habitually confounds his interlocutors, is naturally one of offense. The genuine learner, on the other hand, seems to be capable of learning from the incarnate god no less than from an encounter with Socrates, because in both cases what prepares him for learning the truth is the love of wisdom. To the extent that Climacus is receptive to the gift of faith as well as to the philosophical occasion, it would seem to be this love that makes him so.

[14] *Postscript*, 47. "God is not to be faulted," he adds, "if habit and routine and lack of passion and affectation and chatter with neighbors right and left gradually corrupt most people, so that they become thoughtless...."
[15] On this matter cf. *Postscript*, n. on 170–1: "What is developed here by no means pertains to the simple folk, whom the god will preserve in their lovable simplicity.... On the other hand, it does pertain to the person who considers himself to have the ability and the opportunity for deeper inquiry."

8

Climacan Interlude

On Historical Necessity

Having discussed the situation of the contemporary follower in Chapter Four, Climacus will go on to examine that of the follower at second hand in Chapter Five. The two kinds of follower, of course, are necessarily separated by a period of time. "How long the intervening period should be is up to you," Climacus remarks to the reader, "but if it pleases you, then for the sake of earnestness and jest we shall assume that precisely eighteen hundred and forty-three years have passed." Not coincidentally, this is almost exactly how much time has elapsed between the incarnation of God in the person of Christ and the publication of *Fragments*. But this puts Climacus in a literary predicament: how is he to "suggest" this passage of time? His solution is to employ, after the fashion of comic dramas, a light entertainment or "Interlude." In a comedy, he observes, "there may be an interval of several years between two acts," during which "the orchestra sometimes plays a symphony or something similar in order to shorten the time by filling it up." Instead of offering us music, however, Climacus proposes to fill the time between Chapter Four and Chapter Five by examining a certain philosophical question. What is more, the question, which furnishes the subtitle of the Interlude, is to all appearances a serious one: "Is the Past More Necessary than the Future? Or Has the Possible, by Having Become Actual, Become More Necessary than It Was?" (72).

What accounts for the combination of "earnestness and jest" in Climacus's tone (72)? The question he proposes to examine concerns a view of history that Climacus associates with Hegel and his followers.[1]

---

[1] Stewart 2003 maintains that in this chapter Climacus specifically takes aim at Martensen, who used Hegelian principles to argue that the incarnation was necessary (366–8).

Because they loom large in the intellectual landscape of his likely readers, these thinkers must be taken seriously – even though Climacus makes it clear here, as elsewhere, that he regards them as buffoons. Like certain Dostoyevskian characters who reflect the influence of philosophy in ways that are sometimes comic and often tragic, the Hegelians fall far short of the balance and wholeness exhibited by the most admirable human beings.[2] In *Fragments*, as in *Johannes Climacus*, these philosophers exemplify a jarring disharmony of speech and deed. Yet Climacus supposes as a matter of course that they have shaped the attitudes of his intended audience. "I by no means doubt," Climacus tells the reader near the beginning of the Interlude, "that you have fully understood and accepted the most recent philosophy, which, like the most recent period, seems to suffer from a strange inattention, confusing the performance with the caption" (73). For the "performance" – the actual world in all its concreteness – the speculative philosophers substitute abstract pronouncements. This is the theoretical equivalent of reading captions while ignoring the pictures to which they refer, and then claiming to have achieved a full understanding of what was depicted. And it is Climacus's task to show the reader what this means when it comes to thinking about the past, present, and future.

The Interlude is divided into four sections, "1. Coming Into Existence," "2. The Historical," "3. The Past," and "4. The Apprehension of the Past." These sections are followed by an Appendix, subtitled "Application." As a whole, the Interlude is an unusually dense piece of metaphysical reflection that is in certain respects more of a sketch than a fully elaborated argument. But Climacus's general aim is clear: he wants to safeguard faith from the tyranny of philosophical reason. In particular, he hopes to refute the doctrine that history is the unfolding of necessity – a doctrine that in his view makes freedom, and therewith faith, an illusion. Climacus accordingly argues against any attempt to conflate historical

---

Climacus also seems to be criticizing F. A. Trendelenburg's attempt, in *Logische Untersuchungen* (1840), to account for the transition from the self's possibility to its concrete enactment in actuality – a transition that in Climacus's view takes place, like all coming to be, "in freedom" (*Fragments*, 75) – in terms of a kind of "inner" necessity. See Come 1991.

[2] Dostoyevsky's *Crime and Punishment* invites us to compare Raskolnikov, who uses Hegel's account of "world-historical" individuals to justify murder, with the wise and humane detective Porfiry Petrovich. *Demons* presents us with a menagerie of people who have been corrupted by the ideas of German philosophy (these ideas being the "demons" to which the title refers), including the ludicrous and pathetic Stepan Verkhovensky, his vicious son Pyotr Stepanovich, and Kirillov, who commits suicide in an extreme attempt to lay claim to the lordship Hegel describes in chapter 4 of the *Phenomenology of Spirit*.

inquiry, whose object is that which came into existence in the past, with philosophical inquiry into what is eternally true or what exists necessarily. Beyond this, he attempts to show that the incarnation is not an object of knowledge at all. Insofar as it involves coming into existence and not simply existing, it is an object of *belief*; but insofar as coming into existence is in this particular instance uniquely self-contradictory, it is an object of *faith*. Nor can faith be contradicted by knowledge either of what once was or of what is by necessity. It is rather an act of freedom, open to any human being at any time, that answers to the free act of incarnation itself.

COMING INTO EXISTENCE, THE HISTORICAL, THE PAST

Climacus first considers the concept of "coming into existence." In order to clarify this concept, he begins asking how exactly that which comes into existence is thereby changed. "All other change (*alloiōsis*)," he observes, "presupposes the existence of that in which change is taking place." *Alloiōsis* is the Greek word for "alteration" – the quantitative or qualitative change of an object. Thus, all other change involves alteration in a preexisting thing, which gets bigger, smaller, colder, and so on as it changes. Coming into existence, however, is a change that does not presuppose the existence of the thing in which change takes place. Nor does it involve becoming a different *sort* of thing. "If that which comes into existence does not in itself remain unchanged in the change of coming into existence, then the coming into existence is not *this* coming into existence but another" (73, emphasis in original). If a plan, for example, is intrinsically changed in coming into existence, what comes into existence or is actualized is not this plan but another one.

Climacus's insight may be simply expressed as follows: the change of coming into existence is not "in essence" but "in being" – not a change in *what* a thing *is*, but rather a change from nonbeing to existing.[3] But according to Climacus, the nonbeing that is "abandoned" by that which comes into existence also exists: it is "a being that nevertheless is a nonbeing," which is to say that it is *possibility*. A being that is not also a nonbeing, on the other hand, is an actual being or *actuality*. The change

---

[3] The alteration of an *already* existing thing Climacus calls "redoubling" (76), as it is a kind of coming into existence (= qualitative or quantitative change) that presupposes a prior and more primary coming into existence (namely, that of the underlying thing that undergoes alteration).

of coming into existence is thus "the transition from possibility to actuality" (73–4).

Climacus now tries to establish that the necessary, which by definition cannot be otherwise than it is, cannot come into existence. Coming into existence is a change, "but since the necessary is always related to itself and is related to itself in the same way, it cannot be changed at all." In particular, it "cannot suffer the suffering of actuality – namely, that the possible . . . turns out to be nothing the moment it becomes actual, for the possible is *annihilated* by actuality." The possible that is annihilated is twofold, as it consists not only of the possibility that is actualized, but also all those possibilities that are excluded by the transition to actuality (just as, for example, the possibility that a particular child could be a daughter is excluded when a son is born). "The only thing that cannot come into existence is the necessary," Climacus concludes, "because the necessary *is*" (74, emphases in original).

The preceding reflections lead to a number of conclusions that Climacus states without further elaboration. First, "the actual is no more necessary than the possible, for the necessary is absolutely different from both." Second, "no coming into existence is necessary – not before it came into existence, for then it cannot come into existence, and not after it has come into existence, for then it has not come into existence." The necessary therefore exists always, without having come into existence, precisely "because it is necessary or because the necessary is." Finally, and most important, "all coming into existence occurs in freedom, not by way of necessity." While everything comes into existence by way of a cause, every cause ends in a freely acting cause – a cause that could have acted otherwise. This may not be apparent when one considers the proximate or "intervening" causes of a thing's coming into existence, for these "are misleading in that the coming into existence appears to be necessary." Yet these causes, "having themselves come into existence, *definitively* point back to a freely acting cause" (75, emphasis in original). Although Climacus does not say so, this freely acting first cause of all that has come into existence would seem to be God.

Climacus turns next to the concept of "the historical," which he understands in two senses. What makes a thing historical in the most basic sense is simply that it has come into existence. Hence, everything that has come into existence is by virtue of this very fact historical, "for even if no further historical predicate can be applied to it, the crucial predicate of the historical can still be predicated – namely, that it has come into existence" (75). In this basic sense, even nature is historical.

There is nevertheless something odd about the assertion that nature is historical, because history in a more specific sense seems to be peculiar to human life. Put simply, human beings live *in* history in a way that nonhuman, merely natural entities do not. As Climacus remarks, "the historical is the past" and nature is always "immediately present." If nature is immediately present, then in nature the present is not (to use Hegelian terminology) "mediated" or determined by the past in the same way, or to the same extent, as is the case in human life. While evolutionary biologists and other students of natural history might take issue with the latter claim, it is certainly true that only human beings are self-consciously historical, continually redefining themselves in terms of their actual pasts and possible futures. And this "dialectical" process of redefinition, or of mediating the present in the light of actual pasts and possible futures, is a sign of human freedom. Climacus underscores the role of freedom in human history when he introduces the second sense of the historical: the "more special historical coming into existence" that characterizes human life "comes into existence by way of a relatively freely acting cause, which in turn definitively points to an absolutely freely acting cause" (76).

We are finally prepared to take up the guiding question of the Interlude: is the past more necessary than the future, or has the possible, by having become actual, become more necessary than it was? This question springs in part from the observation that, whereas the future seems to be a realm of wide-open possibility, the past is, so to speak, written in stone. "What has happened," Climacus notes, "has happened and cannot be undone; thus it cannot be changed." But is the unchangeableness of the past the unchangeableness of *necessity*? The same question can be put in terms of possibility and actuality. When in the passage of time the possible becomes actual, it seems to take on the air of necessity. The "actual 'thus and so' [of the past] cannot become different," Climacus concedes, "but from this does it follow that its possible 'how' could not have been different?" Could not the past have come into existence in some other way or according to some other "how," resulting in a different "thus and so" – a different set of historical facts? In a word, could the past have been otherwise, or is history the study of the necessary (76–7)?

In raising this question, Climacus asks us to reflect on the guiding assumption of Hegel's philosophy of history. In the Preface to his *Philosophy of Right*, Hegel famously remarks that "the owl of Minerva spreads its wings only with the falling of the dusk."[4] Minerva (or, in the Greek

---

[4] Hegel 1967, 13.

pantheon, Athena) is, among other things, the goddess of wisdom. That the wise owl flies only at dusk – only, that is, at the end of the day – means that the true significance of events becomes visible only in hindsight. Hegel applies this principle to the understanding of human history as a whole, which he claims has reached its ultimate goal of self-conscious human freedom with the emergence, after the French Revolution and the Napoleonic wars, of the liberal democratic state and its attendant religious, political, and social liberties.[5] Seen in the light (or rather, twilight) of the full realization of freedom, he claims, the course of human history reveals itself to have been both rational and necessary.[6]

Climacus has already shown, however, that the past cannot be regarded as necessary because the necessary cannot be changed in any respect, whereas that which is past has at a minimum undergone the change of coming into existence. This is something the speculative philosophers seem to have overlooked. "The past can be regarded as necessary only if one forgets that it has come into existence," Climacus comments wryly, "but is that kind of forgetfulness also supposed to be necessary?" (77).

This is not all. Every past event has been shaped by other past events, and so is "dialectical with regard to an earlier change, from which it results." What is more, the past must also "be dialectical even with regard to a higher change that nullifies it." Here the main point of Climacus's concern with necessity in the Interlude finally becomes clear. He refers to the past as viewed within the context of a human life, and the "higher change" he has in mind is "the change of repentance, which wants to nullify an actuality" (77). While Climacus does not explain this statement, it would appear that the past is "nullified" by repentance in the sense that the one who repents no longer allows his past to determine his

---

[5] "The *final cause of the World at large*, we allege to be the consciousness of its own freedom on the part of Spirit, and *ipso facto*, the reality of that freedom" (Hegel 1956, 19, emphasis in original). The modern democratic state, Hegel writes, "in and of itself is the ethical whole, the actualization of freedom; and it is an absolute end of reason that freedom should be actual" (Hegel 1967, 279, addition to §258).

[6] "The only Thought which Philosophy brings with it to the contemplation of History, is the simple conception of *Reason*; that Reason is the Sovereign of the World; that the history of the world, therefore, presents us with a rational process" (Hegel 1956, 9, emphasis in original). Because this process has its own inner logic or necessity, the philosophy of history "takes for its problem to understand the necessity of every event" (Hegel 1975, 209). What Hegel means by "necessity" in this context is open to debate. Stewart 2003 defends Hegel against the charge of determinism: Hegel claims merely that "any attempt to think of history will display the necessary categorial structure of the Concept," not that "particular historical events are . . . predetermined" (361).

present and future. If the past were necessary, however, it would not be dialectically related to earlier and subsequent changes and could not itself be changed in any respect. The nullification of the actuality of sin through repentance – to say nothing of the nullification of the actuality of untruth, into which we are plunged by sin – would accordingly be impossible. Speculative philosophy, in other words, seems to entail the impossibility of redemption through faith.[7]

Climacus is quick to point out another oddity entailed by the claim that the past is necessary. Simply by having occurred, he maintains, the past "demonstrated that it was not necessary." But *if* the past were necessary, "it would follow that the future would also be necessary." This is because the necessity of the past would not be something that belongs to it *as* past, inasmuch as the change involved in coming into existence, or in the transition from future possibility to present and past actuality, can have no effect whatsoever on the necessary. Because the past and future would be equally necessary, and because the transitions that we take to distinguish the past from the future would furthermore be irrelevant to this necessity, we could then "no longer speak of the past and the future." "Freedom," Climacus adds, "would then be in dire straits . . . [and] would be an illusion . . . freedom would become witchcraft and coming into existence a false alarm" (77–8).

The foregoing conclusions shed new light on the seriousness of the claim of the modern philosophers that so perplexed the young Johannes Climacus, namely, that everything must be doubted. Far from helping us to understand the deeper meaning of human experience, as Socrates tries to do, the speculative philosophers espouse a theory of history that, if thought through, must lead its adherents not only to doubt the most evident features of our experience, but to reject them as utterly illusory. That this consequence is unintentional is little consolation to those who grasp its implications.[8]

---

[7] If the past were necessary, faith would also in principle be reducible to knowledge, inasmuch as reason "might be able to remove the paradoxicalness of the paradox by coming to understand it as necessary" (Evans 1992, 126). Martensen attempted to provide precisely this sort of argument for faith (Stewart 2003, 367).

[8] In a footnote to the foregoing remarks, Climacus notes that the application of Hegel's "absolute method," to history, which "in the historical sciences . . . is a fixed idea," has "distracted" the learner, "with the result that he . . . forgot to examine . . . the correctness of the method." In particular, the speculative philosophers do not speak to the questions of "what . . . it mean[s] that the idea becomes concrete, what is coming into existence, how is one related to that which has come into existence, etc." (n. on 78).

THE APPREHENSION OF THE PAST

The distinctive mark of past, according to Climacus, is its curious "contradiction between certainty and uncertainty." On the one hand, there is no denying the reality of the past (even though we may dispute about the details): the past "has actuality, for it is certain and trustworthy that it occurred." On the other, "that it occurred is . . . precisely its uncertainty, which will perpetually prevent the apprehension from taking the past as if it had been that way from eternity." The past could not have been what it is "from eternity" because it *occurred* or came into existence, and only the necessary – which, as we have seen, cannot come into existence – is what it is "from eternity." The uncertainty of the past is thus the uncertainty that attaches to anything that could be otherwise than it is. And unless this contradiction between certainty and uncertainty is grasped, the past will be misunderstood (79).

The past is not necessary, Climacus reminds us, and did not become necessary by coming into existence. What is more, the past "becomes even less necessary through any apprehension of it." The specific target of this remark is the speculative philosophy of history, which, as noted previously, claims to discern the necessity of the past from the recently achieved vantage-point of the end or goal of history. According to Climacus, this claim involves a fundamental error of perspective:

Distance in time prompts a mental illusion just as distance in space prompts a sensory illusion. The contemporary does not see the necessity of that which comes into existence, but when centuries lie between the coming into existence and the viewer – then he sees the necessity, just as the person who at a distance sees something square as round. (79)

Because of the distortion introduced by "distance in time," the sense of the contemporary witness that events could have been otherwise is more reliable than the retrospective sense of the historian that they could not.

It is important to observe, however, that the conviction that the past is necessary is influenced by other factors besides its remoteness in time. Historians seek to know not only what actually occurred, but also why things happened the way they did. In addressing the latter question, historians often employ the language of causation that is more suited to the natural sciences. The very nature of historical explanation – which frequently involves the construction of long and complex chains of ramifying effects (e.g., bad economic polices caused poor agricultural yields, which caused food shortages, which caused riots, etc.) – therefore tempts historians as such, and not merely speculative philosophers, to regard the past as necessary. This temptation, Climacus suggests, is strengthened as one's remoteness from events increases. But because the past is shot through with uncertainty – an uncertainty that arises in large measure from human freedom – the relationship between historical events, unlike the unvarying and intrinsically predictable relationships that the physicist observes in nature, is *not* genuinely causal. Food shortages do not cause riots in the same sense that an explosive blast causes shock waves: a riot is, after all, an event that could have been otherwise inasmuch as it springs from a multitude of free choices.

Somewhat earlier in the Interlude, Climacus compared the desire to predict the future with the desire to understand the necessity of the past. With the popularity of speculative philosophy in mind, he noted that "only the prevailing fashion makes the one seem more plausible than the other to a particular generation" (77). He now returns to this comparison. "One who apprehends the past, a *historico-philosophus*," he observes, "is . . . a prophet in reverse (Daub)" (80).[9] What is he getting at here?

The historian's work is in one respect admittedly more complex than that of the prophet: the former tries to state what happened in the past *and* to explain why it happened, whereas the latter tries simply to predict what will happen in the future. Yet the analogy is nevertheless well-considered. Out of a great range of possibilities, the prophet must identify those few that will be actualized. This is the mirror image of the historian's first task, namely, that of establishing what happened. On its face, this task appears to be easier than the corresponding task of the prophet, because it seems to consist simply in distinguishing actual events from those that did not in fact occur. But because the "crucial predicate" of the historical is that it has come into existence (75), making even the most basic determination of what happened may involve inquiring into the "how" of the transition from possibility to actuality. As Climacus will make clear in the sequel, moreover, this transition is essentially uncertain and therefore essentially unknowable, from which it follows that the historical sense for the "how" is more like prophecy than science. The most vivid example of this point is one that Climacus does not mention, but that is surely foremost in his mind. A certain man was born in Bethlehem: let us suppose it is ascertained that this event actually occurred. Well and good, but the significance of this event has everything to do with how the

9 Carl Daub's famous remark that the historian is "a prophet of the past" is quoted by the Hongs at *Philosophical Fragments/Johannes Climacus*, 309, n. 33.

man came into being. Did it happen according to nature, or according to divine agency? What exactly transpired here? In this case, it is evident that one cannot fully grasp *what* happened without first determining *how* it happened.

If a prophet possessed the deepest possible insight into the future, he would be able not only to foresee what will happen, but also to understand why these things will happen. This would be the mirror image of the historian's second task, that of explaining why certain things happened and not others. Because this part of historical inquiry involves a kind of double vision, explaining the past is also akin to prophesying. Good history involves putting oneself in the position of those who were present in the past and seeing events unfold through their eyes, for without this sympathetic ability the historian cannot make reasonable judgments about the individuals who took part in past events. At the same time (and this is also crucial to making reasonable judgments), it involves looking *forward* from the present as it was experienced by those individuals, and doing so in such a way as to determine what could and could not have been seen from their vantage-points. In seeing what could not be seen clearly in the past, the historian must attempt to discern the inner connection of events that would naturally, if not inevitably, result in the actualization of certain possibilities (namely, the ones that we now know to have been actualized). And to grasp this inner connection – which has once again to do with the "how" of coming into being – is to see the past through prophetic eyes.

That the historian is a prophet, Climacus writes, "simply indicates that the basis of the certainty of the past is the uncertainty regarding it in the same sense as there is uncertainty regarding the future." This uncertainty resides in "the possibility . . . out of which it [the future] could not possibly *come forth* with necessity" (emphasis in original). In the face of this uncertainty, the historian is "stirred by the passion that is the passionate sense for coming into existence, that is, wonder." This remark reminds us of Climacus's earlier assertion that the paradox is the passion of thought, for wonder is precisely the passion evoked by paradox. This is especially evident in the Platonic dialogues. When the young Theaetetus admits that he sometimes gets "truly dizzy" in thinking about certain philosophical paradoxes, Socrates tells him that "this experience – wondering – is quite characteristic of a philosopher, for there is no other beginning of philosophy than this" (*Theaetetus* 155d). According to Climacus, the philosopher who "wonders over nothing whatsoever" – as must be the case when one is dealing with "a necessary construction," for such constructions, reflecting the inevitability of logic, involve no contradiction and so no paradox – "*eo ipso* has nothing to do with the historical." Such a person, we may add, also has nothing to do with philosophy, inasmuch as Climacus, like Socrates, regards wonder as a passion that is "worthy of and necessary to the philosopher" (80).

BELIEF AND DOUBT

"So much," Climacus writes, "for the apprehension of the past. But if there is indeed knowledge of the past, as is "presumed," how is this knowledge acquired? Put another way, what is "the organ for the historical" – the cognitive power (or perhaps passion) whose proper object is the historical? Climacus begins to address this question by noting that "the immediate impression of a natural phenomenon or an event is not the impression of the historical, for the *coming into existence* cannot be sensed immediately" (emphasis in original). The historical has in itself the "illusiveness" of coming into existence, "an illusiveness whereby that which is most firm is made dubious." The historical, therefore, "cannot become the object of sense perception or of immediate cognition," for these faculties cannot deceive. They merely present the mind with raw immediacy, while it is judgment that introduces the possibility of deception when it tries to declare *what* is being sensed (81).

If there is knowledge (or something like it) of the past, Climacus observes, the organ for the historical must "be formed in likeness" to its illusive or deceptive object. In particular, this organ must "have within itself...something by which in its certitude it continually annuls the incertitude that corresponds to the uncertainty of coming into existence." This "something" is nothing other than *belief*, for belief willingly takes as certain that which it knows to be intrinsically uncertain.

This is precisely the nature of belief [*Tro*], for continually present as the nullified in the certitude of belief is the incertitude that in every way corresponds to the uncertainty of coming into existence. Thus, belief believes what it does not see; it does not believe that the star exists, for that it sees, but it believes that the star has come into existence. (81)[10]

The same, Climacus adds, is true of an event, involving as it does "the transition from nothing, from non-being, and from the multiple possible

[10] Climacus uses the Danish word *Tro* to signify both "belief" and "faith." In the Appendix to the Interlude, he distinguishes ordinary belief or faith from faith or belief in a "wholly eminent," religious sense (see the next section).

'how.' " The occurrence of an event can be known immediately, "but not that it has occurred, not even that it is in the process of occurring, even though it is taking place, as they say, right in front of one's nose" (81–2).

It follows from the aforementioned considerations that belief is the termination of doubt or uncertainty not by knowledge but by an act of will. In this respect belief answers to skepticism, which, properly understood, *sustains* doubt by an act of will. The Greek skeptic understood that sensation and immediate cognition could not be mistaken. "[B]ut, said he, error has an utterly different basis – it comes from the conclusion I draw. If I can only avoid drawing conclusions, I shall never be deceived." The skeptic thus willed to keep himself "continually *in suspenso*," thereby avoiding the risk of forming mistaken judgments. By the same token, belief is "not a knowledge but an act of freedom, an expression of will." In consciously choosing to "annul" uncertainty, belief willingly accepts the risk that the skeptic chooses to avoid (82–3).[11]

What are its concrete implications of Climacus's characterization of belief, particularly with respect to faith? We may begin to answer this question by noting that Climacus seems to be especially interested in the uncertainty surrounding the manner in which a thing has come into existence:

It [belief] believes the "thus and so" of that which has come into existence and has annulled in itself the possible "how" of that which has come into existence, and without denying the possibility of another "thus and so," the "thus and so" of that which has come into existence is nevertheless most certain for belief. (83)

What this means can be illustrated by the example of the star. The star exists, but how did it come into existence? Was it formed by physical processes that originated in the Big Bang? This is one possible "thus and so." Or was the star formed by God, in the manner reported in scripture (Genesis 1:14–6)? This is another possible "thus and so." The acceptance or rejection of either of these alternatives, as Climacus has now rather carefully established, is a matter not of knowledge but of belief. So, too, is the acceptance or rejection of a certain account of how a particular man who is known to have existed came into existence. Did his conception

---

[11] Climacus adds that the risk of error is essential to belief: "One never believes in any other way; if one wants to avoid risk, then one wants to know with certainty that one can swim before going in the water" (n. on 83).

occur according to the ordinary course of nature? Or was he conceived by God, as is reported in scripture (Matthew 1:18, Luke 1:35)? Either "thus and so" is possible, but because both are intrinsically uncertain, both involve belief.

As the foregoing examples illustrate, what one accepts as historical will depend on what one believes about the "how" of that which has come into existence. Although historians might like to think that they have access to purely objective truths, the historical does not exist independently of the belief of the believer. History, in other words, resembles prophecy more than science. Climacus makes this point absolutely clear when he goes on to speak of "that which by belief *becomes* the historical" (emphasis added). Belief determines the historical when it draws from immediate existence (which is "apprehended immediately" by the contemporary) one of many possible conclusions about the "how" of coming into existence. The particular conclusion that belief draws is furthermore a "resolution" rather than a conclusion, as it does not rest upon a logical inference. In this connection, Climacus reminds us that there is no certain inference from effect to cause, for "the cognitive inference is [only] from cause to effect or rather from ground to consequent." For that matter, "I cannot immediately sense or know that what I immediately sense or know *is* an effect, for immediately it simply is" (emphasis added). Hence, when belief terminates the doubt associated with coming into existence and thereby determines the historical, it does so "not by knowledge but by will." Belief is the opposite of doubt, and neither is a cognitive act, for both are passions (83–4).

In concluding his discussion of belief, Climacus returns to the question of the relationship of one who comes later to the contemporary eyewitness. The contemporary eyewitness to events enjoys the immediacy of sensation and cognition, whereas the one who comes later has only the contemporary's report, "to which he relates in the same manner as the contemporaries to the immediacy." But as Climacus has just established, immediate sensation and cognition cannot apprehend the historical, nor can they serve as the basis for a valid inference about the historical. Hence the fact that the one who comes later is not an eyewitness to events is in truth no disadvantage for him with respect to belief:

The one who comes later does indeed believe by virtue of the contemporary's declaration, but only in the same sense as the contemporary believes by virtue of immediate sensation and cognition, but the contemporary cannot believe by virtue of that, and thus the one who comes later cannot believe by virtue of the report. (85)

APPENDIX: BELIEF AND FAITH

In Chapter Four, Climacus showed that faith cannot be an act of will: faith is the condition for understanding the truth, and one who is untruth cannot come to possess this condition simply by willing (62–3). Even though Climacus uses the same word (*Tro*) for both ordinary belief or faith and religious belief or faith, these must therefore be two different things. One of the main tasks of the brief Appendix to the Interlude is accordingly to address this difference.

Climacus begins by "return[ing] to our poem and to the assumption that the god has been." This historical fact is unique in that it is "based upon a self-contradiction," namely, the coming into existence of the eternal. It is thus a historical fact that is "only for faith." In this context, the two meanings of *Tro* become clear. In its "direct and ordinary meaning as the relationship to the historical," it signifies what we may call belief – the willed termination of doubt about coming into existence. But it has another, "wholly eminent" sense, that of religious faith. Ordinary belief is necessary but not sufficient for religious faith, because the object of the latter is not a "direct historical fact," but the "self-contradiction" of the absolute paradox – the unity of the eternal and the temporal, of infinity and finitude, of absolute difference and absolute equality, in the person of the incarnate god (86–7). That the stars came into being through divine agency is a possible object of ordinary belief, for it involves no essential self-contradiction and is intelligible to the understanding. That God came into being in the person of Christ, however, can only be an object of faith in the eminent sense.

Climacus adverts to Socrates in order to clarify the concept of religious faith. "One does not have *faith* that the god exists, eternally understood," he writes, "even though one assumes that the god exists" (emphasis in original). Thus, "Socrates did not have faith that the god existed," for he assumed that the god is (in the sense of eternal being), not that the god came into existence. For the same reason, his assumption about the god was not belief in the ordinary sense. "What he knew about the god he attained by recollection," Climacus adds, "and for him the existence of the god was by no means something historical" (87). The latter remark does not quite harmonize, however, with the earlier discussion of Socrates in *Fragments*. As Climacus himself observes, the god is the necessary *presupposition* of the philosophical "voyage of discovery" that Socrates represents as recollection (44). What is more, the very little that Socrates "knows" about the god independently of this presupposition comes to him not by way of recollection, but through the god's active engagement – initially and primarily by means of the oracle – in his life.

In the last analysis, the Interlude leaves open basic questions about the nature of faith, including questions about divine grace and its relationship to the will. Nor are these questions settled elsewhere in *Fragments.* Commentators have long disputed whether Climacus means to suggest that faith is a gift of God, an act of human freedom, or somehow both.[12] The existence of such a debate, which reproduces the same sorts of questions about human and divine agency that are provoked by the phenomenon of Socratic eros, is not surprising. Given that faith is "just as paradoxical as the paradox" (65), one would expect that the matters at issue cannot be fully resolved from a theoretical point of view. Attempts to achieve such a resolution have nonetheless been philosophically worthwhile.[13] But perhaps, as Lee Barrett suggests, the need for "a theoretic integration of divine and human agency" dissolves once one understands that the concepts of grace, freedom, and responsibility are meant to help the individual *exist* in faith, in which case what is needed is "clarity about the appropriate contexts for the use of each of these Christian themes."[14]

As we saw at the beginning of this chapter, the purpose of the Interlude is to shorten the time that Climacus imagines separates the follower at second hand from the contemporary follower. Climacus's introduction to the Interlude prepares us for a light comic entertainment, but he instead provides us with some rather difficult and serious philosophizing. His deconstruction of the concept of historical necessity nevertheless succeeds in achieving its main goal: it "shortens" to the point of insignificance the elapsed time that distinguishes the two types of followers, because neither follower is contemporary with the god's incarnation. What is more, the noncontemporaneity of the two types of follower is itself twofold. In the first place, the "historical fact" of incarnation "has no immediate contemporary" because coming into being, which cannot be known immediately, has no immediate contemporary. It is, as Climacus puts the point, "historical to the first power (faith in the ordinary sense)." But it also "has no immediate contemporary to the second power, since it is based on a contradiction (faith in the eminent sense)." The temporal

---

[12] Barrett 1994, 262–3.
[13] See for example the stimulating reflections in Ferreira 1998.
[14] Barrett 1994, 268.

differences between the two types of follower are thus "absorbed" in the "equality" of immediate noncontemporaneity (87–8).

As will soon become fully apparent, Climacus's outwardly humorous but inwardly serious shortening of time is an attack, not only on historical necessity, but also on the general significance that the speculative philosophers attach to history as such. Hegel taught that our access to truth is mediated by history, so that what could never have occurred to human beings in one historical epoch may be well understood in another. This presupposition is contrary to Socrates' philosophical assumption that the truth, being eternal, is equally accessible to all human beings at all times. It is also contrary to the assumption of faith, which attaches the greatest possible significance to one particular historical event, but insists that the truth of that event – a truth that is neither eternal nor historical, but both simultaneously – is equally accessible in every subsequent historical epoch. In taking up the question of the follower at second hand, Climacus will accordingly make a claim that is clearly intended to surprise and provoke: *there is no follower at second hand.* To state what this means, and what its implications are for our understanding of faith, will be one of the main tasks of the next chapter.

9

The Follower at Second Hand and The Moral

Prior to Chapter Five, Climacus has established that neither historically contemporary followers nor followers at second hand are automatically true contemporaries of the god. This does not mean, however, that there are no significant historical differences between these two groups – for there are such differences, and they stem to a great extent from the astonishing success of the god's early followers. In particular, the circumstances in which the first followers encountered the god and wrestled with the question of faith are radically different from those in which followers at second hand do so. The former inhabited a world that was hostile to their faith, whereas the situation is quite otherwise for most of the latter. Indeed, Climacus's first readers (not to speak of his latest readers, who live in a world that bears little resemblance to the Denmark of 1844) were citizens of a Christian nation, and were almost all Christians themselves. They would thus have been inclined to regard themselves as followers of the god before ever having read *Fragments*, and as having been such more or less from birth – even though they might have previously given little or no thought to what it means to *be* a follower.

Do these historical differences between contemporary followers and followers at second hand have any bearing on the decision of faith? And are there historical differences *among* the followers at second hand that may also bear on this decision? These are the primary questions that Climacus addresses in the final chapter of *Fragments*.

Chapter Five reflects the dialectical form of *Fragments* as a whole, in that it reveals the underlying unity of that which initially presented itself as a fragmented totality, namely, the category of the follower. For in the last analysis, Climacus argues, there is no follower at second hand; with respect to the question of becoming a believer, all individuals stand in the same relationship to the god. In the course of developing this argument, he has occasion to clarify the nature of the awareness that must precede the decision of faith, and to speak of something new – the "terror" involved in what he had previously described as the "happy passion" of faith (59). Like the quest for wisdom that Socrates refused to abandon as long as he could still draw breath, faith turns out to be a lifelong struggle. What is more, Climacus makes it clear that the basic structure of this struggle is also Socratic: the individual is left to his own resources in that he cannot rely on the authority of any other human being in coming to understand the truth. The last chapter of *Fragments* thus reaffirms the continuity of genuine philosophy with that which goes beyond it. In so doing, it prepares us for the suggestion of The Moral that Socrates himself somehow holds the key to this continuity.

BECOMING AWARE

Climacus begins Chapter Five, "The Follower at Second Hand," by asking his "dear reader" two questions. First, how does the follower at second hand differ from the contemporary follower? Second, is this a "proper" question, or does one run the risk of "talking like a fool" in raising it? The reader – who was also addressed at the outset of the Interlude, but who did not then respond – now pipes up: not only should the question of the differences between the two kinds of followers not be dismissed as improper, he insists, but there is a further question about whether it makes sense to lump all of the followers at second hand into one group. Should one really "separate such an enormous time span into such unequal parts: the contemporary period – the later period"? On hearing this further question, Climacus rather testily breaks off his imagined conversation with the reader, insisting that distinctions between "a follower at fifth, at seventh hand, etc." should "be subsumed under one rubric in contrast to the category: the contemporary follower." Yet he nonetheless promises to take into consideration the reader's comments (89–90).

Climacus's promise is immediately reflected in the first of the two sections of Chapter Five, "1. Differences Among the Followers at Second Hand." He introduces his discussion of these differences by noting that he will avoid the tendency of speculative philosophy to obscure genuine distinctions by talk of "a certain degree etc. etc.," a tendency that he finds deplorable: "what antiquity regarded negatively – 'to a certain degree' (the mocking toleration that mediates everything without making petty distinctions) – has become the positive, and what antiquity called the positive, the passion for distinctions, has become foolishness." As in his discussion of the contemporary follower in Chapter Four, Climacus will try to cut through "loose chatter" – including the chatter of philosophical mediation – by making such distinctions as will allow the decision of faith to stand forth in all its clarity. Because "opposites show up most strongly when placed together," he proposes to compare the first generation of secondary followers with the latest, all the while keeping in mind the historical differences that distinguish both of these groups from the contemporary follower (91).

The first generation of secondary followers "has (relatively) the advantage of being closer to the immediate certainty, of being closer to acquiring exact and reliable information about what happened." But this is a dubious advantage, inasmuch as "the person who is not so close to the immediate certainty that he *is* immediately certain is absolutely distanced" (emphasis added). Nor is even the contemporary himself immediately certain, for the god, as we have seen, cannot be known immediately. Thus, if a man with the power and passion of a tyrant were to interrogate "all the contemporary witnesses who were still alive and those who were closest to them," and thereby managed to obtain "a complicated report in agreement down to the letter and to the minute," he would have attained greater certainty than even the contemporary eyewitness to events – but he would not thereby be a follower. What the tyrant hopes to see directly, Climacus reminds us, is visible only to faith: "divinity is not an immediate qualification, and the teacher must first of all develop the deepest self-reflection in the learner, must develop the consciousness of sin as a condition for understanding." In sum, all talk about the divinity of the god and the wondrousness of his acts "is nonsense here and everywhere, is an attempt to put off deliberation with chatter" (91–3).

The first generation of secondary followers does, however, enjoy one advantage over those who come later: it is closer than later generations to the "jolt" (*Rystelse*) of the realization that all attempts to see and hear the god as his contemporaries did merely postpone necessary deliberation. "This jolt and its vibrations," Climacus observes, "serve to arouse awareness." By "awareness," Climacus means a clear understanding of what is involved in faith, and in particular the recognition of faith's absolutely paradoxical nature. Awareness, however, "is by no means partial to faith, as if faith proceeded as a simple consequence of awareness." Indeed, awareness may lead to offense at the paradox just as well as to faith. But its advantage is "that one enters into a state in which the decision manifests itself ever more clearly." Although this is "the only advantage [of the first generation of secondary followers] that means anything," the state of awareness is by no means a comfortable one. On the contrary, the prospect of embracing the absolute paradox of the god's appearance in human form is "terrifying" (93–4).

Climacus clearly believes faith is ill served by anything that obscures its true nature. To think and speak about faith in such a way that the possibility of offense is minimized (as do those who offer proofs of its probability, about which more below) is thus to act in a way that increases the difficulty of faith. Yet Climacus suggests that, for later generations of followers, faith has indeed been made more difficult in just this way – that is, precisely by seeming to have been made easier. He introduces this suggestion by way of a counterfactual statement. If the fact that faith is terrifying "never falls stupidly and senselessly into the human rut," he writes, "every succeeding generation will evince the same relation of offense as did the first, because no one comes closer to that fact immediately." As we know, however, succeeding generations (of Europeans, at any rate) have *not* generally evinced offense at the proclaimed divinity of Jesus, and have tended to regard themselves as Christ's faithful followers. Hence, we may infer that the terror involved in faith has, perhaps inevitably, fallen into the "human rut" in such a way that most people have overlooked it. Indeed, one who is "well read" is especially at risk, for such a person particularly likely to have become "a well-trained babbler in whose mind there is neither a suggestion of offense nor a place for faith" (94).

It is at this point that Climacus turns to the latest generation of followers, that of his own readership. This latest generation in the first place "has the consequences to hold on to, has the probability proof of the outcome." By "the consequences," Climacus means the historical transformation of the world brought about by the followers, or would-be followers, of the god. The most obvious consequence of this admittedly remarkable transformation is that it is normal, and indeed expected, that one will profess faith. In a Christian world, there seems to be nothing paradoxical about the Christian faith. But this gives one precisely *nothing* to "hold on to" with respect to faith – unless, that is, "it is assumed that the consequences . . . gained retroactive power to transform the paradox." The assumption that these consequences could make more probable the

absolute paradox, which is utterly improbable, would be "just as acceptable as the assumption that a son received retroactive power to transform
his father." Historical success, after all, is no measure of truth, nor is faith
"partial to probability"; indeed, "to say that about faith would be slander"
(94–5).[1]

"The advantage of the consequences," Climacus notes, "seems to be
that that fact [i.e., the historical fact of the incarnation] is supposed
to have been *naturalized* little by little" (95, emphasis in original). It is
supposed that we acquire faith as easily as children learn the language of
their parents. But this is contrary to the nature of faith:

> That fact [the incarnation], however, has no respect for domestication, is too
> proud to desire a follower who joins on the strength of the successful outcome of
> the matter, refuses to be naturalized under the protection of a king or professor –
> it is and remains the paradox and does not permit attainment by speculation.
> That fact is only for faith. (96)

This is not all. It is true that faith may become "second nature" to an individual, but the individual for whom it is second nature "must certainly
have had a *first* nature" (emphasis in original). If the fact of the incarnation is naturalized, then "it may be said that the individual is born with
faith – that is, with his second nature." But "to be born with one's second
nature, a second nature that refers to a given historical fact in time, is
truly the *non plus ultra* in lunacy" (96).

Climacus illustrates his objection with reference to the Socratic
assumption that the individual "has existed before he came into existence and recollects himself." On the Socratic assumption, consciousness
is eternal, and one's nature "is defined in continuity with itself." If the
individual is born with a second nature, however, there is no such continuity, or, put another way, there is no first nature – unless one assumes
that one is born with both a first and a second nature simultaneously.
But if one assumes this, a strange consequence follows for those who are
born at a time when faith has, as a result of a historical transformation,
become second nature for human beings: "birth is no longer *birth* but
is also *rebirth*, such that he who has never been is reborn – when he is

---

[1] In a note to 94–5, Climacus observes that "the idea...of seriously wanting to link
a probability proof to the improbable...is so stupid that one could deem its occurrence impossible....What Epicurus says of the individual's relation to death (even
though his observation is scant comfort) holds for the relation between probability and
improbability: When I am, it (death) is not, and when it (death) is, I am not."

born" (emphasis in original). In that case, we must also suppose that "the [human] race, after the supervention of that fact [the incarnation], became an altogether different race and nevertheless is defined in continuity with the former" (96–7).

Finally, Climacus points out that the transformation of the world brought about by the followers of the god is in fact a disadvantage for faith precisely insofar as it encourages the erroneous assumption that faith is easily acquired, inasmuch as it can be "passed on like real estate." Such an assumption obscures the fact that the hard work involved in acquiring faith must be performed anew in every generation and by each and every individual. Climacus offers an analogy to illustrate the danger that the latest generation of followers faces with respect to faith. Although Venice is built on the sea, one could imagine a generation that "finally . . . did not notice this at all," and that persisted in its ignorance "until the pilings began to rot and the city sank." Those who attempt to build faith upon the historical success of previous generations of followers resemble these forgetful Venetians, for "consequences built upon a paradox are built upon the abyss" (97–8).

Climacus concludes his comparison of the first generation of secondary followers with the latest generation by observing that the former has the advantage of difficulty and the latter of ease. "When it is the difficult that I am to appropriate," he writes, "it is always an advantage, a relief, to have it made difficult for me." As for the latest generation, the supposed advantage of ease that results from the naturalization of faith in fact makes the acquisition of faith more difficult, so that "this ease is the very dubiousness that begets the difficulty." Once this is recognized, "this difficulty will correspond to the difficulty of the terror, and the terror will grip the last generation just as primitively as it gripped the first generation of secondary followers" (98–9).

Climacus's reflections in the first half of Chapter Five help us to see that, in undertaking the task of clarifying the nature of faith in *Fragments*, he serves faith in precisely the same way that Socrates serves philosophy. Both Climacus and Socrates are essentially in the business of revealing the difficulty of that which previously seemed so easy that most people hardly gave it a second thought. In so doing, both seek to bring the individual into a state of awareness – a state that involves terror (inasmuch as the recognition of one's own ignorance can also be terrifying) and that may just as well result in offense (at the absolute paradox, or at philosophy, or at Socrates himself) as in the decision to embrace either philosophy or faith.

These points of resemblance between Climacus and Socrates are not unexpected, inasmuch as Climacus had stated earlier that "once the condition is given, that which was valid for the Socratic is again valid" (63). But it is only in the second half of Chapter Five that the full implications of this statement become visible.

THE STRUGGLE WITH FAITH: ECHOES OF SOCRATES

Having established that there are no relevant differences between the various followers at second hand with respect to the problem of becoming a believer, Climacus is now prepared to examine the relationship between the follower at second hand and the contemporary follower. He begins the second section of Chapter Five, "2. The Question of the Follower at Second Hand," by reminding us that the god's appearance in human form is neither a simple historical fact (in which case the contemporary would have a distinct advantage over those who come later) nor an eternal fact (in which case "every age is equally close to it"). It is rather simultaneously eternal and historical, and as such is an "absolute" fact. It is furthermore, Climacus maintains, "a contradiction for time to be able to apportion the relations of people" to the absolute. To hold otherwise would be to "imply that the absolute itself is a *casus* in life." The Latin *casus* means "accident" in the general sense of what befalls one, but it is also the word for a "case" in grammar. Climacus seems to have both meanings in mind. In Latin, nouns, pronouns, and adjectives are declined or inflected in a series of cases. The notion of "declension" derives from the comparison of the primary case (the nominative) to a perpendicular line, with the "oblique" cases (genitive, dative, etc.) falling further and further away from it. The absolute, although "declinable in all the *casibus* of life," is not itself a case or accident; it is not an event that befalls one because it stands outside the sphere of time. It is thus "continually the same" and in the same relationship to all else – like a line that is always perpendicular to the plane of individual existence – and is no more affected by the vicissitudes of history than by the modulations of language. This is true even though the absolute fact "is indeed also historical" (99–100).

What, then, is the difference between the historical contemporaries of the god and those who come later? Climacus's answer is this: for the former, the historical event is itself the occasion for becoming a follower, whereas for the latter, this occasion is provided by the report of the contemporaries. The hypothesis of faith presupposes, however, that in both cases the potential follower receives the condition for understanding the truth (= faith) from the god himself. But given that "one who has what one has from the god himself obviously has it at first hand," what sense does it make to speak of a follower at second hand (100)?

That the god himself must directly give the learner the condition for understanding the truth becomes clear also from what follows if one assumes otherwise. Suppose that the contemporary generation of followers received the condition from the god, and that later generations "are to receive the condition from these contemporaries." In that case, "the contemporary becomes the object of faith for the one who comes later, because the one from whom the single individual receives the condition is *eo ipso* (see the foregoing) himself the object of faith and is the god" (100–1).

The preceding observation brings us back to Climacus's assertion that "the highest relation a human being can have to another" is to serve as an occasion for the other to learn the truth (10). This is of course a Socratic insight, and Climacus is quick to point out that his project "went beyond Socrates only in that it placed the god in relation to the single individual." The "Socratic relation" between individuals "will return," he observes, if we assume that the one who comes later also receives the condition from the god – "but, please note, within the total difference consisting of that fact [of the incarnation] and the relation of the single individual . . . to the god." The assumption that the contemporary provides later generations with the condition for understanding the truth, however, entails the absurdity that a human being is a god in relation to another human being. "Who indeed would dare come to Socrates with such nonsense," Climacus wonders – thereby explicitly indicating for the first time that he has written *Fragments* precisely with the intention of producing something that *would* be worthy of presenting to Socrates (101).

Climacus insists that it "takes boldness" to appreciate the "heroism" with which Socrates understood how one human being is related to another. It is not hard to grasp what he means. In the Socratic view, the individual is left to himself; others are at best mere occasions for him to undertake the hard work of learning on his own. Just so, faith is also not for the faint of heart: the terror it provokes arises in large measure from the fact that here, too, we stand alone (although in this case we stand before the god and not the beings) and cannot rely on the help of others. "[T]he point," Climacus writes, "is to acquire the same understanding [as Socrates had] within the formation as assumed – namely, that one human being, insofar as he is a believer, is not indebted to someone else for some-thing but is indebted to the god for everything." This is not an easy task, "especially when it comes to preserving this understanding continually," for "anyone who begins to exercise himself in this understanding no doubt will frequently enough catch himself in a misunderstanding." In the Socratic case, one must see firsthand and with one's own eyes – the eyes of the mind. Faith reflects the same structure: there "cannot be any question of a follower at second hand, for the believer . . . does not see with the eyes of others and sees only the same as every believer sees – with the eyes of faith" (101–2).

Given the foregoing reflections, it is natural to ask what a histori-cally immediate contemporary can do for someone who comes later. Climacus maintains that there are only two ways he can help. First, "he can tell someone who comes later that he himself has believed that fact [of the incarnation]." According to Climacus, this is "not a communication . . . but merely an occasion." The occasion – which, like the Socratic occasion, is essentially a provocation – receives its proper form when the contemporary says "I believe and have believed that this happened, *although it is folly to the understanding and an offense to the human heart*" (emphasis in original). If I speak this way, no communication is possible because there is no question of another sharing an understand-ing with me on the basis of what I have said: I have "done everything to prevent anyone else from making up his mind in immediate continuity with me and to decline all partnership" (102). To speak in this way is to use paradox in the same way that Socrates was accustomed to use it, namely, in order to awaken the learner to his ignorance and to cut him free of his reliance on others.

Second, the contemporary can "in this form [i.e., by speaking of his belief and of its folly . . . tell the content of the fact [of the incarnation]." "[I]n any other form," however, "he is only talking nonsense and perhaps inveigles the one who comes later to make up his mind in continuity with idle chatter" (102).

Does it matter whether the contemporary actually had the faith that he testified he had? According to Climacus, the answer is no: even if one who comes later could determine the truth of the contemporary's testimony – which is impossible – this would be "of no benefit to him . . . in coming to faith himself." For if someone "believes (that is, fancies that he believes) because many good, honest people here on the hill have believed . . . then he is a fool." The object of faith, after all, "cannot be communicated by one person to another" – at least, "not in such a way that the other believes it." And if it is communicated "in the form of faith" (i.e., with emphasis on its being folly to the understanding and an offense to the human heart), the one who communicates "does his very best to prevent the other from adopting it directly" (103).

According to Climacus, the contemporary generation would have done "more than enough" in providing for those who come later had it left behind only these words: "We have believed that in such and such a year the god appeared in the humble form of a servant, lived and taught among us, and then died." This statement is sufficient because it captures the "heart of the matter," which is "the historical fact that the god has been in human form"; the other historical details "are not even as important as they would be if the subject were a human being instead of the god." "Lawyers say that a capital crime absorbs all the lesser crimes," Climacus notes; "so also with faith: its absurdity completely absorbs minor matters" (103–4).

Because the immediate contemporaneity of the first generation is no more or less than the occasion for one to become a believer, "the first and the latest generation are essentially alike." "There is no follower at second hand," Climacus concludes (104–5). This does not mean, however, that immediate contemporaneity might not be an advantage for one who has *already* come to believe. Yet it does seem to confirm Climacus's intuitions about the god. As "the reconciler," he asks, would the god "bring about a reconciliation with some human beings such that their reconciliation with him would make their difference from all others blatantly flagrant?" Would the god "allow the power of time to decide whom he would grant his favor," or rather, would it be "worthy" of him "to make the reconciliation equally difficult for every human being at every time and place?" (106).[2] With regard to this difficulty, Climacus reiterates that faith is a lifelong struggle. "[T]he task [of faith] is identical," he writes, "and faith is always in conflict, but as long as there is conflict, there is the possibility of defeat" (108).

At the very end of Chapter Five, Climacus for the first time speaks of Christianity by name. He envisions the possibility of writing a "next section" of his pamphlet, in which he will "call the matter by its proper

---

[2] These questions are perhaps more than rhetorical, because the god *does* seem to discriminate between those who lived before the incarnation and those who come after. For some discussion of this problem see Rudd 2000/2002, 2.267–70.

name and clothe the issue in its historical costume." This means that he will explicitly discuss Christianity, "the only historical phenomenon that...has wanted to be the single individual's point of departure for his eternal consciousness... [and] has wanted to base his happiness on his relation to something historical." This is an idea, Climacus maintains, that "no philosophy...no mythology...no historical knowledge...has ever had," and one "that did not arise in any human heart." In the present pamphlet, however, he has "to a certain extent...wanted to forget this," and has instead chosen to employ "the unrestricted judgment of a hypothesis...one that I did not wish to abandon before I had thought it through" (109). *Fragments* is accordingly a work of philosophical reflection – but only "to a certain extent," for Climacus has by no means *completely* forgotten about Christianity. Indeed, he draws attention throughout *Fragments* to the fact that he is not the true author of his thought-project, and in particular to his debt to scripture (21, 35–6, 53, 68). He thereby acknowledges that the roots of this thought-project lie in Jerusalem, so to speak, as well as Athens. And if *Fragments* succeeds in helping us to gain a deeper understanding of what Jerusalem might have to do with Athens, this accomplishment springs from nothing other than Climacus's ability to fit together a receptivity to the claims of revelation with a deeply philosophical disposition.

THE MORAL

On the very last page of *Fragments* stands The Moral (*Moralen*), which is worth quoting in full.

This project indisputably goes beyond the Socratic, as is apparent at every point. Whether it is therefore more true than the Socratic is an altogether different question, one that cannot be decided in the same breath, inasmuch as a new organ has been assumed here: faith; and a new presupposition: the consciousness of sin; and a new decision: the moment; and a new teacher: the god in time. Without these, I really would not have dared to present myself for inspection before that ironist who has been admired for millennia, whom I approach with as much ardent enthusiasm as anyone. But to go beyond Socrates when one nevertheless says essentially the same as he, only not nearly so well – that, at least, is not Socratic. (111)

That Climacus's inquiry has a moral – as though it were something like a fable of Aesop – is in itself a strange thing. Perhaps Climacus intends to underscore that *Fragments* is meant to be relevant to how we should live as well as what we should think. But *Fragments* is more like a Platonic dialogue than an Aesopean fable. It is too complex and open ended to contain any easily formulable life-lessons. It may be significant, however, that Climacus adverts in The Moral to Socrates' famous irony – a "cloak," as he suggested in Chapter Three, that is both "concealing and revealing" (32). Could The Moral itself be ironic, in that it contains more than meets the eye? What depths of meaning might lie beneath its seemingly simple surface?

The last sentence of The Moral says something puzzling. To go beyond Socrates when one says just what he said, only not as well, is not Socratic.[3] But what exactly is not Socratic about it? The answer seems to be that one who acts in this way does not in fact go beyond Socrates at all, for one thing that we already know not be Socratic is the failure to do what one says one is going to do. Those who behave in this way fall short of exemplifying the harmony of speech and deed that is one of the hallmarks of Socrates.[4] Climacus's project, on the other hand, "indisputably goes beyond the Socratic" – even if what emerges is just "old-fashioned orthodoxy in its rightful severity" (*Postscript*, note on 275). What is more, Climacus makes it clear that he would not have dared to present himself to Socrates were this not the case. *He*, at least, acts in a way that *is* Socratic. In part, this is doubtless because, unlike the modern philosophers in general and the speculative philosophers in particular, he actually does what he says he is going to do.

But this is not all. It must also be the case that going *beyond* Socrates, as Climacus does, is not in itself un-Socratic – for if it were, this, too, would have prevented him from approaching Socrates.

If it is not un-Socratic to go beyond Socrates, is it positively Socratic to do so? Could it be that going beyond as such, and in particular going beyond *oneself*, is essential to the Socratic? This suggestion seems to be confirmed by everything we have seen of Socrates so far. Socrates represents the perfection of eros. To live Socratically is accordingly to be fundamentally dissatisfied with oneself as one is. It is to be prepared to abandon one's habitual assumptions and attachments in the name of the passionate pursuit of a transcendent truth. It is fearlessly to admit one's

---

[3] This is "a barb that is hurled not only against the Hegelians," but also "against all the nineteenth-century theologies that in one way or another eliminate from their versions of Christianity those elements that logically differentiate it from pagan thought: faith, sin-consciousness, the moment, and most importantly, the incarnation" (Evans 1992, 170–1).

[4] See ch. 1.

ignorance, to open oneself up to that which is unknown, and to embrace paradox – no matter what the cost. Indeed: if Climacus is correct, to live Socratically is in the last analysis to be able to acknowledge that the quest to know oneself and that which is depends upon the guidance of an other that transcends human understanding.

The upshot of The Moral now seems clear: Socrates can "inspect" Climacus and his project only because going beyond Socrates is itself a quintessentially Socratic gesture. If *Fragments* could be reduced to a fable, its life-lesson would be exemplified by the characters of Socrates and Climacus. The lesson would have to do with the self-transcending power of the analogous passions of eros and faith in relation to the truth. For *Fragments*, much like a fable, displays the fruits of Climacus's "ardent enthusiasm" while exposing those who speak without passion about religious or philosophical truth as the proud fools they are.

In the Preface to his book *Beyond Good and Evil*, Nietzsche explains that Europe has experienced a multimillennial "nightmare" induced by Platonism and Christianity, and he indicates that the soporific influence of the dogmas of philosophy and religion can be counteracted, if at all, only by "we, *whose task is wakefulness itself*."[5] Nietzsche's characterization of his task in *Beyond Good and Evil* is noteworthy as a strange and distorted echo of Climacus's project in *Fragments*. To grasp this resemblance, one must look past the surface of what Climacus explicitly says about his undertaking. "My pamphlet seems to be least reminiscent of the beating of an alarm drum," he writes in the Preface, "and its author is least of all inclined to sound an alarm" (7). Having now reached the end of *Fragments*, we can savor the irony of these words. When an alarm is sounded, its purpose is to rouse people and call them to the work at hand, and this is precisely what Climacus sets out to accomplish in his book. The goal of *Fragments*, like that of *Beyond Good and Evil*, is to awaken readers from a sleep brought on by the established forms of philosophy and religion. But Climacus does not characterize this sleep as a nightmare. It is rather a complacent slumber into which his contemporaries have been lulled by the historical success of Christianity on the one hand and speculative philosophy on the other. This complacency is bought at the cost of passion and a sense of paradox, for neither is necessary when faith is second nature and the truth can be learned from every assistant professor. *Fragments* accordingly uses paradox to dispel the loose and thoughtless

---

5 Nietzsche 1966, 3, emphasis in original.

talk that has put his readers to sleep, and to provoke in them a passion for what he, following Socrates, regards as the foremost human responsibility – the urgent and difficult task of coming into the presence of the truth.

Throughout *Fragments*, Socrates serves as a model of the passion that Climacus hopes to arouse in his readers. By virtue of his philosophical eros, Socrates has what young Johannes called "authority": his deeds match his speech, and he is able to hold thinking together with existing in a way that exemplifies what it means to live a philosophical life. Socrates is thus free of the "detestable untruth that characterizes recent philosophy" (*Johannes Climacus*, 117); he is a true philosopher because his life expresses the highest possible fidelity to his ideas. Last but not least, Socrates' experience of eros opens him up to the possibility that faith, like philosophy, is not a purely subjective projection of the self – which is how it is inevitably regarded by offended partisans of reason – but rather a daimonic passion of the soul in which one's own agency becomes indistinguishable from action on the part of the divine.

There are nevertheless certain significant inconsistencies in Climacus's presentation of Socrates, inconsistencies that result in part from the abstract manner in which he first introduces philosophy. In *Fragments*, Climacus confirms the authority of Socrates and the existential truth of his philosophy, but at the same time the religious hypothesis that he develops implies that Socrates is in untruth insofar as he lacks "the consciousness of sin" – something that "only the god could teach" (47). Furthermore, his emphasis on Socrates' commitment to existing philosophically does not sit easily with his characterization of the Socratic project as essentially one of achieving transcendence through recollection. This characterization suggests that Socratic philosophizing is a one-way flight from temporality to eternity; the philosopher who flees temporality for eternity, however, has no special interest in *existing* philosophically, for existence is a time-bound and finite mode of being.

Climacus addresses both of these inconsistencies in the second of his two books, *Concluding Unscientific Postscript to Philosophical Fragments*. He makes it clear in *Postscript* that Socrates expresses "the highest truth there is" for an existing person, and that he is able to do so because of the passion with which he attempts to live in the light of the eternal truth. What is more, Climacus's exploration of the role of passion in Socratic philosophizing turns up another analogue to religious faith above and beyond Socrates' unquestioning adherence to the word of the god at

Delphi. In particular, Socrates' paradoxical attempt to relate the universal, eternal truth to his radically particular and time-bound existence calls for something very close to faith.

In order to complete our examination of the relationship between philosophy and faith in *Fragments*, we must take time to reflect on at least the main elements of Climacus's discussion of Socrates in *Postscript*.

Socrates in *Postscript*

The epigram that introduces *Fragments* is a saying that Climacus attributes to Shakespeare: "Better well hanged than ill wed."[1] Climacus interprets this statement at the very beginning of the Preface of *Postscript*: "better well hanged than by a hapless marriage to be brought into systematic in-law relationship with the whole world" (5). This explanation serves more than one function, for in adverting to the epigram of *Fragments*, Climacus indirectly calls attention to that of *Postscript* – a remark by the sophist Hippias in Plato's *Greater Hippias*. Hippias complains that Socrates has confronted him with nothing but "scrapings and clippings of speeches" (304a). In the immediate sequel to the quoted passage, Hippias advises Socrates to produce big and beautiful discourses and to refrain from the "little speeches" of philosophical question and answer; in this way, he explains, Socrates will avoid seeming "exceedingly unintelligent" by engaging in "nonsense and babble" (304b). Taken together with the epigram of *Fragments*, the meaning of the *Postscript* epigram could hardly be clearer: the proponents of the Hegelian system are sophists or sham-philosophers, and Climacus will extend the Socratic critique of them that he initiated in *Fragments*.

At the end of *Fragments*, Climacus mentions his intention to produce another "section" of his "pamphlet," in which he will "clothe the issue [of Christianity] in its historical costume" (109). This intention is fulfilled in the first part of *Postscript*, which presents the "promised sequel"

---

[1] This is Kierkegaard's rendering of a German version of the Clown's comment in *Twelfth Night*, I.5: "Many a good hanging prevents a bad marriage." See the Hongs' note at *Philosophical Fragments/Johannes Climacus*, 274.

to *Fragments*. The second part of *Postscript*, however, goes beyond the promised sequel: it is "a renewed attempt in the same vein as the pamphlet, a new approach to the issue of *Fragments*." The distinction between the first and second parts of *Postscript* may be put another way: the first part concerns the "objective issue" of the truth of Christianity, whereas the second part concerns "the subjective issue ... [of] the individual's relation to Christianity" (17). It is the latter issue that absorbs Climacus's attention in *Postscript*, as is clear from the fact that the second part of the book takes up more than ninety percent of the whole.

As we shall see, Climacus uses Socrates in *Postscript* both as a riposte to the speculative philosophers and as the primary illustration of what it means to exist and to think "subjectively." Climacus's reflections on Socrates are thus crucial to the new approach he develops in *Postscript*. This new approach establishes that Socratic philosophizing is in certain respects even closer to religious faith than *Fragments* had suggested. It also helps us to see Climacus's understanding of faith in a larger perspective and to bring into focus its limitations.

A LUNAR PHILOSOPHY

The issue in *Fragments* is clearly stated in the questions on its title page, which pose the problem of how the individual can achieve eternal happiness. As Climacus explains in *Postscript*, the issue is therefore "not about the truth of Christianity but about the individual's relation to Christianity" (15). To ask only about the truth of Christianity is to proceed "objectively." An objective approach to Christianity – one in which "the inquiring subject ... is not infinitely, personally, impassionedly interested in his relation to this truth concerning his own eternal happiness" (21) – does not inquire into the meaning of Christianity for the individual. But the meaning of Christianity for the individual is nothing less than the essential meaning of Christianity as such. This is because Christianity is not fundamentally a theoretical doctrine, but a practical one. Its goal is individual salvation, and it therefore "attaches an enormous importance to the individual subject; it wants to be involved with him, him alone, and thus with each one individually" (49).

Speculative thought takes an objective approach to Christianity, for the "inquiring, speculating, knowing subject" is neither "so immodest" nor "so vain" as to ask about his own prospects for eternal happiness (21). "'What matchless audacity,' I hear a thinker say, 'what horrendous vanity, to presume to attach such importance to one's own little self in this world-historically concerned, this theocentric, this speculatively significant nineteenth century'" (16). This thinker is on to something, inasmuch as it takes more boldness for one to imagine that God might be concerned with one's eternal happiness than for a lowly maiden to imagine that the king could be in love with her. Yet Climacus justly protests that Christianity *itself* compels him to be "audacious," for it attaches "an entirely different sort of importance [than the thinker attributes] to my own little self and to every ever-so-little self" (16).

Climacus claims to approach Christianity as "an outsider" who asks how he can share in the happiness that it promises (16). But sincerely posing this subjective question, we may note, puts him closer to the heart of Christianity than "all the others [who] do have faith already as something given, as a trifle they do not consider very valuable, or as a trifle amounting to something only when decked out with a few demonstrations" (17). These others include the speculative thinkers, who assume Christianity as "given" simply because it is an objective fact of one's existence in a Christian nation (50–1).

In truth, the speculative philosopher is an outsider to his humanity as well as to Christianity. "The speculative thinker, "Climacus writes, "has become too objective to talk about himself." He instead talks about speculation "as if this were a man or as if a man were speculation"; hence, "he does not say that *he* doubts everything but that *speculation* does it" (emphasis added). But it is illegitimate to treat thought as if it existed independently of a human thinker. "Socrates states that when we assume flute playing," Climacus writes, "we must also assume a flutist, and consequently if we assume speculative thought, we also have to assume a speculative thinker" (51). The speculative thinker, however, assumes the independent existence of Spirit or self-developing Reason – an absolute being in relation to which the existing individual is in every respect relative, accidental, and insignificant.[2] Such an idea could never occur to Socrates, in whose view, as Climacus so aptly remarks, "every human being is himself the midpoint, and the whole world focuses only on him because his self-knowledge is God-knowledge" (*Fragments*, 11). Nor could it occur to anyone who, in faith, embraces the conviction that the god resolves to love the learner as his equal. In his objectivity, the speculative thinker seems to have forgotten what it means to be a human being.

---

[2] Climacus is not alone in questioning this assumption. Cf. the lengthy criticism of speculative philosophy in Marx 1975.

Climacus goes on to explain just what this forgetfulness entails. The speculative philosopher is exclusively concerned with thinking the eternal truth. His aspiration is to the condition of pure contemplation with which Aristotle identifies the highest divinity (*Metaphysics* 12.7). His task consists in "going away from himself more and more and becoming objective and in that way disappearing from himself and becoming the gazing power of speculative thought." In other words, he "wants to be exclusively eternal within time." "Therein lies the speculator's untruth," Climacus observes, for a human being is nothing other than "a synthesis of the temporal and the eternal." The "impassioned, infinite interest in one's personal eternal happiness" is accordingly "higher" than speculation, and is so "precisely because it is truer, because it definitely expresses the synthesis" (56).

Climacus offers the following vivid image of the speculative philosopher:

> If a dancer could leap very high, we would admire him, but if he wanted to give the impression that he could fly – even though he could leap higher than any dancer had ever leapt before – let laughter overtake him. Leaping means to belong essentially to the earth and to respect the law of gravity so that the leap is merely the momentary, but flying means to be set free from telluric conditions, something that is reserved exclusively for winged creatures, perhaps also for inhabitants of the moon, perhaps – and perhaps that is also where the system will at long last find its true readers. (124)

As we have seen, both Climacus and Socrates dance to the honor of the god.[3] But neither claims to overcome the force of gravity. In the *Phaedrus*, in which Socrates imagines the soul to be endowed with wings of eros that are nourished by the vision of beauty, even the most fortunate human souls are said to be able to catch a mere glimpse of the beings above the roof of the cosmos before they sink back down toward the earth (248a). Wings, after all, do not exempt even the most powerful birds from the law of gravity.[4]

Climacus's description of the speculative thinker is nevertheless reminiscent of certain passages in the Platonic dialogues in which Socrates describes the nature and activity of the philosopher. In the *Republic*,

---

[3] Cf. *Fragments*, 7 with *Postscript*, 89.

[4] Cf. Climacus's comment in the note on 206–7: "The difficulty . . . is that no human being is speculation, but the speculating person is an existing human being, subject to the claims of existence. To forget this is no merit, but to hold this fast is indeed a merit, and that is precisely what Socrates did." The consequences of speculative forgetfulness are vividly spelled out in the first chapter of Marino 2001, "The Objective Thinker is a Suicide."

Socrates says that the genuine lover of learning, being absorbed in contemplating that which truly is, "has no leisure to look down toward the affairs of human beings" (500b–c). In the *Theaetetus,* he represents the philosopher as one whose body alone resides in the city, but whose thought flies in the heavens and below the earth, "letting itself down to none of the things nearby" (173d–e). Both of these passages present the philosopher as a human being who aspires to be a god. They accordingly bring to mind Aristophanes' *Clouds,* a comic drama (produced in 423 B.C.E.) in which Socrates comes on stage suspended in a basket high above the ground, from which he looks down on gods as well as men.[5] This echo of Aristophanes is not incidental: both Platonic passages are clearly intended as caricatures, insofar as neither one acknowledges, or can account for, Socrates' own comprehensive engagement with the affairs of his friends and fellow citizens.[6]

As we have already observed, Climacus's presentation of Socratic philosophizing in *Fragments* is not altogether dissimilar to these caricatures. It is true that Climacus emphasizes Socrates' ignorance as well as his humility before the god, points that have escaped the notice of some commentators.[7] But Climacus also introduces Socratic philosophizing as essentially the recollection of eternal truth – a process in which "the temporal point of departure is a nothing" (*Fragments,* 13). Viewed from this angle, Socratic philosophizing would seem to involve the same flight from temporality to eternity that characterizes speculative thought.

One of Climacus's significant accomplishments in *Postscript* is to correct the misleading impression of Socrates left by *Fragments.* In particular, Climacus takes pains to amend his suggestion that Socrates somehow denies the significance of life in time. He does so by developing an account of what it means to be a subjective thinker – an account in which Socrates figures as the primary example.[8]

---

[5] See *Clouds,* lines 223–7: "*Socrates:* Why are you calling me, ephemeral one? *Strepsiades:* First, I beseech you, tell me what you're doing. *Soc.:* I tread on air and contemplate the sun. *Strep.:* Then you look down on the gods from a perch and not from the earth? – if that's what you're doing." Cf. also 247–8, where Socrates tells Strepsiades that "we don't credit gods" in his philosophical school. I have used the translation of West and West 1984.

[6] For further discussion see Howland 2004, 147–9 and Howland 1998, 53–75.

[7] See, e.g., Rubenstein 2001, who supposes that "readers of *Fragments* might . . . be surprised to see Socrates' *ignorance* highlighted in the *Postscript*" (452, emphasis in original).

[8] While *Postscript*'s account of subjectivity is merely hinted at in *Fragments,* the thesis that *Fragments* and *Postscript* are two stages in the "evolution" of Climacus's understanding of Socrates (Rubenstein 2001) is contradicted by Climacus himself. In *Postscript,* Climacus

SOCRATES AND THE APPROPRIATION OF TRUTH

Although Socrates is in *Postscript* the subjective thinker *par excellence*, he is not the first example cited by Climacus in his discussion of subjectivity. That honor belongs to the playwright, aesthetician, and theologian Gotthold Ephraim Lessing (1729–81), to whom Climacus dedicates an expression of gratitude (63–71).[9] This expression of gratitude pertains to Lessing's having written in such a way as to prevent anyone from "enter[ing] into an immediate relation to him" with regard to the religious. "[H]e closed himself off in the isolation of subjectivity," Climacus observes, for "he understood ... that the religious pertained to Lessing and Lessing alone ... understood that he had infinitely to do with God, but nothing, nothing to do directly with any human being" (65). Like Socrates, who "artistically arranged his entire mode of communication so as to be misunderstood" (note on 70), Lessing used a mixture of jest and earnestness "in declining partnership or, more accurately, guarding himself against it in relation to that truth in which the cardinal point is precisely to be left alone with it" (69). Hence, he was nothing more or less than a midwife of ideas. Climacus could no more be his follower than he could be Socrates', and for the same reason: "just as he himself is free, so, I think, he wants to make everyone free in relation to him" (72).

Like Lessing, Climacus also wants to preserve the freedom of his readers. Yet he nevertheless takes the risk of ascribing to Lessing certain "possible and actual theses" – theses that the latter might not acknowledge as his own, but that Climacus "in teasing exuberance could easily be tempted to want to foist upon him as something he said, although not directly" (72). Note the cautious playfulness of these words – a playfulness that particularly suits the content of the first thesis, which has to do with the impossibility of communicating subjectively appropriated truth as opposed to objective truth.

---

admits the "dubiousness" of his presentation of Socrates in *Fragments*, but explains that it resulted from a conscious choice to avoid "complications" that would result from "mak[ing] the matter as dialectically difficult as it is." "By holding Socrates to the thesis that all knowing is recollecting," he adds, "one turns him into a speculative philosopher instead of what he was, an existing thinker who understood existence as the essential" (n. on 206–7). Climacus explains that it is Plato, not Socrates, who forgets about existing, clings to the thesis that all knowing is recollecting, and thus "loses himself in speculative thought" (205).

9 Note, however, that "in a chapter ostensibly devoted to Lessing, Climacus refers to another shadowy pedagogue [Socrates] even more frequently than he mentions Lessing" (Rubenstein 2001, 442).

The first thesis reads as follows: "*The subjective existing thinker is aware of the dialectic of communication*" (72, emphasis in original). Unlike objective thinking, which involves reflecting on the truth but not on the thinking subject and his existence, subjective thinking involves what Climacus calls "double-reflection." Climacus explains double-reflection as follows: "in thinking, he [the thinker] thinks the universal, but, as existing in this thinking, as acquiring this in his inwardness, he becomes more and more subjectively isolated." The movement by which one attempts to apprehend the truth – the movement Socrates represents as recollection – is thus only the first stage of reflection for the subjective thinker. This is because "the subjective thinker as existing is essentially interested in his own thinking, is existing in it." Hence, the subjective thinker must make another movement, whereby he attempts to appropriate the truth by applying it to his concrete existence. This second movement is "another kind of reflection, specifically, that of inwardness, of possession, whereby it [his thinking] belongs to the subject *and to no one else*" (73, emphasis added).

In sum, the double-reflection of subjective thinking involves thinking the universal, eternal truth and then bringing this truth into the thinker's particular, time-bound existence. This entire process is, as we shall see directly, deeply paradoxical.[10] For now, however, let us consider Climacus's claim that the knowledge that is gained through the appropriation of the truth "cannot be stated directly, because the essential in this knowledge is the appropriation itself" (79).

Climacus's point could be put as follows: there is the truth, and then there is the question of how each existing human being understands or inwardly appropriates the truth. Nothing prevents me from attempting directly to communicate to you how I personally understand the truth – but precisely in doing so, I will have implicitly acknowledged that what really matters is how *you* personally understand the truth. And while I may imagine that my communication may assist you in appropriating the truth, I can have no confidence that you will understand me as I intend you to. For you are entirely on your own also when it comes to appropriating or interpreting my communication of my personal understanding of the truth.

---

[10] The process, as Westphal observes, is both epistemological and ethical. "In either the ethical or the epistemological case," he writes, "the paradox is the tension between my immersion in time, on the one hand, and my transcendence of time, my belonging to eternity, on the other" (Westphal 1996, 122).

There is, in fine, a zone of silence and irreducible privacy at the core of subjective understanding. To attempt to receive pure truth without altering it is to forget that one exists, whereas to appropriate this truth is inevitably to make it conform to the contours of one's particular existence. Put another way, "all receiving is producing" – a thesis that would be confirmed even, or rather precisely, if an effort were made to receive this pronouncement in a manner entirely free from "production" or inward appropriation – for example, if the thesis "came to be used as copy in teaching penmanship" (78).

Climacus is well aware of the contradiction involved in attempting to speak about the inward appropriation of truth. "Suppose, then," he writes, "that someone wanted to communicate the following conviction: truth is inwardness; objectively there is no truth, but the appropriation is the truth." If such a person succeeded in getting others "to proclaim this teaching to all people," he would thereby have failed to become understood – for "the inwardness of the understanding would indeed be that the single individual would understand this by himself" (77). According to Climacus, Socrates appreciated this contradiction: his self-isolation "on account of his daimon . . . from any and every relation" is to be understood as an indirect communication about the problem of communication. For in speaking about the divine sign or voice that comes to him in private, Socrates indicated that "everything subjective, which on account of its dialectical inwardness evades the direct form of expression, is an essential secret" (80).

There is another consequence of the double-reflection of subjective thinking that must be emphasized: "the truth is not the truth but . . . the way is the truth, that is . . . the truth is only in the becoming, in the process of appropriation" (78). Climacus expands on this thought in an earlier passage:

Whereas objective thinking invests everything in the result and assists all humankind to cheat by copying and reeling off the results and answers, subjective thinking invests everything in the process of becoming and omits the result, partly because this belongs to him, since he possesses the way, partly because he as existing is continually in the process of becoming, as is every human being who has not permitted himself to be tricked into becoming objective, into inhumanly becoming speculative thought. (73)

"The perpetual process of becoming," Climacus observes, "is the uncertainty of earthly life, in which everything is uncertain (86)."[11] This

---

[11] Cf. Climacus's comment on 118: "System and conclusiveness correspond to each other, but existence is the very opposite."

ineluctable uncertainty, which applies to both movements of the double-reflection, springs from the paradoxes involved in relating the universal, eternal truth to one's particular, time-bound existence. First, the existing person cannot fully succeed in knowing the truth that he is supposed to apply to his existence, if only because he is asked, as Westphal has observed, "to apprehend eternity from a radically temporal standpoint."[12] "A system of existence cannot be given," Climacus writes; "existence itself is a system – for God, but it cannot be a system for any existing spirit" (118). Hence, the truth that one apprehends will always be to some degree uncertain. Second, the existing person must apply the universal truth to the concrete particulars of his life. He must, to borrow from a Platonic image, bring what he can make out in the sunlit uplands of truth back into the darkness of the cave. This appropriation of the truth into one's own existence calls for judgment, which always involves uncertainty.

To acknowledge uncertainty as the subjective thinker does, and to accept that one has never yet arrived at one's destination but is always *en route*, is to confront "the illusiveness of the infinite in existence." It is to give oneself over to endless striving – an approach to life that does not allow one to derive a "positive, cozy joy" from it. Being a "genuine subjective existing thinker" is therefore too difficult for most people, who "must out of decency finish something, must have results." Most people are capable of acknowledging to the tenuousness and incompleteness of human existence only "once in a while" (although even then, Climacus asserts, they do so without genuine understanding), for to do so continually "could bring a sensate person to despair" (85–6).

While the subjective thinker eschews "results," he does not fall prey to the negativity of despair or cynicism about life. He is thus "continually just as negative as positive, and vice versa"; and while he is "never a teacher," he is nonetheless still "a learner" (85). Put another way, the subjective thinker understands that existence as striving "is just as pathos-filled as it is comic" – just as serious as it is laughable. It is pathos-filled "because the striving is infinite, that is, directed toward the infinite, is a process of infinitizing, which is the highest pathos." The subjective thinker strives to come into the presence of the eternal truth and to exist in the light of this truth. But this striving is also comic, because the attempt to embody the infinite and eternal within one's finite and time-bound existence is a "self-contradiction" (92). This is what Climacus means by "the illusiveness of the infinite in existence."

---

[12] Westphal 1996, 122.

Climacus's description of the genuine subjective existing thinker fits Socrates to perfection – he who was never a teacher, but always a learner; who never despaired of achieving wisdom even though, at the end of his life, he claimed to know only that he knew nothing; and whose profound seriousness of purpose was graced with the lightness of wit and laughter. As Climacus acknowledges, moreover, the key to Socrates' understanding of existence is the conception of eros one finds in the *Symposium*:

According to Plato, Poverty and Plenty beget Eros, whose nature is made up of both. But what is existence? It is that child who is begotten by the infinite and the finite, the eternal and the temporal, and is therefore continually striving. This was Socrates' view – therefore love is continually striving, that is, the thinking subject is existing. (92)

The *Symposium* teaches that the paradoxical passion of eros makes a whole out of the disparate elements of the cosmos (cf. 202e), and that every endeavor to hold being together with becoming in the sphere of existence is at bottom a labor of love. But the highest human manifestation of eros, Climacus suggests, is the subjective thinker's faithful perseverance in the forever uncertain and incomplete task of binding together, in his own existence, the temporal and the finite with the infinite and the eternal. It must also be noted that, because eros is daimonic, it involves a degree of objectivity that is obscured by the term "subjective thinking": according to Socrates, the enthused erotic thinker is acted upon by the divine no less than he acts in response to it.

Although what we already know about Socrates allows us to put a face to Climacus's discussion of subjective thinking, we must not fail to appreciate how this discussion expands our understanding of Socratic philosophizing. It is now clear that Climacus's account of Socratic philosophizing in *Fragments* is essentially one-sided. Climacus stresses in *Fragments* that Socrates endeavored to "recollect" the eternal truth – a process, as is suggested by Socrates' admission of ignorance at his public trial, that is never finished. Yet the inaccessibility of the whole of the eternal truth is only one reason why the philosopher is *philosophos* and not *sophos*, a lover of wisdom rather than a wise man. For Climacus has now explained that wisdom involves not just the apprehension of the truth by the thinker, but also its subjective appropriation. The erotic ladder to the truth of which Diotima speaks in the *Symposium* is not meant to be tossed aside once it has been climbed.

The Socratic philosopher is thus perpetually and simultaneously stretched in two directions: while his mind reaches out from existence toward the truth, he also seeks to bring what he has grasped of the truth back into his existence. This process, moreover, is doubly unfinished, for neither movement is complete. Hence, philosophy shuttles ceaselessly between being and becoming, truth and life – an up-and-down process that is reflected in the dialogues of Plato, which always begin with, and return to, questions that arise within the sphere of daily existence, but which never quite reach satisfactory answers. The Socratic philosopher is in this respect akin to the mythical Sisyphus, who must push his rock down the hill as well as up, and can never cease from either labor because neither is ever permanently completed. So great is the philosopher's passion for existence, however, that he confronts his endless labor with undaunted enthusiasm.

"[T]o become subjective," Climacus writes, "should be the highest task assigned to every human being, just as the highest reward, an eternal happiness, exists only for the subjective person" (163). From what we have seen, it is clear that Socrates is engaged in the highest human task. It is passion that makes possible the infinite self-concentration of subjectivity in itself, and "passion is existence at its very highest" (197). Socrates, who "minded his own business" in that he "was occupied solely with himself" (note on 147), manifests the passion of infinite self-concentration in the form of philosophical eros. And Socratic philosophizing embraces the task of existence, because it – like Christianity – aims at the achievement of eternal happiness, and understands such happiness to be a consequence of learning and appropriating the truth (cf. *Fragments*, 12).

So far, so good. Yet Climacus asserts in *Postscript* that the "highest passion of subjectivity" is not philosophical eros, but *faith* (132). In the last analysis, Socrates falls short of the subjectivity and inwardness involved in Christian faithfulness. This is true even though, as Climacus will make clear, the Socratic or philosophical *appropriation* of the truth – like Socrates' *ascent* to the truth, which could not proceed without the help of the god – involves a kind of faith.

FAITH AND PHILOSOPHY

According to Christianity, the achievement of eternal happiness is a consequence of the individual's appropriation of the truth, which, as we know from *Fragments*, occurs when he embraces the paradox through faith. Individual subjectivity is not, however, prepared "as a matter of course" to receive eternal happiness, and is initially no more than "the possibility of appropriation." Christianity is accordingly concerned with the "development or remaking of the subjectivity, its infinite concentration in itself under a conception of the infinite's highest good." Hence, "the truth of Christianity, if it is at all, is only in this [developed subjectivity]; objectively, it is not at all" (130). It is important to understand just what Climacus is claiming here. By "truth," he means the essential significance of Christianity for an existing human being. In saying that "objectively, it [the truth of Christianity] is not at all," he is not maintaining that the story of God's incarnation in the person of Jesus Christ is false. He means rather that the question of its objective truth or falsity is utterly irrelevant to the individual who is unprepared subjectively to appropriate the fact of the incarnation.

As it turns out, both the appropriation of the Christian truth by faith and the appropriation of philosophical truth by the intellect involve paradox. If there is a difference between the passions of faith and religion, it will therefore have to do with the nature of the paradox to which each passion answers.

We may begin to explore this difference by reflecting on the following statement about truth and paradox.

> At its highest, inwardness in an existing subject is passion; truth as a paradox corresponds to passion, and that truth becomes a paradox is grounded precisely in its relation to an existing subject. In this way, the one corresponds to the other. In forgetting that one is an existing subject, one loses passion, and in return, truth does not become a paradox; but the knowing subject shifts from being human to being a fantastical something, and truth becomes a fantastical object for its knowing. (199)

In this passage, Climacus makes it clear that truth becomes paradoxical only when it enters into relation to an existing subject. In the deepest sense this holds true for Christianity as well as for philosophy, for even though the truth that faith embraces is the absolute paradox, its paradoxical character is not intrinsic to the truth (= God) but is rather a consequence of the absolute difference introduced by our fall into untruth. However, let us set aside Christianity for a moment and reflect on the roles of paradox and passion in the Socratic situation.

"Viewed Socratically," Climacus notes, "the eternal essential truth is not at all paradoxical in itself, but only by being related to an existing person" (205). In other words, paradox enters into the picture only when one attempts to cognize and appropriate the truth. From the Socratic point of view, the truth is wholly intelligible in principle, but not in practice; nevertheless, one must strive to exist in its light. As Climacus puts this point, the truth is objectively uncertain, yet the individual must nonetheless subjectively appropriate this objectively uncertain truth. This is one dimension of the paradox that faced by the genuinely Socratic philosopher. In the process of subjective appropriation, moreover, the individual does what would be paradoxical even if he had no objective uncertainty, for he brings the universal and eternal truth into relation to his particular existence in time. This is another dimension of the paradox.

In Climacus's account, passion is both the origin of, and answer to, paradox. It is passion that gives birth to paradox, for it motivates the individual to relate the truth to his own existence. Yet it is also passion that allows the subjectively existing thinker to hold fast to paradox. Objective uncertainty, Climacus observes, "is precisely what intensifies the infinite passion of inwardness." The more one experiences the truth as uncertain, the more passion is required to hold fast to it. But Climacus does not stop there, for he explains that truth is itself a function of passion. "[T]ruth, he writes, "is precisely the daring venture of choosing the objective uncertainty with the passion of the infinite." Or in another formulation, "*an objective uncertainty, held fast through appropriation with the most passionate inwardness, is the truth*, the highest truth there is for an *existing* person" (203, emphases in original).

The latter claim amounts to a rather striking retraction of the plain implication of *Fragments* that the condition of even one so faithful to philosophy as Socrates is, from the religious point of view, that of untruth.[13] To see this, let us first consider the more nuanced account of truth and untruth that Climacus now offers:

If someone who lives in the midst of Christianity enters, with knowledge of the true idea of God, the house of God, the house of the true God, and prays, but prays in untruth, and if someone lives in an idolatrous land but prays with all the passion of infinity, although his eyes are resting upon the image of an idol – where, then, is there more truth? The one prays in truth to God although he is worshiping an idol; the other prays in untruth to the true God and is therefore in truth worshiping an idol. (201)

This passage by no means denies the significance of objective truth, for Climacus continues to distinguish the true God from idols. Furthermore, he asks not where there is *truth* but where there is *more* truth, which implies that the whole truth is realized by neither the one who prays in truth to

---

[13] Cf. *Fragments*, 47: "What did he [Socrates] lack, then? The consciousness of sin, which he could no more teach to any other person than any other person could teach it to him."

an idol nor the one who prays in untruth to the true God.[14] Nevertheless, Climacus makes it clear that being a Christian is not primarily a matter of getting things right *objectively*. The one who prays "in untruth" prays without passion and inward concentration; in a word, he prays without faith, and so remains unprepared to appropriate the objective truth and to refashion his existence in accordance with it. The one who prays "in truth," on the other hand, prays with the infinite inwardness of faith. Even though the object of his prayer is an idol, his subjective condition is precisely that which is required in order to appropriate the truth from God. He has become genuinely subjective and thereby fulfilled "the highest task assigned to every human being" (163); having done so, he has essentially answered the call of the true God.

While prayer and philosophical inquiry are distinct activities, both may manifest the subjective truth of passion's striving for the infinite. In the case of Socrates, the paradoxical relation of the eternal truth to an existing person was expressed by ignorance, which he "firmly maintained with all the passion of inwardness." "Yet it is possible that in the Socratic ignorance," Climacus writes, "there was more truth in Socrates than in the objective truth of the entire system . . . " (202). Indeed, Climacus now explicitly acknowledges the reflection of the Christian conception of truth in the Socratic:

The thesis that subjectivity, inwardness, is truth contains the Socratic wisdom, the undying merit of which is to have paid attention to the essential meaning of existing, of the knower's being an existing person. That is why, in his ignorance, Socrates was in the truth in the highest sense within paganism. (204)

Perhaps the most powerful illustration of Socrates' attainment of truth through passion is furnished by his approach to the question of immortality. Socrates "poses the question objectively, problematically: if there is an immortality." But he has no objective certainty about this matter.

So, compared with one of the modern thinkers with the three demonstrations [of the soul's immortality], was he a doubter? Not at all. He stakes his whole life on this "if"; he dares to die, and with the passion of the infinite he has so ordered his life that it might be acceptable – *if* there is an immortality. Is there any better demonstration for the immortality of the soul? (201, emphasis in original)

Socrates' "demonstration" is a practical one: he lives his life according to a conviction that is supported by passion rather than reason – in other words, according to his *faith* in the soul's immortality. Socrates' fidelity

---

[14] This is noted in Westphal 1996, 118–19.

to the thesis that the soul is immortal (a thesis that, as we have seen, underwrites his belief in the possibility of philosophy)[15] does not, of course, demonstrate the objective fact of its immortality. But it does prove that at least one human soul can in fact live up to the infinite and the eternal, can actualize them in its own existence and in this sense *live* immortally.

For Climacus, Socrates exemplifies the highest truth there is for an existing person because he refuses to follow the path of speculation, holds fast to his human existence, and stakes his life on what he cannot know. Yet Climacus (who claims, as in *Fragments*, merely to be "imaginatively constructing") nevertheless insists that Christianity, while it presupposes the "Socratic standpoint" of the subjective existing thinker, is "a category of thought that actually does go beyond [Socrates]" (204). He furthermore maintains that there is ultimately an "infinite" difference between the faith manifested by Socrates and Christian faith (note on 206–7). What are his reasons for these assertions?

According to Climacus, the definition of truth as "an objective uncertainty, held fast through appropriation with the most passionate inwardness," is "a paraphrasing of faith" (204). Here, it seems, Climacus directly acknowledges the continuity between Socratic philosophizing and Christian faith. But beneath this apparent continuity there is a deeper discontinuity. In the Socratic case, the truth that is to be appropriated is, as we have seen, objectively uncertain. This objective uncertainty exerts a "repulsion" that the Socratic philosopher overcomes with a passion akin to faith. In the case of Christianity, however, "there is only the certainty that it [the truth that is to be appropriated] is absurd." The truth is the absolute paradox, which is unintelligible to reason. To appropriate this truth, which strikes the understanding as patently absurd, therefore requires "infinitely greater resilience in the inwardness." The Socratic inwardness in existing is accordingly "an analogue to faith, except that the inwardness of faith, corresponding not to the repulsion exerted by ignorance [of that which is objectively uncertain] but to the repulsion exerted by the absurd, is infinitely deeper" (205).[16]

In comparison with the paradox involved in Socratic philosophizing, Climacus suggests that the degree of paradox in the case of Christian faith

---

[15] See ch. 2, 42.

[16] Cf. Climacus's note on 206–7: "the truth as paradox is an analog to the paradox *sensu eminentiori* [in the more eminent sense]; the passion of inwardness in existing is then an analog to faith *sensu eminentiori*"; nevertheless, "the difference is infinite." Climacus will later express this difference in terms of Religiousness A and Religiousness B.

is, so to speak, squared. Whereas Socrates sought to bring into relation to his existence a truth that, considered in itself, is unparadoxical, Christianity seeks to bring into relation to one's existence that which is intrinsically absolutely paradoxical – namely, the unity of absolute difference and absolute equality in the incarnate god. Instead of objective uncertainty and the corresponding Socratic ignorance, Christianity involves objective absurdity and the (understanding's) corresponding certainty that it is absurd. This absurdity is, of course, a consequence of the untruth into which the individual has fallen through sin, for it is sin that introduces the absolute difference that God seeks to overcome through the incarnation (see *Fragments*, 46–7). "If it is already paradoxical that the eternal truth is related to an existing person," Climacus notes, "now it is absolutely paradoxical that it is related to such an existing person." Because the learner is untruth, moreover, "the back door of recollection is forever closed" as an avenue to the eternal truth; the intensity and depth of the passion of inwardness is for this reason, too, even greater than in the case of Socrates (208).

As illuminating as these reflections may be, they nevertheless obscure certain important differences between Socratic philosophizing and Christian faith. For the person of faith, the upward journey toward the truth that characterizes philosophy need not be undertaken at all, because the truth has come down into the cave of human life in the form of Jesus Christ. Both philosophy and faith presuppose what Anthony Rudd has called "a relatedness to reality, an openness to it, which enables reality to become manifest, to find expression,"[17] yet their initial endeavors are quite different: whereas philosophy is engaged in the task of *questing to discover* the truth, faith concentrates on *accepting* a truth that is *given*. The challenges involved in these distinct activities are bound to be rather different. It is also necessary to qualify Climacus's remarks about the difficulty of relating the Christian truth to one's existence. We may grant that this task is absolutely paradoxical for one who stands outside of Christianity, as Climacus claims to.[18] But the Christian who has repented of sin and been reborn – who has, in other words, become a follower of God incarnate – is no longer absolutely different from God, because the absolute difference is a consequence of the condition of untruth that sin produces. What is more, the Christian has an advantage that is not

---

[17] Rudd 1993, 65.
[18] Cf. 16, 617. At 451, Climacus states that "having my life in immanence, [I] am seeking the Christian-religious."; at 557, he claims to exist within the boundaries of Religiousness A.

available to the Socratic philosopher as he attempts to relate the truth to his existence: he has the model of Christ.

We shall return to the latter point shortly. For now, we may ask why Climacus maintains that the difference between Socratic eros and Christian faith is an *infinite* one. It is hard to know how to approach this question, since Climacus furnishes no argument to back up this assertion (even though he claims that such an argument would be easy to provide).[19] He furthermore acknowledges that both Socratic eros and Christian faith manifest the passion of infinity that characterizes the genuinely subjective existing thinker. In both cases, in other words, "the striving is infinite, that is, directed toward the infinite, is a process of infinitizing," which is the highest pathos (92). Nor is it clear how Socratic eros could be analogous to Christian faith if the difference between the two were really infinite. Perhaps this particular concern springs from a misunderstanding, and what must be grasped is that an infinite difference is in any case not an *absolute* one. Yet Climacus later makes the proposed analogy even more tenuous than it already seems to be: while Socratic ignorance is "a kind of analogy to faith," he states, there are in fact "no analogies to the paradoxical-religious in its entirety" (566).

In the last analysis, Climacus never fully clarifies in *Postscript* the relationship between philosophy and faith. As in *Fragments*, philosophical eros is an analogue of the passion of faith, and a stepping stone to understanding this passion. Yet one is left with the paradoxical impression that, while Socratic eros and Christian faith approach each other asymptotically, they nonetheless remain worlds apart.

For the author of *Postscript*, faith is an endless struggle. Strangely, however, Climacus persists in seeing it as a passion that is in its own way "happy." Both of these dimensions of faith are highlighted in the following poetic image:

Sitting calmly on a ship in fair weather is not a metaphor for having faith; but when the ship has sprung a leak, then enthusiastically to keep the ship afloat by pumping and not to seek the harbor – that is the metaphor for having faith. Even if the image ultimately contains an impossibility, this is merely the imperfection of the image, but faith holds out. While the understanding, like a desperate passenger, stretches its arms toward land, but in vain, faith works vigorously in the depths – joyful and victorious, against the understanding it rescues the soul. (note on 224–5)

[19] "That the difference is infinite . . . I can easily show" (n. on 206–7).

In this image, the organs of faith and the understanding sit in the soul like passengers in a leaky ship. Instead of despairing or vainly reaching out toward land – either of which would allow the ship to sink – faith "rescues the soul" by tirelessly bailing water. For this reason, faith is a "battle" that is characterized by extraordinary "strenuousness" (note on 224–5).[20] But even though there will clearly be no end to its labor, faith does its task enthusiastically and joyously.

Two observations are suggested by Climacus's image. First, it applies to Socrates' philosophical passion no less than to faith. If the soul is a ship, it belongs in the water; this is the proper medium of its existence. Hence, to climb out onto *terra firma*, as the understanding longs to do, would be to abandon the soul. In Climacus's image, the understanding displays the impulse of speculative thought, which forsakes human existence for the solid ground of objective truth and certainty. Socrates, on the other hand, seeks to hold truth and existence together, which is to say that he seeks to remain in the water while attempting to reproduce in the ship something like the stability of the land. Enthusiastic bailing is thus also a metaphor for Socratic philosophizing.

Second, and most important, Climacus's poetic image amounts to something like a romantic idealization of existing in faith (and by the same token, of existing in Socratic passion) as heroic striving.[21] For Climacus, both forms of existence essentially involve maintaining and perfecting passion in the face of a perpetually unfinished task.[22] But how is one to maintain enthusiasm and joy in the face of the Sisyphean endeavor to keep one's leaky boat afloat, as Climacus says earlier, "out on 70,000 fathoms of water" (204)? How does one go about "acquiring daily the certain spirit of faith" (55)? Climacus has no answers, and in fact admits that he is "still far from having fully understood the difficulty of Christianity." Nevertheless, this extreme difficulty is in his view no argument against faith: "Whether anyone has done this [existed in

---

[20] Cf. 449–50: "it . . . seems to me that to be known *in time by God* makes life enormously strenuous. Wherever he is present, every half hour is of infinite importance. But to live in that way cannot be endured for sixty years; one can hardly endure three years of strenuous study for an examination, which still is not as strenuous as a half hour like that" (emphasis in original).

[21] Perhaps Climacus takes his cue from Socrates, who suggested that his service to the god took the form of a heroic quest (*Apology* 22a, 28b–29a).

[22] At 565, Climacus speaks of the believer's "daily efforts to keep himself in the passion of faith, which presses its way forward against the understanding (which is like rolling a weight up a mountain)." Cf. 55: the believer "daily acquir[es] the certain spirit of faith."

faith], whether anyone is doing it – of what concern is that to me, if this is indeed what it is to have faith?" (note on 224–5).[23]

A full exploration of Climacus's relation to Christianity would require an examination of *Postscript* as a whole. It may nonetheless be worthwhile to hazard some tentative suggestions on this score.

In *Fear and Trembling*, Johannes de Silentio seeks to understand the remarkable faith of Abraham, whose love of God was so great that he did not hesitate to take his son Isaac up Mount Moriah in order to sacrifice him. Silentio thinks that Abraham's story, worn dull by time and familiarity, has become a kind of cliché whose potentially transformative force is no longer felt. He accordingly begins with an "Exordium" and a "Eulogy" that are designed to underscore the magnitude of Abraham's achievement and evoke a sense of awe before his example. In the course of the Eulogy, Silentio takes pains to show that, of those who were great, "Abraham was the greatest of all" (16). The more he praises Abraham, however, the more he increases the difficulty of making sense of Abraham's faith. The problem is that everything Silentio says about Abraham's extraordinary greatness expresses *our* perspective on him as we look up, so to speak, from below – not *Abraham's* understanding of his relationship to God, which is what we sought to understand in the first place. The Eulogy furthermore builds up Abraham to such an extent that we can only despair at achieving the kind of faith he manifests.

Climacus seems to experience a similar difficulty in relation to Christian faith. Looking back from the vantage-point of *Postscript*, he explains that in *Fragments* he sought to introduce Christianity "by making it difficult, as difficult as possible, yet without making it more difficult than it is" (381). One may wonder whether, at least in *Postscript*, he hasn't exceeded the limits he set for himself. Like Silentio's praise of Abraham, Climacus's characterization of faith has a certain aesthetic purity, but this purity is apparently purchased at a high price. As Climacus describes faith, it would seem to be beyond the reach of anyone whose passion for existence falls short of the heroic – including himself. "Johannes Climacus," he declares in the Appendix to *Postscript*, "does not make it out that he is a Christian;

---

[23] This remark is reminiscent of Kant's response to the question "whether any genuine virtue is actually to be encountered in the world." "Even if there never have been actions springing from such pure sources," he writes, "the question at issue here is not whether this or that has happened . . . on the contrary, reason by itself and independently of all appearances commands what *ought* to happen" (Kant 1964, 75, emphasis added).

for he is, to be sure, completely preoccupied with how difficult it must be to become one" (617).[24]

When all is said and done, Climacus's name may be deeply ironic: by his reckoning, both faith and philosophy seem to be so high that, for most human beings, there is no ladder that could possibly reach them. But the most profound irony is that Climacus seems to ignore the teaching of the man for whom he is named. The essential insight of St. John Climacus is that the person of Christ provides human beings with a ladder to God where none existed previously. According to *The Ladder of Divine Ascent*, Christianity makes possible a gradual ascent to God, and so to existence in faith, through the imitation of Christ. If this is correct, Kierkegaard's Climacus seems to overlook a decisive difference between Christian faith and Socratic philosophizing. For the erotic ascent of Socratic philosophizing must be distinguished from the participatory ascent of Christianity, just as the learner must be distinguished from the follower. In particular, Christ presents himself to his followers not only as an authoritative guide for their lives ("I am the way, the truth, and the life," John 14:6), but also as a helping hand to lift them up when they stumble in attempting to walk in his footsteps. Socrates, on the other hand, leaves the learner essentially on his own. The love of wisdom is for the learner who would live Socratically what Christ's compassionate example is for the learner who would live Christianly. Yet the intensity and focus of Socrates' philosophical passion is utterly unparalleled, from which it seems to follow that the philosophical life *as lived by Socrates* is indeed beyond our reach.

While the problem of living Socratically surfaces repeatedly in Plato's writings, it is felt most urgently in the *Phaedo*, the dialogue that concludes with Socrates' death.[25] The *Phaedo* dramatizes the acute anxiety of

---

[24] Like Silentio, who is struck with awe by the "knight of faith," Climacus confers heroic status on the individual who combines in the "incognito" of humor "absolute religious passion" with "spiritual maturity": such a person is a "knight of hidden inwardness" (506). Lippitt 2000, however, argues that Climacus's self-presentation is part of a deliberate rhetorical and pedagogical strategy that bears comparison with Socrates' employment of irony. According to Lippitt, Climacus *himself* uses humor as an incognito "that both protect[s] ... inwardness in the ... religious person, *and* enable[s] something of the nature of this inwardness to be indirectly communicated" (95, emphasis in original; cf. *Postscript*, 451 with 504–11). If this is correct, Climacus's characterization of faith as a passion of heroic dimensions might be part of his humorous incognito.

[25] See also Plato's *Clitophon* and the last part of the *Symposium*, in which Alcibiades' ambivalent "indictment" of Socrates on the charge of *hubris* (219c) is clearly fueled by his awareness of his own erotic deficiency (cf. 216b).

Socrates' friends as they confront the question of how to continue philosophizing in his absence. For his part, Socrates does his best to discourage
any slavish dependence on him. When asked how he should be buried,
he replies "any way you like, if indeed you can catch me and I don't get
away from you" (115c). But this playful admonition does not change the
fact that Socrates' friends are at a loss as to how to carry on. "We felt that
he was just like a father," Phaedo explains, "and that, having lost him, we
would live like orphans for the rest of our lives" (116a).

The foregoing reflections on the prospects for living Socratically and
Christianly echo ideas that Kierkegaard develops in his journals. It seems
fitting to conclude this study by turning from Climacus to Kierkegaard,
in order to see what light the latter can shed on these prospects as well
as on Climacus's understanding of philosophy and faith.

Epilogue

Kierkegaard on Christ and Socrates

Kierkegaard mentions the name of Socrates in the Hong edition of his journals and papers well over two hundred times. Some of his remarks revolve around themes familiar from the pseudonymous works, such as Socrates' existential "proof" for the immortality of the soul, the significance of his example for the Christian dialectician, his exemplary use of indirect communication, his attention to the single individual, his negativity, and his emphasis on doing as the proper criterion of knowing.[1] On other occasions, Kierkegaard reflects on the Socratic nature of his own task. "I wonder if it did not go with Socrates in his age as with me," he muses in a typical entry. "He came to be regarded as representing evil, for in those days ignorance was looked upon as evil – and yet Socrates was in truth the physician."[2] Yet another significant set of entries explores Socrates' anticipation of Christian existence – a theme that is especially prominent in Kierkegaard's later years. "This Socratic thesis is of utmost importance for Christianity," he writes in 1850:

Virtue cannot be taught; that is, it is not a doctrine, it is a being-able, an exercising, an existing [*Existeren*], an existential [*existentiel*] transformation, and therefore it is so slow to learn, not at all as simple and easy as the rote-learning of one more

---

[1] On the soul's immortality see JP 73, 1.27 (X.2 A 406), JP 255, 1.108 (IX A 32), and JP 4280, 4.214 (X.3 A 315); on Socrates' dialectical example JP 373, 1.153 (VIII.1 A 547) and JP 390, 1.161 (X.2 A 453); on his use of indirect communication JP 649, 1.267–76 (VIII.2 B 81); on his attention to the single individual JP 2030, 2.413 (X.3 A 476) and JP 4295, 4.219 (X.5 A 133); on his negativity JP 754, 1.350–351 (III A 7); on knowing as doing JP 895, 1.400 (IV C 86) and JP 4765, 4.457–8 (X.4 A 138).
[2] JP 4555, 4.355 (X.2 A 401); cf. JP 6532, 6.251 (X.2 A 195), JP 6839, 6.472–5 (X.5 A 104), and JP 6901, 6.524–6 (XI.1 A 439).

language or one more system. No, in respect to virtue there is always particular emphasis on *the internal*, the inward, "the single individual."[3]

And in 1854, Kierkegaard observes that "just as Socrates is said to have talked continually only about pack asses and leather tanners etc. . . . so Christianity uses the same words and expressions we human beings use and yet says something entirely different from what we say."[4]

Socrates' efforts to reach the single individual inevitably suggest a comparison to Christian reformers, and ultimately to Christ himself. In comparison to Socrates, Kierkegaard writes in 1850, Luther "took the matter too lightly." "He ought to have made it obvious that the freedom he was fighting for . . . leads to making life . . . infinitely more strenuous than it was before." Instead, Luther "swung off too hastily":

> Jubilantly . . . the contemporary age embraced his cause, joined the party – Luther wants to topple the Pope – bravo! Well, all I can say is that this is pure political bargaining. . . . I have the deepest respect for Luther – but was he a Socrates? No, no, far from that. When I talk purely and simply about man I say: Of all men old Socrates is the greatest – Socrates, the hero and martyr of intellectuality. Only you understood what it is to be a reformer, understood what it meant for you yourself to be that, and were that.[5]

In another entry from the same year, Kierkegaard writes: "Outside of Christianity Socrates stands alone – you noble, simple wise man – you were actually a reformer."[6] And in 1849, he asserts that Socrates "is the only one, is 'the martyr' in the eminent sense, the greatest man." Christ, on the other hand, cannot be called a martyr because he "was not a witness to truth but was 'the truth.'"[7]

This is not all. In an entry from 1853, Kierkegaard muses on the situation of philosophy after Socrates and Christianity after Christ. "They say," he writes, that whereas "in Socrates philosophy was *as yet merely* a life," it subsequently becomes doctrine and then scientific scholarship, from whose heights we now "look back on Socrates as inferior." So, too, "in Christ, in the apostles, in the first Christians Christianity was . . . *as yet merely* a life . . . and now we stand at the pinnacle of scientific scholarship and look back on the first Christians, for in them Christianity was as

---

[3] JP 1060, 1.463 (X.2 A 606), emphasis in original.
[4] JP 3532, 3.615–616 (XI.1 A 19); cf. JP 4264, 4.209 (VII.1 A 65) and JP 4290, 4.218 (X.4 A 497).
[5] JP 2514, 3.80 (X.2 A 559).
[6] JP 6871, 6.508 (XI.1 A 133).
[7] JP 2651–2, 3.160 (X.1 A 119–20).

yet merely a life."[8] How, then, can we recover the Socratic or the Christian life? This question leads directly into Kierkegaard's most provocative reflections on Socrates.

SOCRATES' UNIQUENESS

In a journal entry from 1849, Kierkegaard explains the nature of the example that Christ furnishes for his followers.

[I]t must be firmly maintained that Christ has not come to the world only to set an example [*Exempel*] for us. In that case we would have law and works-righteousness again. He comes to save us and to present the example. This very example should humble us, teach us how infinitely far away we are from resembling the ideal. When we humble ourselves, then Christ is pure compassion. And in our striving to approach the prototype [*Forbilledet*], the prototype itself is again our very help. It alternates; when we are striving, then he is the prototype; and when we stumble, lose courage, etc., then he is the love which helps us up, and then he is the prototype again.

It would be the most fearful anguish for a person if he understood Christ in such a way that he only became his prototype and now by his own efforts he would resemble the prototype. Christ is simultaneously "the prototype," and precisely because he is that absolutely he is also the prototype who can be approached through the help of the prototype himself.[9]

Kierkegaard makes it clear in this passage that Christ provides not only the prototype or archetype of the Christian life, but also a ladder, so to speak, to help one climb up to the archetype. Christ is thus not only the truth but the way to the truth, in that his example furnishes us with the condition for understanding and appropriating the very truth that he exemplifies.

In the Socratic case, as we have seen, the condition for understanding the truth is not just reason. It is more fundamentally the desire to learn the truth. In a word, it is the passion of philosophical eros. But eros makes possible more than understanding, for it is also the condition for existing in the light of this understanding. Eros is the way to the truth that answers to the example of Christ in Christianity.

The condition for understanding the truth is in the Socratic case one that all human beings are already supposed to possess. But Climacus makes it clear in *Postscript* that Socrates' philosophical passion is extraordinary. Kierkegaard agrees. In his journals, he indicates that Socrates is

[8] JP 3317, 3.522 (X.5 A 113), emphasis in original.
[9] JP 334, 1.140 (X.1 A 279).

unique in being able, without following Christ's example, to live up to his understanding of the truth and thus to actualize the ideal. Others simply lack the condition of genuinely philosophical eros that makes this possible. Nor can Socrates give this condition to anyone else, for in order to do so he would have to be a god. For Kierkegaard, the problem with Socratic philosophizing is thus not that it is too low in comparison with faith, as would be the case if it were untruth, but that it is too high for ordinary human beings. Because ordinary human beings lack the means to appropriate the truth on their own, Christ compassionately gives them a ladder with which to climb up to his example. Socrates, however, can furnish no such aid.

While Kierkegaard frequently refers to Socrates in his journals, his mature understanding of Socrates is most fully spelled out in a long entry from 1854, the year before his death.[10] The general theme of this entry is the difference between poetry and actuality, a theme Kierkegaard introduces by observing that the extraordinary wittiness of Socrates' speeches in the *Apology* can make us "read him as if he were an author" and thereby forget that "the stakes are life and death." Socrates seems to combine poetry and actuality in his own person in a way that is altogether unique:

Socrates is the only one of his kind! Such a cultivated intellect, so very subtly educated and sharpened that presumably such a man would need all the coddling and all the remoteness from actuality that a poet, an artist, needs – and then to be the toughest character in Greece, one who does not produce in a study but in the most crucial actuality, with everything at stake and face to face with death, infuses this subtle intellect so subtly into every line, so magnificently into even the most unimportant turn.

What my pseudonyms frequently say could be said of Socrates: His life is not a drama for men but for the gods; spectators such as he required are found almost as rarely as a Socrates.

In this passage, Kierkegaard suggests that Socrates' speeches and deeds, even in the midst of exigent circumstances, reflect the sort of poetic perfection one normally associates with a carefully composed text. But this point alone does not explain why most human beings are not fit spectators of his life's drama. What does Kierkegaard mean to say here?

[10] JP 4301, 4.221–3 (XI.1 A 430).

Kierkegaard makes himself more clear in the immediate sequel, in which he reflects on "the Socratic principle" that "to understand, truly to understand, is to be."

For us more ordinary men this divides and becomes twofold: it is one thing to understand and another to be. Socrates is so elevated that he does away with this distinction – and therefore we are unable to understand him, understand him in the most profound, the Socratic, sense.

Socrates' life is graced by an extraordinary integrity of understanding and existing. In him, speech and deed, logos and ergon, are one; his actions are fully in harmony with his grasp of the truth. But if understanding and being are one and the same – and this is what is expressed in the Socratic principle that virtue is knowledge, or, as Climacus puts it, that "all sin is ignorance" (*Fragments,* note on 50) – then one who falls short in the domain of being will also fall short in the domain of understanding, and vice versa. If, for example, my deeds fail to reflect my understanding of justice, it would follow that I do not truly understand justice. By the same token, those "more ordinary men" whose existence reflects a division between understanding and being cannot truly understand Socrates. In Kierkegaard's imagination, Socrates' life is properly a spectacle for the gods because they, too, do what they know and know what they do, for which reason only they can fully appreciate his godlike integrity.

The upshot of these reflections is something quite surprising. As we have seen, Climacus claims that Socrates lacked "the consciousness of sin." "Sin" in this context must be understood as the perversity of will that drives a wedge between what we do and what we understand – something that, according to Climacus, "only the god could teach."[11] For his part, Kierkegaard suggests another reason why Socrates might have lacked this consciousness: he was one of the only human beings ever to have been *without* sin.

Outside of Christianity Socrates is the only man of whom it may be said: he explodes existence, which is seen quite simply in his elimination of the separation between poetry and actuality. Our lives are such that a poet portrays ideality – but actuality is a devil of a lot different. Socrates is an ideality higher than any poet is able to poetize it, and he actually is this, it is his actuality. This is why it is all

---

[11] *Fragments,* 47. Cf . Rudd 2000/2002, 2.264: "What constituent, then, does Socrates lack for the defining of sin? It is the will, defiance." Of course, Socrates is acutely conscious of "sin" in the Socratic rather than the Christian sense, i.e., as ignorance.

wrong for Oehlenschläger to want to poetize Socrates.[12] In relation to Socrates "the poet" is a completely superfluous person who can only become an object of ridicule, a laughing-stock, when he does not keep the proper distance but even wants to poetize him. What does it mean to poetize? It means to contribute ideality. The poet takes an actuality which lacks something of ideality and adds to it, and this is the poem. But, good God, Your Lordship, there is no need at all to add anything here; Socrates' ideality is higher, and it is that precisely by being actuality.

If Socrates did not acknowledge the will's perversity, it is simply because he had no experience of this phenomenon. It is true that he was not a Christian, but he did not need Christianity. He was able to hold the truth together with existence, the ideal together with the actual, because his will was completely in accord with his understanding of the good. This unity of willing and understanding, of knowing and being, is nothing other than eros. At the same time, the knowledge of ignorance that is intrinsic to genuinely philosophical eros protected him from the sin (and sinful consequences) of intellectual pride.

Kierkegaard suggests that Socrates' extraordinary eros puts him, both existentially and intellectually, beyond the reach of ordinary human beings.[13] By the same token, however, it puts the rest of us beyond *his* reach. As the only man outside of Christianity to explode existence, Socrates would seem to combine ideality and actuality in a manner reminiscent of Christ. Not being a god, however, he was limited by his experience and so could not know what Christ knew – and what we know – about sin. Without this knowledge, it could not occur to him that others might lack the condition for understanding the truth, much less that this condition cannot be supplied in the absence of a concrete example that would both give them something to imitate and teach them how to imitate it.

[12] Adam Oehlenschläger was the author of a book called *Sokrates* (Copenhagen: 1836). On poetizing Socrates, Climacus adds the following in the same journal entry: "What a wonderful Socratic difficulty! In order to poetize a man it is surely necessary first to understand him. But Socrates himself says: 'To understand is to be.' O dear poet, if you were able to understand this it would never enter your head to poetize it. Consequently it can be poetized only if it is not understood, or to poetize Socrates is *eo ipso* a misunderstanding, and to praise a poet for having poetized Socrates in a masterpiece makes a fool of him."

[13] This point is disputed by Silentio. "If there were no final lines from Socrates," Silentio writes, "I could have imagined myself in his place and created some, and if I had been unable to do so, a poet would have managed it, but no poet can find his way to Abraham" (*Fear and Trembling*, 118).

PHILOSOPHY IN IDEALITY AND ACTUALITY

So far, we have treated at face value Kierkegaard's portrait of Socrates as a godlike figure who was free from original sin. It would be remiss to conclude without noting that there is reason to doubt both the sincerity and the accuracy of this portrait. In the first place, Kierkegaard's private musings, like his pseudonymous writings, frequently have an experimental quality. His characterization of the Athenian philosopher might even be regarded as playful, for it turns out to contain a deep ambiguity. Kierkegaard insists that Socrates' actuality cannot be poetized; his "is an ideality higher than any poet is able to poetize it, and he actually is this, it is his actuality." His Socrates, however, is the Socrates of Plato's dialogues, and Plato himself warns us in his *Second Letter* that "there are no writings of Plato nor will there ever be, but those now said to be his are of a Socrates grown beautiful and young" (314c). If in the dialogues Socrates has grown beautiful and young – whatever this might entail – has he not been poetized? And if neither Oehlenschläger nor anyone else can poetize Plato's Socrates, might this not be because Plato has essentially *already* poetized Socrates to the utmost extent?[14]

The present line of thought might lead one to infer that Kierkegaard "plagiarizes" Plato in fashioning his portrait of Socrates, much as Climacus admittedly "plagiarizes" scripture in characterizing the god.[15] But the relationship between Kierkegaard and Plato – a subject of great interest, especially given that both depart from the model of Socratic existence in choosing to make writing central to their philosophical endeavors – is more complicated than first appearances might suggest.[16] For Kierkegaard elsewhere effectively admits that he cannot avoid poetizing Socrates in the course of attempting to grasp his actuality. In an entry from 1848, he notes that whereas Christ is "eternally present," Socrates "is present only historically"; for this reason, "it certainly does not help me to pray to Socrates: what I am to know about him I must learn from history or shape it out of my own head."[17] As for learning from history,

---

[14] Except that even Plato's Socrates is occasionally susceptible to a Typhonic or "sinful" assertion of self-love (cf. *Phaedrus* 242c with ch. 5, 113).

[15] I owe this suggestion to Denise Schaeffer.

[16] This subject has yet to be adequately explored. Richard Purkarthofer has observed in conversation that Kierkegaard is "the new Plato" in relation to Socrates. One should note that, unlike the old Plato – who appears in the dialogues only in the *Apology*, and furthermore in a nonspeaking role – Kierkegaard is quite comfortable writing about himself.

[17] JP 318, 1.133 (VIII.1 A 565).

Kierkegaard observes in another entry from 1848 that "no one can really learn anything from the past . . . because it is the past and consequently can only be comprehended by the imagination. But imagination and the medium of imagination is a medium of ideality." And in the sequel, he adverts to Socrates in the course of noting that "ideality is the very contradiction of being in actuality; only in the medium of ideality can a man be so ideal that he is ideal at every moment – in actuality this is impossible."[18]

To press this line of thought somewhat further, the Socrates of Kierkegaard's journals, like that of Climacus in *Fragments* and *Postscript*, seems to have been poetized – at least in comparison with Plato's Socrates – in one revealing respect: both Kierkegaard and Climacus tend to represent Socratic philosophizing as the heroically independent endeavor of a solitary individual.[19] Both thereby encourage the impression that the Socratic philosopher's relationship to the truth, like Abraham's direct and immediate relationship to God in *Fear and Trembling*, is an internal one involving no third term. This is the case even though Climacus recognizes the irreducibly social or political character of Socratic inquiry.[20] For Socrates, the erotic, philosophical quest unfolds in dialogue; while learning is ultimately the act of an individual soul, the soul's orientation and movement toward the truth may be decisively influenced by the participation of others in this quest. In this crucial sense, Socrates does not leave the learner *entirely* on his own. It is true that the learner may flag and fall short of the task of living philosophically, just as the follower may, in Kierkegaard's words, "stumble, lose courage, etc." As Socrates makes clear in the *Phaedrus* and *Symposium*, however, it is the beauty and nobility of other souls that awaken one's eros, and it is through dialogue with others that one approaches wisdom. While a separate study would be required to clarify the exact nature of this dynamic, the power of dialogue to invigorate and fructify philosophical eros is arguably the solution to the problem confronted by Socrates' companions in the *Phaedo*. Socrates' friends mistakenly cling to the memory of his speeches and deeds in an effort to sustain their philosophical existence. They would do better to

---

[18] JP 1054 1.458–459 (IX A 382).
[19] In both cases, this may be explained by the pedagogical intention to counteract the influence of the crowd and turn the reader inward. But it is worth noting that Kierkegaard's characterization of Socrates in the late journals and papers reflects his tendency to imagine or poetize *himself* as a solitary martyr. On the implications of Kierkegaard's literary self-fashioning for a full understanding of his writings, one should begin with Garff 2005.
[20] See ch. 3, 77 and ch. 4, 81–2.

consider how they can jointly help themselves by continuing to converse with one another after the manner of their teacher.

In spite of the aforementioned difficulties, Kierkegaard's reflections on Socrates and Christ help us to see that the question of the relationship between philosophy and faith is in a fundamental sense relative to the individual for whom these are possible modes of existence. Our examination of The Moral of *Fragments* suggested that going beyond Socrates, as Climacus attempts to do, is itself a quintessentially Socratic gesture. It is now possible to hazard the further suggestion that Climacus's thought-project is motivated by a Socratic awareness of his own limitations. This critical self-awareness is not in itself an indication of the inadequacy of the Socratic, philosophical life. Rather, it acknowledges Climacus's personal inability to match what he takes to be Socrates' accomplishment in maintaining and perfecting his passion for the daily task of holding the truth together with his existence.

What are we to make of the fact that even one with Climacus's passion for wisdom and love of discursive thinking falls short of fully living up to his best understanding? On one hand, it might help to underscore the extent of the human need for a non-Socratic relationship to the truth. Alternatively, it might be meant to call attention to the practical impossibility of living up to the heroic ideals of faith and philosophy advanced by the likes of Climacus and Silentio. Climacus presents himself as one who fails to recognize, and is therefore unable to grab hold of, the ladder of truth that is constituted by what Kierkegaard describes as the compassionate prototype of Christ. Although Climacus is remarkably open to both philosophy and faith, he consequently gives the impression of being caught in between them. Perhaps Kierkegaard – and Climacus, too, if he is indeed a closet Christian[21] – intends to suggest that overlooking the role played by the prototype in relating the individual to God is an error akin to that of overlooking the role of dialogue in Socratic philosophizing. The fact of sin entails that to live in faith is to approach God the Father by giving oneself over to the compassionate prototype of Christ (cf. John 14:6). So, too, to live philosophically is to approach the truth in and through dialogue with others. To suppose that one could dispense with either of these modes of mediation is in its own way to fancy oneself "free from telluric conditions" (*Postscript*, 124) and thus essentially to repeat the mistake of the speculative philosophers. In any case, there is good reason to question Climacus's characterization of faith as a passion even

---

[21] See Lippitt 2000.

more difficult to sustain than Socratic eros. Such judgments are likely to tell us more about the one who makes them than about the intrinsic nature of either philosophy or faith.

One of Kierkegaard's last journal entries on Socrates is a wistful expression of the mystery of his human accomplishment, a mystery that moves away from us and toward eternity, and thus in the opposite direction of revelation.

Socrates is the only person who solved the problem: he took everything, everything, with him to the grave. Marvelous Socrates, you performed a feat which remains eternally just as difficult, if anyone should want to repeat it; you left nothing, nothing, nothing, not even the thinnest thread of a result which a professor could grab onto; no, you took everything along to the grave. This way you kept the highest enthusiasm closed up airtight in the most eminent reflection and sagacity, kept it for eternity – you took everything along.[22]

---

[22] JP 4303, 4.224 (XI.1 A 449).

Works Cited

Allison, Henry E. 1967/2002. "Christianity and Nonsense." *Review of Metaphysics* 20.3: 39–58. In Conway 2002, 3.7–29.

Barrett, Lee. 1994. "The Paradox of Faith in Kierkegaard's *Philosophical Fragments*: Gift or Task?" In Perkins 1994, 261–84.

Benardete, Seth. 1984. *The Being of the Beautiful: Plato's Theaetetus, Sophist, and Statesman.* Chicago: University of Chicago Press.

Borges, Jorge Luis. 1964. *Labyrinths: Selected Stories and Other Writings.* Ed. Donald A. Yates and James E. Irby. New York: New Directions Publishing Corporation.

Brickhouse, Thomas C. and Nicholas D. Smith. 1989. *Socrates on Trial.* Princeton, NJ: Princeton University Press.

Cappelørn, Niels Jørgen, Hermann Deuser, and Jon Stewart, ed. 2004. *Kierkegaard Studies Yearbook 2004.* Berlin: Walter de Gruyter.

Climacus, John. 1982. *The Ladder of Divine Ascent.* Trans. Colm Luibheid and Norman Russell. New York: Paulist Press.

Come, Arnold B. 1991. *Trendelenburg's Influence on Kierkegaard's Modal Categories.* Montreal: Inter Editions.

Conway, Daniel W., ed. 2002. *Søren Kierkegaard: Critical Assessments of Leading Philosophers.* Four vols. London: Routledge.

Cooper, John M. 1997. "Introduction." In *Plato: Complete Works*, vii–xxvi. Ed. John M. Cooper. Indianapolis/Cambridge: Hackett Publishing Company.

Daise, Benjamin. 1999. *Kierkegaard's Socratic Art.* Macon, GA: Mercer University Press.

Delatte, Dom Paul. 1950. *The Rule of St. Benedict.* Trans. Dom Justin McCann. Latrobe, PA: The Archabbey Press.

Derrida, Jacques. 1981. "Plato's Pharmacy." In *Dissemination*, 61–171. Trans. Barbara Johnson. Chicago: University of Chicago Press.

Dostoyevsky, Fyodor. 1994. *Demons: A Novel in Three Parts.* Trans. Richard Pevear and Larissa Volokhonsky. New York: Alfred A. Knopf.

Dunning, Stephen N. 1994. "The Illusory Grandeur of Doubt: The Dialectic of Subjectivity in *Johannes Climacus.*" In Perkins 1994, 203–22.

Emmanuel, Steven M. 1996. *Kierkegaard and the Concept of Revelation.* Albany: State University of New York Press.

Evans, C. Stephen. 1983. *Kierkegaard's Fragments and Postscript: The Religious Philosophy of Johannes Climacus.* Atlantic Highlands, NJ: Humanity Books.

———. 1992. *Passionate Reason: Making Sense of Kierkegaard's Philosophical Fragments.* Bloomington: Indiana University Press.

———. 2004. "The Role of Irony in *Philosophical Fragments.*" In Cappelørn, Deuser, and Stewart 2004, 63–79.

Ferreira, M. Jamie. 1998. "Faith and the Kierkegaardean Leap." In Hannay and Marino 1998, 207–34.

Garff, Joakim. 2005. *Søren Kierkegaard: A Biography.* Trans. Bruce H. Kirmmse. Princeton, NJ and Oxford: Princeton University Press.

Green, Ronald M. 1992. *Kierkegaard and Kant: The Hidden Debt.* Albany: State University of New York Press.

———. 1994. "Kierkegaard's *Philosophical Fragments*: A Kantian Commentary." In Perkins 1994, 169–202.

Griswold, Charles L., Jr. 1986. *Self-Knowledge in Plato's Phaedrus.* New Haven, CT: Yale University Press.

Hackforth, R. M. 1933. *The Composition of Plato's Apology.* Cambridge: Cambridge University Press.

Hannay, Alastair. 2001. *Kierkegaard: A Biography.* Cambridge: Cambridge University Press.

Hannay, Alastair and Gordon D. Marino, ed. 1998. *The Cambridge Companion to Kierkegaard.* Cambridge: Cambridge University Press.

Hegel, G. W. F. 1956. *The Philosophy of History.* Trans. J. Sibree. New York: Dover Publications.

———. 1967. *Hegel's Philosophy of Right.* Trans. T. M. Knox. London: Oxford University Press.

———. 1969. *Hegel's Science of Logic.* Trans. A. V. Miller. London: Allen & Unwin.

———. 1974. *Hegel's Lectures on the History of Philosophy.* Three vols. Trans. E. S. Haldane and Frances H. Simson. New York: The Humanities Press.

———. 1975. *Hegel's Logic.* Trans. William Wallace. Oxford: Oxford University Press.

———. 1977. *Hegel's Phenomenology of Spirit.* Trans. A. V. Miller. Oxford: Oxford University Press.

Heidegger, Martin. 1975. *Early Greek Thinking.* Trans. David Farrell Krell and Frank A. Capuzzi. New York: Harper and Row.

Horkheimer, Max and Theodor W. Adorno. 1991. *Dialectic of Enlightenment.* Trans. John Cumming. New York: Continuum.

Houe, Poul and Gordon D. Marino, ed. 2003. *Søren Kierkegaard and the Word(s): Essays on Hermeneutics and Communication.* Copenhagen: C. A. Reitzel.

Howland, Jacob. 1991. "Re-reading Plato: The Problem of Platonic Chronology." *Phoenix* 45.3: 189–214.

———. 1993. "The Eleatic Stranger's Socratic Condemnation of Socrates." *Polis* 12: 15–36.

———. 1998. *The Paradox of Political Philosophy: Socrates' Philosophic Trial.* Lanham, MD: Rowman & Littlefield.

————. 2000. "Xenophon's Philosophic Odyssey: On the *Anabasis* and Plato's *Republic.*" *American Political Science Review* 94: 875–89.

————. 2002a. "Love of Wisdom and Will to Order in Plato's *Timaeus*: On Peter Kalkavage's Translation." *Interpretation* 30: 93–105.

————. 2002b. "Plato's Politic Writing and the Cultivation of Souls." In *Plato as Author: The Rhetoric of Philosophy,* 77–98. Ed. Ann Michelini. Leiden: E. J. Brill.

————. 2004. *The Republic: The Odyssey of Philosophy.* Philadelphia: Paul Dry Books.

————. 2005. "Storytelling and Philosophy in the *Republic*: The Ring of Gyges." *American Catholic Philosophical Quarterly* 79: 213–32.

Kant, Immanuel. 1964. *Groundwork of the Metaphysics of Morals.* Trans. H. J. Paton. New York: Harper & Row.

————. 1965. *Immanuel Kant's Critique of Pure Reason.* Trans. Norman Kemp Smith. New York: St. Martin's Press.

Kierkegaard, Søren. 1962. *Philosophical Fragments.* Trans. David Swenson and Howard Hong. Introduction and commentary by Niels Thulstrup. Princeton, NJ: Princeton University Press.

Lippitt, John. 2000. *Humor and Irony in Kierkegaard's Thought.* New York: St. Martin's Press.

Mackey, Louis. 1971. *Kierkegaard: A Kind of Poet.* Philadelphia: University of Pennsylvania Press.

Marino, Gordon. 2001. *Kierkegaard in the Present Age.* Milwaukee, WI: Marquette University Press.

Marx, Karl. 1975. "Critique of Hegel's Doctrine of the State." In *Karl Marx: Early Writings,* 57–198. Trans. Rodney Livingstone and Gregor Benton. Harmondsworth, England: Penguin Books.

Muench, Paul. 2003. "The Socratic Method of Kierkegaard's Pseudonym Johannes Climacus: Indirect Communication and the Art of 'Taking Away.'" In Houe and Marino 2003, 139–50.

Mulhall, Stephen. 1999. "God's Plagiarist: The *Philosophical Fragments* of Johannes Climacus." *Philosophical Investigations* 22: 1–34.

Nielsen, H. A. 1983. *Where The Passion Is: A Reading of Kierkegaard's Philosophical Fragments.* Tallahassee: University Presses of Florida.

Nietzsche, Friedrich. 1966. *Beyond Good and Evil: Prelude to a Philosophy of the Future.* Trans. Walter Kaufmann. New York: Vintage.

————. 1967. *The Birth of Tragedy and the Case of Wagner.* Trans. Walter Kaufmann. New York: Random House.

Pangle, Thomas L., ed. 1987. *The Roots of Political Philosophy: Ten Forgotten Socratic Dialogues.* Ithaca, NY: Cornell University Press.

Petersen, Anders Klostergaard. 2004. "*Philosophical Fragments* in a New Testament Perspective." In Cappelørn, Deuser, and Stewart 2004, 39–62.

Perkins, Robert L., ed. 1994. *International Kierkegaard Commentary: Philosophical Fragments and Johannes Climacus.* Macon, GA: Mercer University Press.

Poole, Roger. 1998. "The Unknown Kierkegaard: Twentieth-century Receptions." In Hannay and Marino 1998, 48–75.

Possen, David. In press. "Kierkegaard and F. C. Baur." In *Kierkegaard and his German Contemporaries.* Ed. Jon Stewart. Berlin: Walter de Gruyter.

Reeve, C. D. C. 1989. *Socrates in the Apology: An Essay on Plato's Apology of Socrates.* Indianapolis, IN and Cambridge: Hackett Publishing Company.

Roberts, Robert C. 1986. *Faith, Reason, and History: Rethinking Kierkegaard's Philosophical Fragments.* Macon, GA: Mercer University Press.

Rocca, Ettore. 2004. "Die Wahrnehmung des Glaubens." In Cappelørn, Deuser, and Stewart 2004, 18–38.

Rubenstein, Mary-Jane. 2001. "Kierkegaard's Socrates: A Venture in Evolutionary Theory." *Modern Theology* 17: 4: 441–73.

Rudd, Anthony. 1993. *Kierkegaard and the Limits of the Ethical.* Oxford: Oxford University Press.

————. 2000/2002. "The Moment and the Teacher: Problems in Kierkegaard's *Philosophical Fragments.*" *Kierkegaardiana* 21: 92–115. In Conway 2002, 2.257–76.

Schaerer, René. 1941. "Le Méchanisme de l'Ironie dans ses Rapports avec la Dialectique." *Revue de Métaphysique et de Morale* 48: 181–209.

Steinsaltz, Adin. 1989. *The Talmud: The Steinsaltz Edition. A Reference Guide.* New York: Random House.

Stewart, Jon. 2003. *Kierkegaard's Relations to Hegel Reconsidered.* Cambridge: Cambridge University Press.

Strauss, Leo. 1988. "What is Political Philosophy?" In Leo Strauss, *What is Political Philosophy? And Other Studies,* 9–55. Chicago: University of Chicago Press.

Taylor, A. E. n.d. *Plato: The Man and His Work.* New York: The Humanities Press.

Taylor, Mark C. 1975. *Kierkegaard's Pseudonymous Authorship: A Study of Time and the Self.* Princeton, NJ: Princeton University Press.

Thompson, Josiah. 1973. *Kierkegaard.* New York: Alfred A. Knopf.

Vlastos, Gregory. 1991. *Socrates, Ironist and Moral Philosopher.* Ithaca, NY: Cornell University Press.

Watkin, Julia. 2001. *Historical Dictionary of Kierkegaard's Philosophy.* Lanham, MD: Scarecrow Press.

West, Thomas G. 1979. *Plato's Apology of Socrates.* Ithaca, NY: Cornell University Press.

West, Thomas G. and West, Grace Starry. 1984. *Four Texts on Socrates: Plato's Euthyphro, Apology, and Crito and Aristophanes' Clouds.* Ithaca, NY: Cornell University Press.

Westphal, Merold. 1996. *Becoming a Self: A Reading of Kierkegaard's Concluding Unscientific Postscript.* West Lafayette, IN: Purdue University Press.

————. 1998. "Kierkegaard and Hegel." In Hannay and Marino 1998, 101–24.

Index

Christianity (*cont.*)
  participatory ascent of, versus erotic
    ascent of philosophizing, 207
  as philosophical deduction, 28
  possibly a human invention, 52
  proclaims incarnation of God, 79
  truth of, is subjective, 199
  is unintelligible to philosophy, 21
  uniqueness of, 183
  versus philosophy, 28
Cicero, *Tusculan Disputations*, 36
Climacus (*see also* faith; ignorance;
    indirect communication; ladder;
    Nietzsche, Friedrich; paradox;
    Plato; playfulness; St. John
    Climacus; wonder)
  and beginning of philosophy, 20–21
  Christianity and, 190, 206–207, 217
  as dancer, 39–40
  is no deconstructionist, 135
  as fictional character, 143
  goes beyond scripture in his poem,
    80
  has no opinions, 38
  ignores teaching of eponymous
    saint, 207
  imagination of, 17–18
  instances self-ironizing of
    understanding, 123
  irony of, 33
  as loafer, 35
  as midwife, 40
  nourished by ideality, 18
  as pamphleteer, 34, 37
  philosophy and faith in relation to,
    32, 55, 102, 155–156, 183, 204,
    217
  as plagiarist, 97–98, 134–135, 215
  as poet, 84, 91, 140
  precedes the god, 139–140
  serves the god, 39
  Socrates and, 106, 178–179, 184,
    192, 197, 217
  Socratic character of, 5–6, 16–18,
    25–26, 36–39, 55, 57, 103–104
  sounds the alarm, 185–186
  thought-project not invented by, 51

comedy, 157, 158, 192, 196
Croesus, 62

Derrida, Jacques, 7, 135
Descartes, René, 20, 118
difference, absolute, 119–125
  annuled by repentance, 203–204
  cannot be grasped by
    understanding, 103, 119–128
  does not prevent understanding the
    god *as* god, 123
  the god not simply characterized by,
    122–124
  paradox of communicating, 123
  produces self-ironizing of
    understanding, 121
Diotima, 17, 73–75, 83, 197
Dostoyevsky, Fyodor, 5, 158
doubt
  as beginning of philosophy, 20
  not beginning of philosophy,
    24–25

eros (*see also* Aristophanes; love;
    passion), 12, 26
  can overcome moral error
    (*hamartia*), 113, 125
  cannot be grasped technically, 74
  as condition for understanding, 78,
    211
  culminates in perplexity, 114
  daimonic structure of, 59, 71
  does not occur in *Apology*, 69–70
  exceeds understanding, 80
  faith and, 59, 98, 103–104, 139,
    147, 155–156
  and the god, as roots of philosophy,
    59
  is not projection of subjectivity,
    68–69
  lies at bottom of self-love, 112–113
  opens soul to mystery, 69, 74, 115
  as paradoxical passion, 78
  and philosophical prophecy, 72–73,
    75–76, 110, 120, 125–126
  rescues Socrates from depravity,
    105

and thumos, 69, 73–74, 112, 131–132

unity of immanence and transcendence in, 93

as way to truth, answers to example of Christ, 211

eternity (*see also* learner; moment, the)
confused with history, 21
as seen from each hypothesis, 145

Evans, C, Stephen, 2

faith (*see also* belief; Christianty; Climacus; eros; jolt of faith; ladder; New Testament; paradox; passion; Socrates; speculative philosophy; untruth; wonder)
absurdity of, 182
assumes Socratic relation between individuals, 180
autopsy of, 153
cannot be derived from order of world, 118
cannot become second nature, 176–177
Climacus on difficulty of, 178, 205–206
converges with philosophy, 100
difficulty of, obscured for later generations, 176
double vision of, 138, 150–151
as enthusiastic bailing, 204–205
existential transformation of, 3, 123
eyes of, 181
as folly to the understanding, 181
imposters of, 154
involves accepting given truth, versus philosophic quest of discovery, 203
is happy, 146, 204
jolt of, 175–176
is not knowledge, 147–148
a lifelong struggle, 174, 182, 205
not an act of will, 148–149
not communicated by one person to another, 178, 181–182

of Socrates, 68, 76, 198, 202
shared by the god and the learner, 146
terror of, 4, 174, 176
trust essential to, 88
wedding analogy of, 151–152

Feuerbach, Luwig, 132

follower, the (*see also* learner, the), 51
distinctions within the category of, 175–178
may also be a learner, 141
owes divine teacher everything, 53
receives condition from the god himself, 179–180
at second hand, does not exist, 172, 173, 182
should use paradox to awaken others, 181
is often unreflective, 173

freedom, *see* history

God, *see* Chrisitanity; love; philosophical argument; self-knowledge; truth, the

god, the (*see also* Climacus; difference, absolute; eros; faith; follower, the; learner, the; love; passion; teacher, the)
ambiguity of, 29, 39–40
is absolutely different, 103
can teach those who come later, 153
cannot be known immediately, 149–150, 175
descends to learner, 94, 96
exemplifies human possibility, 138
expresses love as servant, 95, 139
genuine contemporary sees and hears magnificence of, 151
guarantees meaningfulness of Socrates' philosophical quest, 119
incarnation of, an absolute fact, 179
irony of, 93–96
life of, reminiscent of Socrates', 137, 142–144

For EU product safety concerns, contact us at Calle de José Abascal, 56–1°,
28003 Madrid, Spain or eugpsr@cambridge.org.

www.ingramcontent.com/pod-product-compliance
Ingram Content Group UK Ltd.
Pitfield, Milton Keynes, MK11 3LW, UK
UKHW010041140625
459647UK00012BA/1530